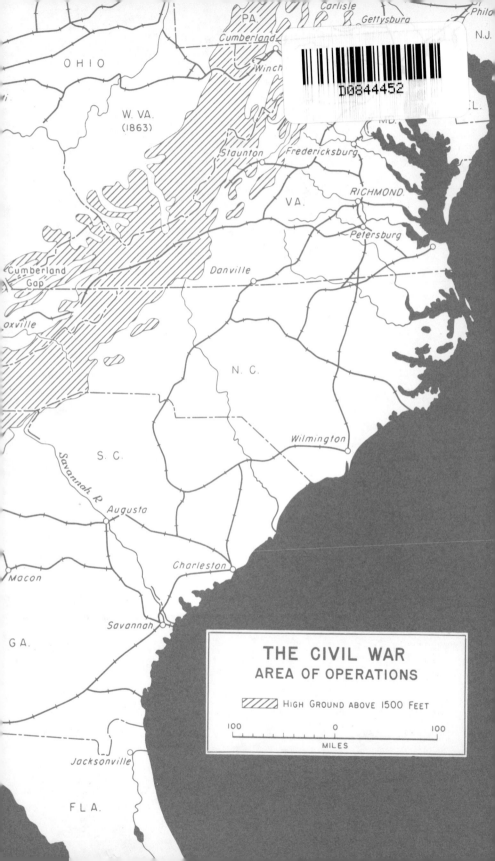

THE CIVIL WAR
AREA OF OPERATIONS

▨ High Ground above 1500 Feet

100   0   100
MILES

THE POLITICS
OF COMMAND

THE POLITICS
OF COMMAND

Factions and Ideas in Confederate Strategy

Thomas Lawrence Connelly
Archer Jones

LOUISIANA STATE UNIVERSITY PRESS/BATON ROUGE

ISBN 0–8071–0228–8
Library of Congress Catalog Card Number 72-89113
Copyright © 1973 by Louisiana State University Press
All rights reserved
Manufactured in the United States of America
Printed by Edwards Brothers, Inc., Ann Arbor, Michigan
Designed by Albert Crochet

Contents

Acknowledgments

The authors express appreciation to the staffs of many archives who assisted in preparation of this book. Special assistance was provided by staff members of the Library of Congress, the National Archives, the Virginia Historical Society, Washington and Lee University Library, Howard-Tilton Memorial Library at Tulane University, the Department of Archives at Louisiana State University, Emory University Library, Duke University Library, and the Southern Historical Collection at the University of North Carolina.

Several individuals offered criticism, advice, and encouragement for this project. Special gratitude is due to Professor T. Harry Williams of Louisiana State University, Professor Frank Vandiver of Rice University, Professor Grady McWhiney of Wayne State University, Professors Robert Ochs, O. S. Connelly, and Kenneth Toombs of the University of South Carolina, Professors A. S. Britt and James Morrison of the United States Military Academy, and Professor Donald F. Schwartz of North Dakota State University. Special thanks are owed to Dennis Lindemeier who executed the diagrams, and to the office of the Chief of Military History, United States Army, Washington, D.C., from which the authors acquired the Map of the Area of Operations used on the end papers.

Introduction

In the library at Morristown National Historical Park is a letterbook used by General P. G. T. Beauregard during the last months of the Civil War. Written in the back of the volume, perhaps by Beauregard himself, is a curious "Epitaph of the Confederate States." This bitter obituary notes that the Confederacy was "murdered by Jefferson Davis—aided and abetted by Benjamin, Seddon, Mallory, Memminger, Northrop and Gorgas." The principal pallbearers are noted as "Generals Cooper, Bragg, Kirby Smith, Lt. Generals Hood, Holmes and Pemberton." The epitaph concludes that the South was "buried with military honors by Lee, Johnston and Beauregard."

This acid indictment of the administration's war policy was symptomatic of the continual wrangling within the Confederate high command during and after the Civil War. All Confederate historians are familiar with the long list of famous quarrels such as those between Jefferson Davis and Joseph E. Johnston, or Davis and Beauregard.

Too often some historians have viewed these disputes as merely personal matters, and no doubt some of them were. Johnston's postwar *Narrative of Military Operations* contains personal attacks upon a number of men, particularly upon Jefferson Davis, just as General John B. Hood's *Advance and Retreat* was a ferocious postwar assault upon Johnston. Obviously the dislike between Davis and Beauregard resulted in part from a strong conflict of personalities, as did much of the serious opposition to General Braxton Bragg within the Army of Tennessee.

For almost a half century following the war, former Rebel commanders continued to rekindle their quarrels. General James Longstreet's memoirs, published scarcely a decade before World War I, evinced his undiminished dislike of Bragg. General Jubal Early's memoirs, also published long after the war, marked the culmination of his thirty-year personal assault upon the reputation of Longstreet. Dozens of battles were refought, not only in books of reminiscence, but in such organs as *Century Magazine* and its subsequent *Battles and Leaders* compendium, the *Southern Historical Society Magazine,* William Dawson's *Historical Magazine,* and elsewhere.

Historians have seen such quarrels as being conducted by only two groups within the Confederate civil and military leadership—proadministration and antiadministration. Thus Bragg becomes stereotyped as a pro-Davis general, while Joseph E. Johnston is labeled an antiadministration man. Although there is some basis for these assumptions regarding command conflict, it is not accurate to cast a total stereotyping on them as merely personal or strictly pro- or anti-Davis in nature. For example, within the congressional opposition to Davis there was great variation in motivation, in timing, and in the intensity of personal dislike. Robert Barnwell Rhett opposed Davis from the beginning for a number of reasons which included personal jealousy and a philosophical disagreement on the matter of states' rights. Senator Louis T. Wigfall and other Davis opponents, initially his supporters, changed sides for a number of reasons, ranging from disagreement with Davis' conduct of the war to petty jealousies. Wigfall was apparently motivated by anger over not being consulted about a vital cabinet change in late 1862.

Nor can the infighting among Confederate generals be disposed of in any simple fashion, for too many facts deny the existence of an elementary pattern. For example, where would one place Generals Braxton Bragg and Leonidas Polk? Both were warm personal friends of the President, yet both differed with Davis in overall policy on strategy. They held similar viewpoints as to the vital importance of the Confederate West but were themselves bitter enemies. Thus, on some issues, Bragg and Polk were proadministration generals; in others, such as strategy, they often disagreed with Richmond.

In short, the continual infighting among the Confederate leadership had deeper sources than personal conflicts and anti-Davis sentiment. It involved a continuing debate over basic war policy, particularly the Confederacy's proper strategic course.

This book reevaluates this debate through a discussion of Jefferson Davis' strategic policy and the major influences which helped to mold his decisions. In the process it addresses itself to a number of familiar questions about the American Civil War. One of these is the role and significance of Robert E. Lee. The treatment here will hardly end such well-argued controversies as whether Lee's propensity for the offensive generated a level of casualties which the Confederacy could not sustain, or whether his view of the war was limited by his preoccupation with Virginia. The major thrust is not these familiar points but rather detailed examination of his influence on the shaping of Confederate strategy.

To a marked degree Rebel strategy was shaped by the personality and influence of the South's most successful field general. Lee's field success, his rapport with President Davis, and other factors combined to make him a powerful voice in wartime planning. The effect—and wisdom—of Lee's advice in widescale matters of strategy needs reexamination. His obsession with the war effort in Virginia, his admitted lack of knowledge of the western front, and his seemingly parochial attitude as a Virginian produced two questionable effects. First, Lee succeeded in drawing Richmond's attention more often toward the Virginia front; even when Davis evinced concern for other areas, Lee usually managed to obtain a special status for his Army of Northern Virginia by having it maintained and supplied apart from the general Confederate reinforcement reserve.

Of course Lee's stress on the importance of Virginia was opposed by officers in the West, and, as Sir Frederick Maurice has pointed out, there was a struggle between easterners and westerners quite analogous to that among allied leaders during World War I. This struggle is perceived as more than a parochial one between Lee with his loyalty to Virginia and to his army, on the one hand, and officers of western extraction or army assignment and loyalty on the other. The western bloc is analyzed and found to be a heterogeneous ad hoc aggregation with divergent interests, objectives, and loyalties. This group of politicians and generals, many of them private enemies, were, however, united in several common interests. They were concerned with the central Confederacy, particularly with the successful defense of the Chattanooga–Atlanta corridor to the South's munitions complex in Georgia and Alabama. To protect this area, the western bloc advocated a Napoleonic concentration and offensive in the West. Although dominated by Beauregard's influence, the western bloc contained such varied personalities as Braxton Bragg, Joseph E. Johnston, and James Longstreet. This clique was more influential than some historians have indicated. Its pressure on Confederate strategy can be seen at several critical points in the war, in particular the 1862 invasion of Kentucky, the 1863 concentration prior to the battle of Chickamauga, and in the 1864 planning for the spring campaign.

This debate involves principles of strategy. We agree with T. Harry Williams—up to a point—that it was not that Jomini's strategy was out of date but that it was rather a question of the "national application of the one Jominian principle that might have brought success." Agreeing that Lee was primarily a "field or theatre strategist," we contend that he opposed a national application of Jomini, while the westerners advocated just such an application. Furthermore, we contend that just as Lee's strategic successes resulted from an application of Napoleon's and Jomini's principles, so successes in the West were derived from much broader applications of the same principles, culminating in the truly nationwide concentration of Chickamauga.

The western bloc's strategic mentor was P. G. T. Beauregard, and his ideas were clearly derived from his study of Jomini and Napoleon. Jomini is usually represented as an advocate of limited war and the place-oriented strategy characteristic of eighteenth-century warfare. Further study of Jomini's writings indicates that his ideas were very close to those of Napoleon and to accepted modern strategy. Beauregard had fully absorbed these ideas and used them in understanding the strategy of the war, and applied them to the era of railroad and telegraph, ultimately giving unity to Confederate strategy.

Beauregard and Bragg showed clearly by word and deed that they were disciples of Jomini and Napoleon. Although Lee's operations, as well as many of Davis' decisions, are in full harmony with the Europeans' principles, the thesis is not confirmed "that many a Civil War general went into battle with a sword in one hand and a Jomini's *Summary of the Art of War* in the other."[1]

This, however, is not pertinent to the interpretation, since it is clear that Beauregard was so influenced and many Confederate generals followed his lead in strategy. Nor, for that matter, is it really essential to the interpretation that Jomini was not an exponent of Austrian ideas since the influence of Napoleon on Beauregard is clear as is the influence of Beauregard on Confederate strategy. That Beauregard had served in both Virginia and Mississippi and advocated his strategy from the neutral ground of South Carolina reinforces the thesis that his ideas were derived from principles rather than from any geographical allegiance. His ideas provided the rationale for the partisans of western concentration and provided a principle for Confederate strategy which could constantly be pressed on Davis. In several significant respects this bloc was successful in overcoming Lee's influence, and Davis seems to have absorbed many of Beauregard's ideas.

The western bloc is also important because it was representative of a fourth vital influence upon Rebel strategy—the broad network of informal associations within the Confederacy. Much research remains to be done on these cliques. Associations were based upon family ties, prewar friendships, state interests, or acceptance of common strategic ideas. Although there were many informal groups, four seem predominant. The Abingdon-Columbia bloc was a vast network of family ties, friendships, mutual dislikes, and common ideas. It linked such generals as John B. Floyd, Joseph E. Johnston, P. G. T. Beauregard, William Preston, John C. Breckinridge, and

---

[1] T. Harry Williams, "The Military Leadership of North and South," in David Donald (ed.), *Why the North Won the Civil War* (Baton Rouge, 1960), 23–46. See also: Frank Vandiver, "Jefferson Davis and Confederate Strategy," *The American Tragedy* (Hampden-Sydney, Va., 1959), 19–32. For differing views of Jomini and Civil War strategy, see David Donald, *Lincoln Reconsidered* (New York, 1956), 82–102; Archer Jones, "Jomini and the American Civil War, a Reinterpretation," *Military Affairs*, XXXIV (December, 1970); J. D. Hittle, *Jomini and His Summary of the Art of War* (Harrisburg, Pa., 1947), 2.

Wade Hampton, and political figures such as William Porcher Miles and Louis T. Wigfall.

The Kentucky bloc, a powerful lobby for the Confederate occupation of that state, saw a continual coalition of men such as Generals John C. Breckinridge, John Hunt Morgan, Willam Preston, Joseph Lewis, and Simon Bolivar Buckner. The Beauregard bloc was a personal association, resting upon the Creole general's broad personal connections with many civil and military leaders. In a definite pattern Beauregard dispensed his viewpoints on strategy to Bragg and Longstreet, to state leaders such as Francis Pickens, Isham Harris, and Joseph E. Brown, and to congressional friends such as Charles Villeré, Louis Wigfall, William Porcher Miles, and Roger Pryor.

The anti-Bragg bloc was another powerful informal clique. It was based mainly upon local antipathy for Bragg within the Army of Tennessee, but also indicated the frequent cross-pattern of informal associations. It included such men as Generals Leonidas Polk and William Hardee, who actually were allied with Bragg on strategy. It also included generals of the Kentucky bloc, particularly Simon Buckner, John C. Breckinridge, and William Preston.

The importance of this fourth pressure factor—a complex of informal organizations—is vital when considering Confederate strategic planning. These associations provided vital support for the ideas of the western concentration bloc. Also, one is impressed with the number of influential civil and military leaders who were allied in such cliques due to common dislikes, common strategic viewpoints, or other reasons. In fact, when one considers the strength of the western bloc, bolstered by such combines as the Abingdon-Columbia, Kentucky, Beauregard, and anti-Bragg factions, the question of where the Confederate establishment lay takes on new dimensions.

A fifth influence on formulation and execution of strategy was the Confederate departmental system of army administration. Too often historians have believed that Davis viewed the military department as a mere tool by which he could implement policy. Actually, the departmental system was far more important to Davis, and its evolution provides a view of the evolution of Davis' own thinking. Also, the departmental system was something of an arena, within which all other major pressure factors—European ideas, Lee, the western bloc, general informal associations—vied with Davis' own ideas in the formulation of policy. Finally, the resulting strategic policy which developed—departmental command—was essentially Davis' philosophy for conducting the war. For while the departmental system may have been instituted by Davis as an instrument of administration, it gradually became a strategy in itself. Frequently, Davis seemed to shape Rebel policy to fit the needs of the departmental system, rather than the reverse.

This book is not intended to be a comprehensive treatment of the factors influencing Confederate strategy. Political and diplomatic considerations have been omitted as have important personal factors, such as the participants' health and family concerns. Likewise, we have only scratched the surface of the informal relationships that existed among southern leaders.

We have deliberately limited ourselves to those aspects of the topic concerning which we felt we had something new to say or about which we had new hypotheses to propose or new lines of research to suggest. Obviously this book is also intended to raise more questions than it answers. An attempt is made to provide a fresh approach not only to the European heritage of Confederate thought, but to the role of such individuals as Lee and Beauregard in strategic policy. The role of the informal cliques in Confederate military history, especially that of the western bloc, has much potential in Civil War research. Finally, a new approach is sought to the problems of the departmental system, for it was no mere administrative organ. In the evolution of this system, conditioned by these other influences, one may begin to develop new perspectives on the Confederate decision-making process.

Thomas Lawrence Connelly
University of South Carolina

Archer Jones
North Dakota State University

THE POLITICS
OF COMMAND

I
The European Inheritance

The American Civil War was influenced by the military developments of the era of the French Revolution and Napoleon, the
interpretation made of these developments by the military historian
and theorist, Baron Henri Jomini, and by the West Point curriculum
through which most of the higher commanders passed.

The Napoleonic era changed a system which had been evolved
from the seventeenth century until it had culminated in the eighteenth
in the perfection of the management of unitary armies by careful
deployment of troops in what were essentially very brittle formations.
After the development of the bayonet in the eighteenth century,
the careful distribution of the proper mixture of pikemen and
musketeers was no longer necessary. Precise linear formations were
still needed, however, in order to develop full firepower. For this
reason, armies continued to be rigid and difficult to deploy and
to maneuver throughout both centuries. Because these armies were
not often subdivided into separately maneuverable groups, the
operations and deployment were quite slow. Then, too, concentration
of troops became essential in order to prevent an isolated body from
being caught and crushed.

The defensive power of these armies, when properly arrayed, was
enormous. Battles, though infrequent, were bloody. The attacker
was at a great disadvantage because the enemy could easily elude
him while he was deploying for battle and because of the great
defensive strength enjoyed by a deployed army when assaulted in
front. On the other hand, casualties in a defeated army might be
particularly severe if there were any disruption of the rigid and
unarticulated formations; that is, formations which were poorly
subdivided and lacked control. Flanking maneuvers were extremely

difficult because of the danger of leaving gaps in a line. Even after the bayonet had superseded the pike and it was possible to cover small gaps with fire, flanking operations were still difficult because of poor articulation.

As these armies increased in size, they became more tightly bound to a line of communications in order to secure supplies. They often remained in the same locality for long periods of time, quickly exhausting local supplies. By the eighteenth century it was quite difficult for the slow-moving, heavily concentrated armies to live off the land. The strategy of the seventeenth and eighteenth centuries, then, was dictated by the need to keep the troops concentrated and by the supply problems which this situation created. The strength of the defense and the risk of heavy casualties reinforced a policy of accepting battle only when a decisive advantage could be won or, at least, the risks, if defeated, were minimal.

Each contestant was usually represented in each theater of operations by a single unitary army. The armies were kept concentrated, fighting and maneuvering as units. In the eighteenth century, however, a form of dispersal, the cordon, was practiced, particularly by armies on the defensive. Since the objective was to protect territory, these detached forces were placed to protect vital positions or to cover routes of advance into the protected territory and routes leading toward the main army or its flanks. These cordoned detachments usually occupied strong defensive positions and could be expected to hold up an enemy advance until reinforced or until new defensive dispositions could be made. These detachments were essentially separate forces with distinct missions. Although they were used in offensive situations, their spirit was defensive, and they represented a high level of security-mindedness.

The campaigns of the two centuries consisted of maneuvering by unitary armies, each seeking some advantage such as breaking an opponent's supply line or forcing battle on favorable terms. Consequently, there were few battles and even fewer decisive campaigns because the armies were so slow in movement and deployment and so bound to their lines of communications that they either could not force battle on each other or could not prevent a defeated enemy from escaping. The entire operation resembled a chess game in which each opponent has a single piece with nearly identical characteristics. Good generalship, then, largely depended upon the skillful maneuvering of an army as a single chess piece. Such a confining and limited situation is obviously unlikely to produce decisive battles.

In the next period, the wars of the French Revolution and the age of Napoleon, there were changes in both strategy and tactics. Greater power of tactical maneuver was achieved by the increased use of skirmishers, by the subdivision of armies into divisions, by a marked increase in the articulation of smaller units, and by the altered character of the troops. The power of the offensive increased. The greater mobility of the better articulated armies made flanking movements easier and dispersion safer. These changes occurred early in Napoleon's career. Napoleon's armies were dispersed, not in cordons for defense, but in a way to permit their concentration at the enemy's weak points when they were revealed. This dispersion, with the intent and the ability to concentrate at any point, was an essential part of Napoleon's strategy. His iconoclastic dispersion confused his enemies of the Old Regime and masked his intentions which were to provide flexible alternative actions. His strategy was to feel out the enemy, to discover a vulnerable spot, to promote or await any enemy maneuver, and then to take advantage of the opportunity for a rapid concentration and attack.[1]

In this way Napoleon exploited the weaknesses of the cordon system. His army appeared to be dispersed, but actually it only waited to take advantage of the dispersal of the enemy. Napoleon's own apparent dispersal tempted the opposing army to disperse also; but whereas Napoleon's dispersal was a prelude to concentration, the opposition's was a detachment in cordons. Napoleon's approach was equally adaptable to both the offensive and the defensive.

Even though the innovations during the French Revolution and the Napoleonic era destroyed most of the tactical characteristics of earlier warfare, some of the old strength of the defensive remained.

---

[1] Robert S. Quimby, *The Background of Napoleonic Warfare* (New York, 1957), 159–82, 255–57.

As one might expect, the new cohesiveness and articulation of the armies of Napoleon increased their offensive power in the face of the rigid and badly articulated armies of the Old Regime. Against armies similar to Napoleon's, however, the defensive also remained strong, but the course of operations was different. For example, the new flanking movements could be met by previously impossible rapid changes of front.

Some of the old approaches remained useful, or at least available, to a general who wished to employ them. In spite of the possibility of flanking movements and dispersion, armies could be kept concentrated and maintain a high level of security. But if these concentrated armies were forced to remain long in one place dependent on their lines of communication, the problems and techniques of maneuvering a unitary army would again assert themselves.

Thus, these two military traditions in grand tactics and strategy— those of the seventeenth and eighteenth centuries and those of the age of Napoleon—could influence Civil War operations. Some of both of these traditions were transmitted to Civil War generals in the works of Baron Henri Jomini, the interpreter of Napoleon and author of the *Traité des grandes opérations militaires* in 1806 and the *Précis de l'art de la guerre* in 1838. A student of the campaigns of Frederick the Great, Jomini embodied some of the pre-Napoleonic tradition in his theoretical work as well as much that was distinctively Napoleonic.

The important influence of Jomini on the American Civil War generals has often been emphasized; and frequently, both Jomini and the generals he influenced have been judged adversely. It is the pre-Napoleonic elements in his writings which are deemed to be the most influential, and it is also for this element in his writings that he has been most criticized.

The pre-Napoleonic influences in Jomini were limited to elements in his strategy and tactics. Although he acknowledged that his "prejudices" were "in favor of the good old times when the French and English guards courteously invited each other to fire first," he realistically hoped for and expected "a medium between those struggles of populations, and the ancient regular wars, made only by permanent armies." His yearning for "the good old times" was that of a professional soldier who wishes to avoid the complications of a national war. His outlook was conditioned by his experiences in Spain, where he was dismayed by the "organized assassination" of that "frightful epoch when the curates, the women, and the children organized over the whole soil of Spain, the murder of isolated soldiers."

The American Civil War did meet his expectations that a medium between struggles of people and wars of armies could be found. The Confederates were the nation in arms envisioned by Jomini. Unlike the Spanish, they did not, as he hoped they would not, wage a "war of extermination" against the invading Union forces. The Confederate government did uniform its troops and regulate "the part which populations were to take in the controversy," nor was the war "entirely out of the pale of the laws of nations . . . ." Whether or not the Civil War met Jomini's criteria with respect to military attacks upon civilians and their property is uncertain, for he is silent upon the point. He enjoined that an army living off the country should always pay for its requisitions in order to retain the good will of the local people. He did not, however, censure a politically motivated Austrian devastation of Bavaria during the war of the Austrian succession.[2]

[2] J. D. Hittle, *Jomini and His Summary of the Art of War* (Harrisburg, Pa., 1947), 52; Baron de Jomini, *Summary of the Art of War, or a New Analytical Compend of the Principal Combinations of Strategy, of Grand Tactics, and of Military Policy,* trans. Major O. F. Winship and Lieutenant E. E. McLean (New York, 1854), 41–47, 159. For a contrary view, see: David Donald, *Lincoln Reconsidered* (New York, 1956), 94–95; Stephen E. Ambrose, *Halleck: Lincoln's Chief of Staff* (Baton Rouge, 1962), 5–6. For an exploration of some additional ramifications of this reinterpretation of Jomini, see: Archer Jones, "Jomini and the American Civil War, a Reinterpretation," *Military Affairs,* XXXIV (December, 1970); Lieutenant-Général Jomini, *Histoire critique et militaire des guerres de Frederic II, Comparées au système moderne, Avec un Recueil des principes les plus importans [sic] de l'art de la guerre* (troisième édition, 3 vols.; Paris, 1818) I, 22. This is the third edition of the *Traité des grandes opérations militaires,* which includes comparisons with all of Napoleon's campaigns (the *système moderne* of the title). The reference cited can be found in the first English edition of *Treatise on Grand Military Operations or a Critical and Military History of the Wars of Frederick the Great as Contrasted with the Modern System Together with a Few of the Most Important Principles of the Art of War,* trans. Colonel S. B. Holabird (2 vols.; New York, 1865), I, 41. Since the English edition was unavailable prior to the Civil War, the author's

Jomini's last major work, *Précis de l'art de la guerre,* is the one most often cited today and probably the only one that is still read. Almost purely theoretical, it differs from his other works, which are military history. Although Jomini's *Précis* is an effort to treat all aspects of the art of war, from national policy to tactics, the author's most obvious preference for and greatest emphasis is on strategy. More than one-third of the work deals directly with that subject. The chapter entitled "Grand Tactics and Battles" is less than a third of the length of the chapter on strategy, and the grand tactics chapter itself contains many references to strategy.

Apparently this predilection for strategy is based, in part, on the difficulty of reducing the conduct of battles to the same clear and simple rules which he had developed for strategy. Principles do not seem to be possible in the presence of variations in the "precise transmission of orders, the manner in which the lieutenants of the general-in-chief shall conceive and execute them; the too great energy of some, the laxity or the defective *coup d'oeil* of others. . . ." Speaking of the proper moment for a counterattack, for example, Jomini noted that here "theory becomes difficult and uncertain, because it is found then insufficient and will never be equal to natural genius for war, nor the instructive *coup d'oeil* which experience in combats will give to a general brave and of a tried *sang-froid.*" His rule for grand tactics and battles was that the general should "judge soundly of the important point of the field of battle" and "direct his attention upon that point."

Jomini's preference for strategy because it was more suited to analysis was reinforced by his belief that it was more important than grand tactics and battles. Speaking of successful surprise attacks by one army on another, he says that these attacks are "more rare and less brilliant than great strategic combinations which assure

<hr />

translations of the French edition will be quoted. The French will be cited as Jomini, *Histoire,* and the English as Holabird, *Grand Military Operations.* Le Baron de Jomini, *Tableau analytique des principales combinaisons de la guerre, et de leur rapports avec la politique des états pour servir d'introduction au Traité des grandes opérations militaires* (Paris, 1830), was a much shorter initial version of the *Précis de l'art de la guerre* and was intended to serve as an introduction to and be read in conjunction with the *Traité des grandes opérations militaires.*

victory, thus to speak, before having fought." Also, strategy seemed to him more durable, especially since the inventions of his day seemed to forecast a "great revolution in the organization, the armament and even the tactics of armies. Strategy alone will remain with its principles which were the same under Scipios . . . and Napoleon, for they are independent of the nature of arms, or the organization of troops."[3]

In his *Précis* Jomini sought to define the essence of the Napoleonic revolution in strategy and to give rules for its application. His rules were as follow:

1. In carrying by strategic combinations the mass of the forces of an army successively upon the decisive points of a theater of war, and as much as possible upon the communications of the enemy, without endangering its own;
2. In maneuvering in such a manner as to engage this mass of the forces with fractions only of the hostile army;
3. In directing equally, on the day of the battle, by tactical maneuvers, the mass of one's forces upon the decisive point of the field of battle, or upon that of the hostile line which it would be important to overwhelm;
4. In managing so that those masses be not merely present upon the decisive point, but that they be put in action there with energy and concert, in a manner to produce a simultaneous effort.

Jomini recognized the limitations of this last statement, and, after referring his critics to Chapter XXXV of this *Traité des grandes opérations militaires*, agreed that it was "very easy to recommend the carrying one's principal force upon the decisive points, and to know how to engage them thereon; but that the art consisted precisely in recognizing these points." He thus devoted much of his *Précis* to the principles and the "developments necessary" for the "different chances of application to be comprehended."

In seeking to find the means of recognizing the decisive point, Jomini did not follow the present-day approach to analyses of the Napoleonic method—dispersion followed by concentration on the

[3] Jomini, *Summary of the Art of War*, 215, 220, 217, 228, 59: and Le General Jomini, *Histoire, critique et militaire, des guerres de la Révolution* (15 vols.; Paris, 1820–24), IX, 315. For a premonition that the increase in firepower would lead to the tank, see Jomini, *Summary of the Art of War*, 60.

enemy's weak point. True, he advocated concentration, but his approach in strategy was based on the concepts of lines of operation and the use of interior lines. A line of operation refers to the direction in which an army moves in advance or retreat. According to Jomini's concept, the employment of interior lines permitted a concentration of one's troops against a fraction of the enemy's troops. As the diagram below shows, enemy forces A, B, and C are moving on separate lines of operation. Force X, however, is on an interior line of operation: The troops are concentrated and would be able to attack either A, B, or C.

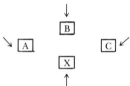

Because the enemy forces are incapable of moving rapidly, C could be defeated before forces B and A could reach it to give assistance. Force X would probably use smaller forces to delay the march of the other enemy forces to the aid of the attacked force. The same interior lines situation prevails in this arrangement:

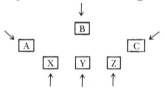

Forces X, Y, Z, on interior lines, can concentrate more rapidly than A, B, and C, and can attack one of them before the others can come to its assistance. This second arrangement is not as convenient as the first and was less likely since Jomini persistently urged concentration.

The essence of Jomini's strategy, then, is in the principle of the interior line "which an army would form to oppose several hostile masses, but to which would be given a direction such that the different corps could be drawn towards each other and their movements connected, before the enemy could possibly oppose to them a greater mass." Another principle was that of moving upon the enemy's communications, either when the enemy was dispersed, as Napoleon did in the Marengo campaign, or when the enemy was more concentrated, as in the second Mantua campaign.

The exception to Jomini's rule of interior lines occurred if there were "immense forces," so large that they "could not be made to act upon the same zone of operations," and so superior that one could "maneuver in two directions without being liable to see one of your corps overthrown by the enemy." Under these circumstances "it would be a fault to accumulate your forces on a single point, and thus deprive yourself of the advantages of your superiority, by rendering it impractical for a part of your forces to act." When operating in this way, however, "it will always be prudent to reinforce suitably the part of the army which . . . would be called upon to play the most important part," and both armies should be under "one chief who would have his headquarters with the principal army."

That Jomini's first historical work was a history and analysis of the campaigns of Frederick the Great seems to have permanently influenced his conception of tactics. Although Jomini served the French army during the Napoleonic era and wrote histories of their operations, he never seemed to shake off the influence of the unitary deployment necessary for and characteristic of the armies of Frederick's day. Jomini's armies were always united and his diagrams show no flanking movement other than the deployment of an entire army on a flank after the manner of Frederick at Leuthen. It may also be true that he applied his strategic concept of interior lines to the grand tactics of battles and for this reason felt that an army must always remain a unit with all of its parts contiguous.[4]

Jomini's tactical model was less influential than his strategic model. In his tactical exposition, Jomini also laid emphasis on the techniques of Napoleon's later campaigns. Here, the wide detached flanking movement was not as much in evidence as the push by superior numbers through a position weakened by the fire of superior artillery. In Napoleon's day, artillery could be brought close to the enemy's lines and injure the troops severely with grape and cannister. Unlike

---

[4] Jomini, *Summary of the Art of War*, 81, 115, 208.

Napoleon, Jomini disparaged field fortifications which had played such a dominant role in the slow positional warfare of Field Marshal von Daun and other eighteenth-century generals. Jomini's antipathy for their strategic method apparently applied as well to the field fortifications which they employed so extensively. Again, tactical realities would make this Jominian prescription irrelevant.

He did, however, apply his principle of masses against fractions to the battlefield, recommending that "in lines of battle too extended and cut up, the centre will be always the most essential to attack; in close lines the centre is on the contrary, the strongest point, since independently of the reserves which are found there, it will be easy to cause it to be sustained by the wings; then the decisive point will be on the contrary, upon one of the wings."[5]

As an interpreter of Napoleon, Jomini missed a good deal. His grand tactics were largely Frederician in that he seems to have permitted his passion for concentration and his study of eighteenth-century unitary armies to cause him to overlook not only the detached flanking movement but also the possibilities for maneuver inherent in the subdivided and well-articulated army of Napoleon's day. More serious, perhaps, was the impact of his effort to distill a set of rules from the campaigns of Frederick and Napoleon. The essential spirit of the Napoleonic method—dispersion and concentration upon the enemy's weak point when the opportunity was presented—was obscured in his *Précis* by his effort to define it in terms of interior lines and central position. Jomini's emphasis upon concentration obscured the necessary dispersion. His entire system of analysis and his emphasis on concentration told a general what to avoid rather than what to do; unless, of course, the enemy made some blunder which was easily discernible in terms of his rules.

Inadvertently the spirit of Jomini's *Précis* is that of "safety first." He is the pillar of "sound" strategy. Although he strove to provide the recipe for victory, he constantly spoke in terms of avoiding defeat,

[5] Quimby, *Background of Napoleonic Warfare*, 296–97; Conrad H. Lanza, *Napoleon and Modern War* (Harrisburg, Pa., 1943), maxims 17, 37, 39–45; Jomini, *Summary of the Art of War*, 169, 209.

insisting that "military science has principles that could not be violated without defeat." Illustrative of this idea is his attitude toward detached turning movements to outflank an enemy line of battle. He recognized them and their merit, but feared "movements too disconnected, in the face of the least respectable enemy." Worried about "the dangers, not only of turning maneuvers, but of every gap left in the line of battle," Jomini recommended "that by adopting in general a system of battles very compact and well connected, we will be found in condition to meet every contingency, and will leave little to chance." Emphasis on what to avoid rather than what to do seems inherent in this kind of military writing. Napoleon's maxims, for example, read much like Jomini's principles.

A study of Jomini's *Précis* could have produced a careful soldier, effective on defense, but one who missed the real spirit of Napoleon's strategy. On the other hand, a study of Jomini would not be misleading; his "bias could be corrected by anyone who followed his clear exposition. . . ." The tactics of the *Précis* were completely out of date by the middle of the nineteenth century, as Jomini had warned they would be. If a study of the *Précis* were coupled with a careful mastery of his histories of Napoleonic and French Revolutionary campaigns, the effect might be quite Napoleonic. The *Précis* abounds with references to history, and if a reader read Jomini's *Vie politique et militaire de Napoléon*, for example, he would find a quite solid and conventional narrative of Napoleon's campaigns which would well support the modern generalizations about Napoleon's strategy and tactics. Like many others of the Enlightenment's would-be Newtons of the social sciences, Jomini failed. Unsuccessful in his attempt to be the Newton of the art of war, Jomini had more success as an analytical military historian. If the student of warfare had concentrated on Jomini's *Traité de grandes opérations militaires,* he would have encountered fewer problems.

The *Traité* might be a better place to begin than the *Précis,* which presumed a familiarity with military history. He sought in his *Précis* "to prove by the history of twenty celebrated campaigns" that his fundamental principles explained all victories and defeats. Even though his twenty campaigns were chosen from the period 1701 to 1831, he apologized for having too frequently "cited the same events as examples." He had used only a few, he said, for "the convenience of readers who have not all the campaigns in their memory or in their library." Even his limited selection requires, as a minimum, a thorough mastery of all of the operations of the Seven Years' War and the wars of the French Revolution and Napoleon. Because of the frequent allusions to various campaigns and battles, none of which are described, a fruitful reading of the *Précis* would have to come after a careful study of the military history of the eighteenth century and of the Napoleonic era. It was for this reason that Jomini thought that none but the "historical form adopted in my treatise on grand military operations" would be "as clear and as strongly demonstrative for young officers. . . ." Even in his *Traité*, in which the principles were derived from a narrative of the Seven Years' War, a thorough knowledge of Napoleon's campaigns would have been, if not essential, at least of great value because of the many comparisons of the operations of Frederick and Napoleon.

The *Traité* was published more than thirty years before the *Précis,* although the *Précis* was translated into English eleven years before the *Traité*. For anyone with a modest reading knowledge of French, however, the *Traité* would have been much more influential because it contained a short and final chapter, the thirty-fifth, which summarized Jomini's principles of war. Even a student with very bad French could translate this brief last chapter. The whole *Traité* is a didactic work, using a comparative approach between the campaigns of Frederick and Napoleon to inculcate Jomini's concept of the Napoleonic or "modern" system. He intended it to teach far more of the principles of war than his history of Napoleonic operations did, and it was his principal theoretical work until the publication of the *Précis*. In American military education the *Traité* was undoubtedly the most influential of his works through the 1840's. Henry W. Halleck, at one time an instructor at West Point, wrote that the *Traité* "is considered by military critics the most important of all his works, as it embodies the main principles of the military art, with numerous illustrations drawn from the campaigns of the great captains of different ages."[6]

It thus seems likely that Civil War generals whose basic military ideas were formed before the 1850's derived what Jominian instruction they received from the *Traité*, either directly or through their instructors. A more careful consideration of this work seems desirable, in view of its potential influence on the Civil War generals.

Jomini's *Traité* was a very detailed and critical history of the Seven Years' War. It went through many editions. Soon after the close of the Napoleonic Wars, the revisions were indicated by a new title which identified the comparisons of Frederick and Napoleon or the *système moderne*. These revisions included footnote references to Napoleonic campaigns which were analogous to those discussed and, occasionally in the discussions of the campaigns, long expositions of how Napoleon might have conducted a particular operation.

The work, like his *Précis*, is analytical, seeking, in the manner of the Enlightenment to induce the principles of the art of war. Tactical and strategic principles receive nearly equal emphasis. Jomini insists that the principles which are applicable to both strategy and tactics are true for the campaigns of Frederick the Great and of Napoleon. He also discerned many differences between the wars of Frederick and of Napoleon: the change in emphasis from position to maneuver; the great increase in the speed of marching; the reduced dependence on supply lines because both dispersion and longer and more numerous marches permitted far greater emphasis on living off the country; and an end to the excessive deliberation which characterized the campaigning of the Seven Years' War. The principles of the art of war are the same, however. In Jomini's view,

---

[6] B. H. Liddell Hart, *The Ghost of Napoleon* (London, 1933), 105–18; Jomini, *Summary of the Art of War*, 29, 209, 214, 224–25, 82, 6, 141, 12–13. Lanza, *Napoleon and Modern War*. See especially maxims 2–5, 7, 11–14, 22, 34, 39, 43–45, 47, 52, 54–55, 62–65. For Napoleon's warning against separating one's force, see maxims 10, 26, and 34; for advice comparable to Jomini's, see maxims 7 and 77. H. W. Halleck, trans., *Life of Napoleon by Baron Jomini* (4 vols.; New York, 1864), 24. The University of South Carolina Library's copy of the 1818 edition of the *Traité*, dating from the days of South Carolina College, had uncut pages in it in 1967. In the margin of the thirty-fifth chapter, however, English words were written in.

a critical narrative of Frederick's operations exemplifies the proper application of the principles of which Napoleon was the master.

A few simple lessons are inculcated throughout the work. They are stated as the principles of war, and are brought together in the last chapter. The didactic effort is quite successful, because the principles are always expounded after the narrative of a campaign which illustrates them. The character and impact of the work are quite different from his *Précis*, where he sought to present the principles out of the context of military history. Compared to the *Traité*, his later work would, for one not a serious student of military history, be analogous to an exposition of physics or chemistry which was abstracted from the phenomena which the laws are intended to explain. The principal value of the *Traité*, however, is in both the history and the commentary.

His reiterated principles and the implicit and explicit lessons of his long critical narrative must have had a significant impact on his reader. His tactical expositions, largely Frederician, are for the most part limited, in their relevance, to the rigid, badly articulated linear system of Frederick's day, and to conditions in which cavalry still had a prominent place on the battlefield. The enduring tactical lesson, like the strategic, is to attack where the enemy is weak: the enemy's flank, unless he is much spread out, in which case the center would be the best point of attack. The tactical system is, however, based entirely upon the maneuvering of a united army. No breaks in line nor any detachments are to be allowed.[7]

---

[7] A summary of the *Traité* was included in the West Point text [S. F. Gay de Vernon], *A Treatise on the Science of War and Fortification Composed for the Use of the Imperial Polytechnick School and Military Schools; and Translated for the War Department for the Use of the Military Academy of the United States: To Which Is Added a Summary of the Principles and Maxims of Grand Tactics and Operations*, John Michael O'Connor, trans. and ed. (2 vols. and vol. of plates and maps; New York, 1817), II, 387–490. The continuing influence of the *Traité* is supported by the publication in Columbia, South Carolina in 1864 of Frank Schaller, trans., *The Spirit of Military Institutions by Marshal Marmont . . . with a New Version of General Jomini's Celebrated Thirty-fifth Chapter of Part I, of Treatise on Grand Military Operations*. The second edition, 1811–16, was entitled *Traité des Grandes Opérations Militaire, contenant l'histoire critique des campagnes de Frédéric II, comparée à celles de l'empereur Napoléon . . . .* The third edition was the *Histoire* cited earlier. The fourth edition of 1851 returned to the

All of the strategic lessons are concerned with the best means of exploiting the weaknesses of the cordon system, particularly favored by the Austrians. Jomini constantly preached the virtue of rapid concentration and the value of a central position from which the bulk of one's forces could attack one of the enemy's cordoned detachments. The same principle is found in grand strategy, using the concept of lines of operation. A single line, i.e. a single army, is better than a double line. This is the concept later embodied in his *Précis.*

Jomini's view of strategy and the lessons which are constantly emphasized in his *Traité* are well illustrated by three operations, one actual and two hypothetical. They are significant because they give concrete illustrations of the application of his principle of interior lines and are essentially models which his pupils might have sought to apply.

Jomini was very critical of Frederick, feeling that he "gave little impulse to the art of war. . . ." Frederick did not understand lines of operations, but on one occasion his campaigns fully exemplified Jomini's principles. The "brilliant results" of Frederick's campaign of 1758 proved "better than all systematic reasoning, the advantage of interior maneuver lines over exterior ones."

Most of Frederick's operations in the Seven Years' War consisted of defending Brandenburg, Silesia, and Saxony. The Austrians, based in Bohemia, with the assistance of forces in South Germany raised by some of the smaller German states, sought to invade Saxony and Silesia. The Russians, based in Poland, menaced Brandenburg and, later, Silesia as well. A small and remarkably inactive Swedish detachment on the Pommeranian coast required a small Prussian detachment to watch it.

After beginning the year 1758 with an unsuccessful invasion of Moravia and a retreat through Bohemia, Frederick marched north with a portion of his forces to hold the Russians in check. Having

---

Traité form of title, retaining the *comparées au système moderne* comparison. Jomini, *Histoire,* III, 346, I, 230–31, II, 276; Holabird, *Grand Military Operations,* II, 449, I, 201–202, II, 43.

defeated the Russian General Fermor at Zorndorf, he marched twenty-two miles a day with a part of these forces to Saxony and raised the siege of Dresden. Surprised and defeated by the Austrians in Saxony, he nevertheless was able to lead a portion of his forces around their flank into Silesia and raise the siege of Neisse. In spite of having sent to Saxony most of his forces which had been opposing the Russians, Dresden was again about to fall to the Austrians. The last act of the campaign was a return march by the king from Silesia to Saxony, again saving Dresden.

Frederick's marches were essentially a series of concentrations of forces at each threatened point, an example of Jomini's principle of "carrying by strategic combinations the mass of the forces of an army successively upon the decisive points of a theatre of war." And the meaning of "successively" is quite clear in the context of these operations of Frederick. The decisive points were not, in this case, the weakest points but those where Frederick's enemies were about to lop off parts of his territory. Since the king's enemies were on an outer ring around Prussia and Saxony, Frederick, in most instances, had shorter marches than his opponents, should they have wished to make corresponding moves. He was aided immensely by the lack of coordination among the forces of the coalition opposing him and by the excessive deliberation and caution of the Austrian commander, Field Marshal von Daun.

On the other hand, Frederick's operations in the next year, 1759, were strongly censured by Jomini. "By his apathy at the opening of the campaign of 1759, he made an extraordinary error" in not taking advantage of the fact that the Russian army was only active for about half of the year. It wintered in Poland and, because of the distance and bad condition of Polish roads, could not menace Brandenburg before June. It had to leave the scene of operations early in the fall because of its long march back to its winter quarters. Being between the Russians and the Austrians, Frederick *"not only possessed the immense advantage of an interior line of operations against two isolated lines at enormous distances; but even the certainty that one of these armies would be paralyzed for half of the year. . . .* What wouldn't Napoleon have accomplished with the advantageous position of Frederick? How different would the results have been if Napoleon's principles had been applied to that position? Look at his campaigns."

Jomini's recommendation for "applying the system of Napoleon to the position of Frederick in 1759," was to concentrate about 80 percent of all Prussian forces in Silesia in the early spring. He estimated that Frederick could have completed this concentration in eight days and that it would have sacrificed to the enemy only temporary success in Pommerania and Saxony. Jomini then offered two alternative operations against the Austrians in Bohemia. One involved a feint with light troops against Glatz while the main Prussian army passed around Daun's left, separating him from his detachments in western Bohemia. The other would have been to penetrate Bohemia via Glatz, passing around Daun's right. In either case, the Austrians would have had either to fight superior numbers to retain their communications or to make a precipitate retreat from Bohemia.[8]

Almost all of Jomini's recommendations for applications of the Napoleonic system have to do with Frederick's situation. Apparently Jomini felt that Frederick's enemies, with their vastly superior forces, really had no legitimate problem which required sophisticated military solutions, since "nothing more was needed to annihilate Frederick than a little coordinated and simultaneous action and a commander above mediocrity." In one instance Jomini offered a plan in which he would "put Napoleon in the place of Daun." He made this substitution in 1761 when the Austrians were delaying their advance until June, when the Russian army would at last be in the theater of operations and able to cooperate.

Although Jomini thought that the idea for a concerted Austro-Russian advance against Silesia was a good one, he deplored the loss

[8]Jomini, *Histoire,* III, 121, II, 221–22, 447–553 (Italics are Jomini's); Holabird, *Grand Military Operations,* II, 278, I, 442–43, II, 170–74. Napoleon in his comments on Frederick's campaign of 1759, advocated the same operations that Jomini did. Napoleon felt that it would have forced Daun to fight a battle, and "disabled him from attempting anything during the remainder of the campaign." *Memoirs of the History of France during the Reign of Napoleon Dictated by the Emperor at St. Helena and Published from the Original Manuscripts Corrected by Himself* (7 vols.; London, 1823–24), VII, 258 (dictated to Count de Montolon).

of time. He further considered that Silesia with its eight fortresses was a poor place to attack Frederick compared to Saxony, where the king then had only one strong point. Feeling that the Austrians had missed a good chance, Jomini recommended an invasion of Saxony rather than Silesia to take place in the spring before the Russians arrived. He advocated an Austrian concentration and a movement around Frederick's left. Had they "attacked Frederick simultaneously, and driven him steadily to the left, he would have been cut off from all of his resources; the loss of a battle would have ruined him." This proposed campaign illustrates the territorial objective in Jomini's thinking since he emphasizes the advantages of invading Brandenburg "for the purpose of destroying the resources of the King." Although Jomini's strategy was directed at the defeat of the enemy army by a combination of battle and maneuver, success would result, not in the destruction of the enemy army, but in what he called "a war of invasion," a deep and rapid penetration of enemy territory.

Frederick's enemies failed to appreciate the opportunities presented by a war of invasion which was "especially advantageous when directed against a small country, whose principal resources are in the theatre of operations itself. . . ." Frederick's enemies "failed to understand this truth, for otherwise they would have needed only one campaign." Frederick's objective was to defend his territory and his Saxon conquest, because these territories would provide the resources to keep up his strength and to continue the war until his enemies were divided or exhausted. The objective, for Frederick's enemies, would have been to cripple his warmaking potential by occupying his territory. Battles are rarely thought of as annihilating the enemy. At most they are envisioned as temporarily disabling the enemy or his operations on a particular front.[9]

The three campaigns discussed here present Jomini at his best as an interpreter of Napoleonic strategy. In grand strategy Jomini's

---

[9] Jomini, *Histoire*, III, 232–37, III, 338–39 (Jomini's words are *un peu d'ensemble*), III, 236, II, 460; Holabird, *Grand Military Operations*, II, 364–67, II, 444, II, 336, II, 179. See also: Jomini, *Histoire*, III, 120–27, 147–48; Holabird, *Grand Military Operations*, II, 278–82.

concept of lines of operation works well to explain the Napoleonic approach. Jomini vividly illustrates the meaning of his concepts of interior lines, of concentration, and of striking the enemy at his weak point. He also, implicitly, shows that battles are intimately related to the maneuvers which precede them or which will result from a victory.

It is not difficult to see the potential impact of this work on Civil War leaders. Both Prussia and the Confederacy were beset on several fronts by separate and not always well-coordinated armies. These similarities would make it difficult for a Confederate thoroughly familiar with these campaigns not to recognize the analogies. The lessons for the Union are not so explicit, but certainly they are there, particularly in Jomini's constant pleas for a concert of action among the allied armies. Furthermore, on the strategic level, there was little difference between the Napoleonic method and the Jominian prescription as long as there was more than one theater of operations.

For the army commander as well as the grand strategist, the *Traité* offered something of value. A good deal of the modern approach to Napoleon is not only embodied in the narrative and commentary of the *Traité*, but is also summarized in the last chapter. In this chapter, "Exposition of General Principles," he laid down a number of measures. One of them, which does not appear in the *Précis*, embodies much of the Napoleonic method. He enjoins us to "direct our movements against the most advantageous weak point. The choice of the weak point depends on the position of the enemy." There was no doubt, in the thirty-fifth chapter, that the decisive point was the enemy's weak point, for he reiterated that "the art of war consists in concerting a superior effort of a mass against the weak point."

In his *Précis* Jomini had devoted chapters to the policy of war and to the problems of adapting military means to political objectives, pointing out that differing military strategies and objectives would be required for various political goals. In his discussion of the appropriate measures for the allies against Frederick he has made ¶ an application of this in recommending a war of invasion as the means for attaining the allied objectives.

This recommendation also illustrates Jomini's conception of the difference between the eighteenth-century strategy of Daun and that of Napoleon. Whereas Daun had given his attention to places and had been more concerned with advantageously avoiding the enemy army than with meeting it under favorable circumstances, the orientation in Jomini's concept of operations was toward the enemy army itself. Although the conquest of territory is the result, he wished to maneuver so as to concentrate superior numbers against a weaker force of the enemy army, defeating it by a combination of maneuver and battle. By rapid concentration of strength against weakness, by aiming at the enemy's communications, by threatening envelopment, and by thus forcing disastrous retreat or battle under unfavorable circumstances, the deep and permanent penetration of the war of invasion could be obtained.

Although Jomini dwelt little on the ultimate objective of the war of invasion, its political potential was noted in his *Précis* when he observed that it could capture "the hostile capital" or "a military province, the loss of which could determine the enemy to peace." In his *Traité des grandes opérations militaires* he expanded somewhat on the objectives of his strategy. The diplomatic importance of territory is assumed. Its military importance is implicit, though, for emphasis, he reiterates that for Frederick the Great the occupation of "the heart of his states" would have "left him no resources for raising men and money." At the close of the Seven Years' War, Jomini emphasized that Frederick's loss of Upper Silesia, Saxony, and Pommerania "left the King no means of recruiting his army which daily melted away. . . ." Implicit in his *Traité* is the assumption that the loss of territory will ultimately destroy the enemy's army by destroying the resources for its maintenance and support. This approach has been called by J. F. C. Fuller the strategy of exhaustion, and defined as the policy of denying "to the enemy what may be called his 'vital area of operations'—that part of his country essential to the maintenance of his forces. . . ." Acquisition of this area has been "even more important than winning victories in the field because it knocked the bottom out of the enemy's fighting power."

The best means of conquering territory, however, was that of

Napoleon, "to dislocate and to ruin the hostile army; certain that states and provinces fall of themselves, when they have no longer organized forces for covering them." Although Jomini did not advocate this as the only method nor rule out reliance on maneuver, implicit in his histories is the assumption that little territory could be gained unless the enemy's army was first defeated, though not necessarily destroyed.[10]

Why should Jomini take the approach of the strategy of exhaustion rather than aim at the strategy of annihilation, the superior efficacy of which he acknowledged? The reason may have been that he had an implicit skepticism about the possibility of achieving the latter. This idea is well indicated by his comments on some prospective battles between Frederick and Daun in his hypothetical campaign in which he had "put Napoleon in the place of Daun." He points out that, if Daun had been unsuccessful in his invasion of Saxony and "had lost one battle," he could have rallied at Dresden and renewed his invasion in eight days. A second defeat would have involved retreating again to Dresden or even to Bohemia, but because of the casualties, "two battles won by the king would have destroyed his own army, without having acquired an inch of territory on that line of operations."

It is clear that Jomini's *Traité* lacked several of the major weaknesses of the *Précis*. The actual and hypothetical historical illustrations put flesh on the bones of the theory and the key Napoleonic concept of the weak point as the decisive point received adequate emphasis and ample illustration. The war of invasion, only briefly alluded to in the *Précis*, was explained and illustrated, with the strategy of exhaustion indicated as the ultimate sanction of the war of invasion,

[10] Jomini, *Histoire*, III, 100, 148, 278, 336, 358; Holabird, *Grand Military Operations*, II, 449, 457, 259, 297, 398. See also: Jomini, *Histoire*, II, 220–21, 344; Holabird, *Grand Military Operations*, I, 442, II, 92; J. F. C. Fuller, *The Second World War, 1939–1945* (New York, 1949), 35. See also Gordon A. Craig, "Delbruck: The Military Historian," in Edward Meade Earle (ed.), *Makers of Modern Strategy* (Princeton, 1952), 273–82. For application to the Civil War, see: Charles P. Roland, "The Generalship of Robert E. Lee," in Grady McWhiney (ed.), *Grant, Lee, Lincoln and the Radicals: Essays in Civil War Leadership* (New York, 1964), 24; T. Harry Williams, *McClellan, Sherman, and Grant* (New Brunswick, 1962), 68–72; Archer Jones, *Confederate Strategy from Shiloh to Vicksburg* (Baton Rouge, 1961), 14–15, 20–22.

should its political impact be inadequate to secure victory. The utility in grand strategy of Jomini's concept of interior lines was frequently and graphically illustrated.

Nevertheless, for an army commander the *Traité* has limited use. Jomini's rules really constitute only an indictment of the cordon system popular with Austrian generals in the eighteenth century and give rules on how to exploit its weaknesses. What happens if the enemy is not so obliging as to divide his forces *en cordon?* Only rarely does Jomini suggest a need or a means to induce the enemy to make the fundamental mistake upon which his system of offense is based. In other words, he has nothing to say about how to create conditions favorable for concentrating against the enemy's weak point. In one of his rare allusions to this problem, he noted that "one of the most efficacious means of applying the general principle which we have pointed out is to make the enemy commit mistakes in terms of the principle." By means of a few bodies of light troops, the enemy may be made so uneasy on "several important points of his communication," that "he will oppose them with numerous divisions, and parcel out his masses."

Thus, as the Napoleonic tradition is interpreted by Jomini, one of his main lessons is to show how one exploits the weaknesses of the cordon system while avoiding its pitfalls. Jomini's advocacy of concentration omits Napoleon's dispersion which necessarily precedes it. His emphasis in his *Précis* on the decisive point omits the means of determining or creating it; and his insistence upon a single objective point obscures the essential Napoleonic feature of concentration upon the weak point as revealed by enemy dispositions or maneuvers. Even though the *Traité* identifies the decisive point, Jomini provides really no means for creating a weak point. This omission and his constant emphasis on concentration without the preliminary dispersion, would prepare army commanders who could avoid defeat but who might well be deprived of the means for achieving victory. The *Traité*, then, reveals much but not all of Napoleon, and the *Précis* obscured some of Jomini and much of Napoleon.

Yet on the grand strategic level the differences between Jomini and Napoleon would be minimal as long as there was more than one theater of operations. Several theaters would assure as many lines of operations, thus mitigating Jomini's failure to indicate means of inducing the enemy to divide his forces.

Because of the difference between Napoleon as revealed in a study of his campaigns and Jomini's interpretation of him and because of the difference between Jomini's *Précis* and his *Traité,* the impact of the military developments of the preceding century were bound to differ among different Civil War leaders. The differences resulted from their temperament as well as from their command of the French language and the depth and breadth of their study of military history and of the literature of the art of war. Nor can one overlook the traditions, the education, and the influences within their own army which must have been influential along with their own military experience before and during the Civil War. Without a staff college to distill this inheritance into an official army doctrine of strategy and operations, the variety in the impact of this inheritance was assured. The one source of uniformity was the curriculum of the United States Military Academy at West Point and the influence of Dennis Hart Mahan.

Modeled on the *École polytechnique,* the West Point curriculum stressed engineering. Most of the military science was concerned with small unit tactics, although strategy was also taught. Dennis Hart Mahan, professor of engineering and the art of war, 1830–1871, was a dominant and influential teacher. He had been educated at West Point himself and also studied extensively abroad, particularly in France. Mahan's teachings combined an emphasis on the value of fortifications and an insistence on celerity in military operations. Mahan, the founder of the Academy's Napoleon Club, also considered military history important. In view of the slight attention given to strategy in the curriculum, it is doubtful that Mahan's teachings in that area had as much influence as his concern with fortifications, an emphasis which correlated well with the engineering orientation of the curriculum. His teaching that the "spade, implementing the terrain, went hand in hand with rifle and bayonet," must certainly have made an impression in such an engineering oriented environment.[11]

It is clear, therefore, that the West Point curriculum did not provide sufficient emphasis on strategy and grand tactics to imbue its graduates with the operational principles of either Jomini or Napoleon. Any fundamental understanding of these ideas would, of necessity, have to come through individual study. Neither the environment and concerns of the army, the conditions of service, nor the availability of suitable libraries were really conducive to this further study. Yet some officers engaged in this study and, in rare cases, revealed its influence in their writings. Two such officers who held responsible Civil War positions, H. W. Halleck and P. G. T. Beauregard, wrote on the art of war. They had similar opportunities to study military science. French was Beauregard's native tongue, and Halleck had taught French at West Point and had traveled for a half year in Europe. Graduating from West Point within one year of each other, Beauregard and Halleck were second and third, respectively, in their

---

[11] Jomini, *Histoire*, III, 233, 235, 350–51; Holabird, *Grand Military Operations*, II, 364, 366, 452. See, however, Rudolf von Caemmerer, *The Development of Strategical Science in the 19th Century*, trans. Karl von Donat (London, 1905), 28–29. Caemmerer feels that "annihilation of the hostile Army in battle and pursuit is the only guiding star for all of his military thinking." With respect to this principle, he equates Napoleon, Jomini, and Clausewitz. See 88, 109, also 273–74. Caemmerer is certainly correct in the sense that the enemy's army was always the objective in Jomini's operations, and Caemmerer is implicitly contrasting him with the territorial system of his predecessor, Bulow. On the other hand, Jomini's historical works convey skepticism that complete annihilation of the enemy army will be achieved. As a military historian, Jomini was well aware of how rare and difficult such an annihilation was, and he may, in his exposition of the merits of the strategy of exhaustion, have been proposing an alternative.

Jomini's strategy is certainly not geographical in the sense of Bulow's and others' in the Daun tradition. Rather he seems to be arguing that even if annihilation is not possible, the enemy army must be aimed at, and this will be definitely more fruitful than a policy of securing and consolidating small territorial gains. He seems to be trying to show why an invasion, made possible by the defeat of the enemy's army, will be decisive, even against so obstinate an opponent as Frederick. Jomini, *Histoire*, III, 350–51; Holabird, *Grand Military Operations*, II, 452; R. Ernest Dupuy, *Men of West Point: The First 150 Years of the United States Military Academy* (New York, 1951), 12–24. Professors J. M. Morrison and T. E. Griess of West Point indicate that only eleven clock hours were devoted to strategy. The Gay de Vernon work with it's 100-page condensation of the *Traité* was dropped in 1832. The *Précis* was not used until 1860.

classes. Both men were commissioned in the corps of engineers.

Halleck's *Elements of Military Art and Science* was heavily indebted to Jomini's *Précis*. The kind of influence exerted can be best appreciated by noting Halleck's injunction that the "first and most important rule in offensive war is, to keep your forces as much concentrated as possible." He went on to point out that this concentration "will not only prevent misfortune, but secure victory,—since by its necessary operation, you possess the power of throwing your whole force upon any exposed point of your enemy's position." Halleck seems to have been influenced also by the writings of the Archduke Charles. In the bibliography for his chapter on strategy, Halleck lists the archduke's *Principes de la stratégie*, "a work of great merit," ahead of Jomini's *Précis*. Perhaps because Halleck found the "technical terms" in the Archduke Charles's work to be "very loosely employed," he chose to use as a model Jomini's chapter on strategy. This chapter, he noted, "embodies the principles of this branch of the art."

There is, thus, strong reason to believe that Halleck's reading of Jomini's *Précis* was conditioned by his study of the French translations of the writings of the archduke. Halleck refers several times to the archduke's campaigns as well as citing him as an authority. The Archduke Charles, an able general and worthy opponent of Napoleon, was an entirely different soldier with his pen. His writings were expositions of the Field Marshal von Daun school of the slow eighteenth-century positional warfare in which he had been trained as a youth. Perhaps it was the archduke's geographically oriented strategy, with its emphasis on security and the value of strategic positions, which made his strategy so congenial to Halleck, a specialist in and proponent of fortifications. On the other hand, Jomini's preference for a war of movement and his feeling that fortifications had but limited value might have influenced Halleck to depart from Jomini. Instead of Jomini, Halleck quoted the Archduke Charles. " 'Possession of strategic points,' says the archduke, 'is decisive in military operations; and the most efficacious means should, therefore, be employed to defend points whose preservation is the country's safeguard. This object is accomplished by fortifications.' " Halleck went on to point out, again quoting the archduke, that during the

Revolution, France "sustained herself against all Europe; *and this was because her government, since the reign of Louis XIII, had continually labored to put her frontiers into a defensive condition agreeably to the principles of strategy;* starting from such a system for a basis, she subdued every country on the continent that was not thus fortified and this reason alone will explain how her generals sometimes succeeded in destroying an army, and even an entire state, merely by a strategic success."[12] Thus Halleck's passion for fortification may

[12] H. Wager Halleck, *Elements of Military Art and Science; or, Course of Instruction in Strategy, Fortifications, Tactics of Battles, etc.; Embracing the Duties of Staff, Infantry, Cavalry, and Engineers* (New York, 1846), 40, 59, 74, 77. For his panegyric on fortifications, see *ibid.*, 78–87. For the character of Archduke Charles's writings, see Rudolph von Caemmerer, *The Development of Strategical Science in the 19th Century,* 56–71. Caemmerer feels that the archduke's theories had their origin in Daun's headquarters. Archduke Charles, *Principes de la stratégie, developpés par la relation de la campagne de 1796 en Allemagne* (3 vols.; Paris, 1818), is the edition cited by Halleck. Its translation was overseen by Jomini, and the introduction and notes are his. There was something of a vogue for Archduke Charles about the time Halleck wrote his *Military Art and Science.* At least five biographies or other works about him appeared between 1840 and 1860.
   Jomini, 30–31, n. 1, objected to the archduke's emphasis on strategic points, defined geographically, insisting that operations "ought above all to be directed against the organized forces of the enemy," that "les points géographiques" will fall "only after the disorganization and destruction of the enemy's means of defense. It was the neglect of these truths that has often led to wars of provinces, rivers, or places and has made wars indecisive."
   Halleck's own operations after Corinth are at variance with his Jomini-inspired writings. An advocate of concentration, he dispersed after Corinth. His great deliberation and careful entrenchment on his advance to Corinth are reminiscent of Field Marshal von Daun. This action, together with his security-mindedness, his eighteenth-century desire to avoid battles, his deployment *en cordon,* and his concern to repair railroads and secure strategic points, all strongly suggest that the writings of Archduke Charles had been the determining influence on Halleck as a field commander.
   Mr. Ambrose, in his *Halleck,* 46–57, feels that the influence of Jomini was decisive in Halleck's conduct. The hypothesis that it was the influence of Archduke Charles has the merit of explaining Halleck's addiction to a cordon approach, and, when he left Buell and Grant with separate armies, his violation of Jomini's rule against two separate armies (or lines of operation) on the same frontier. All of the rules for Halleck's elaborate consolidation after his capture of Corinth are laid down in the section on the base of operation in the *Principes de la stratégie,* 20–30. The base, a series of well-defined, interconnected points perpendicular to the line of operations, should, according to the archduke, have a breadth proportional to the depth of the army's advance. After an advance has been made, it is desirable to develop a new base. It should be established "so that it presents a series of points, having good communications with each other as well as with the original base." The italics were supplied by Halleck. Jomini took strong exception to this statement, saying

have led him, unconsciously perhaps, to embrace a strategic system at variance with that of Jomini, because, in part, it gave a prominent place to the value of fortifications.

Beauregard's *Principles and Maxims of the Art of War,* published as a guide for his officers during the war, was briefer and quite different from Halleck's earlier work. He began by giving his version of Jomini's principles:

> The whole science of war may be briefly defined as the art of placing in the right position, at the right time, a mass of troops greater than your enemy can there oppose to you.
>
> PRINCIPLE NO. 1—*To place masses of your army in contact with fractions of your enemy.*
> PRINCIPLE NO. 2—*To operate as much as possible on the communications of your enemy without exposing your own.*
> PRINCIPLE NO. 3—*To operate always on interior lines (or shorter ones in point of time).*

The differences between these principles and those in Jomini's *Précis* are interesting and perhaps significant. No mention is made of a decisive point: all of the emphasis is on being stronger than the enemy. The word *concentration* is not used and dispersion of forces is envisaged. Although Beauregard urges, for example, that you should "prevent your enemy from bringing the mass of his forces in contact with fractions of your own, or large fractions against small ones," concentration is not enjoined as it is in Halleck's work. The main body of Beauregard's short treatise is a source of this difference. The treatise is composed of thirty-four maxims. The substance as well as the form is Napoleonic; in fact, some of Napoleon's maxims are quoted verbatim. Selection seems to have been made according to those which were valid for 1863 and which were relevant to the duties of officers in his department.

As in the case of Halleck, the influence of Mahan and the West

---

that although "the utility of well fortified strategic points cannot be contested, can it really be said that France triumphed for twenty years only because she had fortresses and her enemies lacked them?" He emphasized that the "best fortresses are patriotism, belief in the established order, governmental vigor, and national unity in support of the government." Archduke Charles, *Principes de la stratégie,* 45–47, 46, *n.* 1.

Point curriculum is exhibited in an emphasis on fortifications. Some additions were also made to Napoleon. For example, in "Maxim 18,—*A position cannot be too strong; lose no opportunity of strengthening it by means of field fortifications.*" But even at a time when Beauregard was commanding a coastal department whose entire *raison d'etre* was the defense of key ports with fortifications as a principal means of defense, the Jominian or Napoleonic influence seemed to predominate. There is no hint of the Archduke Charles, of strategic points, nor of defensive cordons. A war of movement is still envisioned.[13]

Neither Halleck nor Beauregard emerged from their study of the art of war as disciples of Jomini. Halleck had adopted from the Archduke Charles much that was antithetical to Jomini whereas Beauregard's Jominian doctrine was heavily influenced by the writings of Napoleon. From these two cases it is obviously impossible to generalize the impact of either West Point training or individual study. Yet the two individuals themselves are of immense importance in their respective armies. After opposing one another at Corinth in the late spring of 1862, each exerted great influence on the strategy of the war. Halleck, after first ordering operations in the West which seem directed toward establishing a base according to the principles of the archduke, then assumed a position of great formal authority over operations when he began a tenure of nearly two years as Union general in chief. Beauregard, on the other hand, was soon relieved of his western command but assumed a position of considerable informal influence. From his new assignment in Charleston he worked tirelessly and with some effect to influence the course of strategy of the war.

Confederate strategy would also strongly reflect the impact of another West Point graduate, Robert E. Lee, the South's most successful field commander and President Davis' most trusted adviser.

---

[13] P. G. T. Beauregard, *Principles and Maxims of the Art of War—Outpost Service; General Instructions for Battles; Reviews* (Charleston, 1863), 3–4, 7, *passim*. This is reprinted in P. G. T. Beauregard, *A Commentary on the Campaign and Battle of Manassas. . . .* (New York, 1891). There is a third edition, published in New Orleans in 1890. See also Lanza, *Napoleon and Modern War*, XIII, *passim*.

II
Robert E. Lee
and Confederate Strategy

No instance during the Civil War better exemplifies the application of Napoleonic and Jominian concepts than Confederate operations on the Virginia front in 1861 and 1862. This was true even though it is uncertain whether many of the participants were explicitly guided by a knowledge of Napoleonic and Jominian concepts.

Initially both combatants had used two lines of operations. In the summer of 1861 General Joseph E. Johnston's Army of the Shenandoah defended the Virginia-Maryland sector of the Appalachian Valley against a Union force led by General Robert Patterson. East of the Blue Ridge, General P. G. T. Beauregard's Army of the Potomac opposed an advance from Washington by the troops of General Irvin McDowell's Department of Northeastern Virginia.

An advance in July by McDowell, unaccompanied by any corresponding move by Patterson, inspired Jefferson Davis to order a concentration on Beauregard's front against McDowell. Patterson's inertia, together with the increased mobility made possible by rail communication, enabled Johnston to unite successfully with Beauregard. McDowell's defeat at First Manassas had strategic parallels in the campaigns of Frederick and Napoleon.

This first Virginia campaign established a pattern for the Confederate Army of Northern Virginia. In 1862 operations under Generals Robert E. Lee and Thomas Jackson also involved concentration on interior lines. In the Shenandoah Valley campaign, Jackson operated in a style reminiscent of both Frederick and Napoleon as he concentrated successively against the "Austrian" advances of Generals John C. Fremont and Nathaniel Banks. When Lee assumed command in Virginia in June, 1862, he collected reinforcements from the North Carolina department, and then used the railroad to bring Jackson from his line of operations in the Shenandoah Valley, in order to complete his concentration at Richmond against General George B. McClellan. This pattern of rail usage to realize Jominian interior lines was as clear in the Seven Days' campaign as it had been at First Manassas. In addition, the Napoleonic flavor of dispersion and concentration was clearly present, for Jackson's independent valley operations were most effective as both a distraction and a prelude to concentration. Lee most effectively and quite consciously exploited the cordon approach of his opponent.

The Seven Days' campaign of June–July, 1862, like most of Lee's later battles, began with a detached flanking move which may reflect the influences both of Napoleon and of the Mexican War. At First Manassas, Beauregard had recommended that Johnston join him, not for the purpose of reinforcement, but to attack McDowell on the flank. Johnston had rejected this suggestion because he distrusted the capabilities of his green troops to execute such a maneuver. But Lee incorporated this Napoleonic maneuver into his plan for the Seven Days', though even the brilliant Jackson and his seasoned troops were unable to execute it successfully.

After halting McClellan's advance on the eastern or Peninsula line of Federal operations, Lee promptly concentrated against the threat developing from General John Pope's Army of Virginia in the area north and northwest of Richmond. Before the Federals could complete a junction of forces on Pope's line of operations, Lee had concentrated against the hapless Pope and again used the detached flanking maneuver. Thus the strategy of the Seven Days' and Second Manassas were similar to that of First Manassas and Jackson's valley campaign. All resembled Frederick's campaigns in 1757 and 1758 and Napoleon's defense of his Mantua siege. They also demonstrated how well Jomini's concept of interior and exterior lines could generalize the Napoleonic method. Lee's use of Jackson in the Shenandoah Valley, however, transcended Jomini. Lee's strategy included the vital element absent from Jomini—distraction to induce enemy dispersal, the essential prelude to concentration. Jomini had omitted this means to induce an enemy dispersion; Lee, like Napoleon, included it.

Despite such successes, Lee's operations in Virginia need further examination. His penchant for the offensive, at least until the spring of 1864, raises some questions. Clearly Lee's strategy was to protect Richmond and cover his logistical base in Virginia. Yet Lee's frequent offensive thrusts and his almost invariable assumption of the offensive in battle suggest that he believed a stalemate could be avoided by the annihilation of the enemy army.

If Lee was pursuing the strategy of annihilation, he was disappointed. Moreover, his operations were expensive in terms of manpower. Lee's losses in the Seven Days' exceeded the number of effectives in the Army of Tennessee the previous autumn. In the Gettysburg campaign, Lee lost more men in his avowed purpose to prevent an advance on Richmond than Braxton Bragg had in his Army of Tennessee in October of 1862. At Chancellorsville, Lee's casualties almost equaled those of the combined Confederate surrenders of Forts Henry and Donelson. In fact, during his first four months as commander of the Army of Northern Virginia, June–September, 1862, Lee lost almost fifty thousand troops. Such a number far exceeded the total troop strength of the Army of Tennessee in the western theater during the same time span. Considering the South's manpower shortage and basic need for a strategic defensive posture, Lee's tactical losses seem excessive.[1]

If these losses are excessive, in spite of the great tactical and strategic success that accompanied them, it is at least in part because they are judged in the context of the Confederate war effort as a whole. Lee's position in this overall war picture, particularly his role as a strategist, needs careful reexamination. What was Lee's influence in general Confederate strategy, his recommendations for coordinating the South's strategic lines of operations?

Lee actually supplied little general strategic guidance for the South. He either had no unified view of grand strategy or else chose to remain silent on the subject. Two reasons, both debatable, have been

---

[1] Louis H. Manarin, "Lee in Command: Strategical and Tactical Policies" (Ph.D. dissertation, Duke University, 1965), 574; T. Harry Williams, "The Military Leadership of North and South," in David Donald (ed.), *Why the North Won the Civil War* (New York, 1962), 47; J. F. C. Fuller, *Grant and Lee: A Study in Personality and Generalship* (Bloomington, Ill., 1957), 260–65, 286–87.

offered for Lee's not taking a more apparent interest in general war policy. It has been suggested that his rightful concern was the Army of Northern Virginia, thus allowing him neither the time nor the right to suggest policy. Yet many other commanders found such opportunity. Frequently General P. G. T. Beauregard submitted overall strategic plans. Generals Joseph E. Johnston and James Longstreet suggested policies in 1863 and 1864. Even lesser known officers, such as Generals Dabney Maury and Leonidas Polk attempted to construct strategic plans for the entire southern effort. Lee, however, leading the South's largest army and possessing probably more influence than most on the civil authorities, never approached the subject of strategy in this manner. He often suggested specific measures rather than present plans.[2]

A more probable reason given for Lee's approach was that he did not have the power to suggest overall war strategy. Frequently Lee scholars have speculated on what he might have done had he enjoyed genuine authority. The inference is always that he lacked authority to aid the entire Confederate effort in both the eastern or western theaters. These scholars suggest that when Lee was official

---

[2] Charles P. Roland, "The Generalship of Robert E. Lee," in Grady McWhiney (ed.), *Grant, Lee, Lincoln and the Radicals: Essays on Civil War Leadership* (New York, 1964), 35; Otto Eisenschiml, *The Hidden Face of the Civil War* (Indianapolis, 1961), 216. For evidence of other general strategic plans, see Beauregard to Bragg, October 7, 1863, and Beauregard to Pierre Soulé, December 8, 1863, both in P. G. T. Beauregard Papers, Confederate Records, Record Group 109, National Archives; Beauregard to Bragg, September 2, 1862, July 7, 1863, in Braxton Bragg Papers, Western Reserve Historical Society; Beauregard to Louis Wigfall, May 16, 1863, in Wigfall Family Papers, Library of Congress; *The War of the Rebellion: A Compilation of the Official Records of the Union and Confederate Armies* (Washington, D.C. 1880–1901), Ser. I, Vol. XIV, 955. (Hereafter cited as *Official Records,* with all references to Ser. I). By December, 1863, Beauregard had presented six general plans to the government; see *Official Records,* XXXI, Pt. 3, p. 812. See also Polk to Hardee, July 30, 1863, in Leonidas Polk Papers, University of the South Library; Polk to Jefferson Davis, August 9, 1863, in Leonidas Polk Papers, Duke University Library; Polk to Davis, July 26, 1863, in *Official Records,* XXIII, Pt. 2, p. 932; James Seddon to James Longstreet, May 3, 1875, in James Longstreet Papers, Emory University Library; Archer Jones, *Confederate Strategy from Shiloh to Vicksburg* (Baton Rouge, 1961), 206–10; Longstreet to Thomas Jordan, March 27, 1864, Longstreet to Beauregard, March 15, 1864, in *Official Records,* XXII, Pt. 3, pp. 627, 679; H. J. Eckenrode and Bryan Conrad, *James Longstreet, Lee's Warhorse* (Chapel Hill, 1936), 285–87; Longstreet to Lee, September 5, 1863, in *Official Records,* XIX, Pt. 2, p. 699.

adviser to Davis in the spring of 1862, he lacked real power; that his position as army commander further dimmed his chances of any broad direction; and that when in 1865 he was appointed commander in chief, his hands were tied by the jealousy of Davis and by the crumbling fortunes of the South. Thus has Lee been stereotyped as the brilliant but powerless war leader in Virginia.[3]

That Lee had little power is one of the great myths of the Civil War. Quite the contrary, he had a position, both official and unofficial, from which he was able to make known his views throughout the war. When the government was moved to Richmond in 1861, Lee already held a position described by his son as the President's "constant and trusted adviser." In March, 1862, he was summoned to be what his biographers have labeled as a weak military adviser to the President. Such writers often cite Lee's own letter to his wife on March 14, in which he stated that he could see no advantage or pleasure in his duties. But Lee did not deny there—or elsewhere—that he had influence. His orders stated that he was to have charge of the armies of the Confederacy, under Davis' direction. Later, when General John Magruder congratulated him on being advanced to "Commander-in-Chief of the Confederate forces," Lee in his reply made no correction. In fact, Douglas Freeman himself admits that during Lee's three-month official duties in this particular office, he was called upon to pass on operations in every southern state, and that Davis consulted him on larger issues of strategy. Freeman, however, argues that Lee was allowed no free hand on any plan of "magnitude." Lee's failure to produce a plan of magnitude occurred not as a result of lack of power but as a result of his own selection. His correspondence as adviser reveals that he had obvious authority to address and advise generals in all war theaters, but that his interests were largely confined to matters on the Altantic slope. There, in Virginia, Lee's influence as adviser was indicated by his well-known

[3] Clifford Dowdey, *Lee* (Boston and Toronto, 1965), 181, 519; Douglas Southall Freeman, *R. E. Lee: A Biography* (4 vols.; New York, 1935–36), II, 4–7; Walter Taylor, *Four Years With General Lee* (New York, 1878), 37–38; A. L. Long, *Memoirs of Robert E. Lee* (New York, 1886), 391–92, 401; Roland, "The Generalship of Robert E. Lee," 35, 58–59.

role in Davis' decision in May, 1862, to order Joseph E. Johnston's army to assemble on the Peninsula and oppose McClellan.[4]

Also, many historians have assumed that when Lee took command of the Army of Northern Virginia on June 1, he relinquished his position as military adviser. Yet his new orders said nothing of abolishing his former office. Instead, on June 1, Davis told Lee that the new command "renders it necessary to interfere temporarily with the duties to which you were assigned in connection with the general service, but only so far as to make you available for command in the field of a particular army." Lee's son recalled later that "at all times" Lee continued to advise Davis and the War Department as to the disposition of other Confederate armies.[5]

The question of whether Lee officially or unofficially retained his formal position as adviser is academic. What is important is that, beginning at least by 1862, Lee exerted an advisory influence on Confederate military matters. This influence contradicts assertions that he lacked a position of power. Officially or not, Lee advised the government on general strategy and command problems from the summer of 1862 until 1865.

Of what use did Lee make of his position? What sort of advice did he give Davis? In June, 1862, he suggested stripping Georgia and the Carolinas to inaugurate a second front in Virginia under General Thomas Jackson. In July, 1862, he suggested an invasion of Kentucky by the Army of Tennessee. In September he suggested that the Army of Tennessee be sent to hold Richmond while he invaded Maryland. In December he again suggested the reinforcement of Virginia by Bragg's army as well as the reinforcement of North Carolina from South Carolina.

An examination of Lee's 1863 correspondence gives further evi-

[4] Robert E. Lee, *Recollections and Letters of General Robert E. Lee* (New York, 1904), 103; Freeman, *Lee*, II, 6–7; Lee to wife, March 14, 1862, in Clifford Dowdey and Louis H. Manarin (eds.), *Wartime Papers of R. E. Lee* (Boston, 1961), 127–28; Fuller, *Grant and Lee*, 114; Dowdey, *Lee*, 181, 189–90; Magruder to Lee, March 14, 1862, in *Official Records*, IX, 66; Lee to Magruder, March 17, 1862, in *Official Records*, IX, 70–71.

[5] Davis to Lee, June 1, 1862, in *Official Records*, XI, Pt. 3, pp. 568–69; Lee, *Recollections and Letters*, 103; Dowdey, *Lee*, 409.

dence that he did not hesitate to make suggestions regarding other war theaters. In January and February he offered advice regarding the reinforcement of the Department of North Carolina by troops from the neighboring Department of South Carolina, Georgia, and Florida. He conferred with Davis in March regarding what the armies of Braxton Bragg and John C. Pemberton should do in the West. Throughout April and May he was consulted on western problems. In May he suggested how Joseph E. Johnston should contest U. S. Grant in Mississippi, and in June advised President Davis on how and why Bragg's Army of Tennessee should take the offensive against General William S. Rosecrans. After Gettysburg, Lee advised Davis that Beauregard's army should be transferred from South Carolina to Virginia. In August and early September, Lee conferred closely with Davis on the western situation. In September and October, Lee repeatedly offered advice as to how Bragg should deal with Rosecrans. After Bragg's defeat at Missionary Ridge and subsequent resignation, Lee was consulted about the matter of his successor. In fact, on four occasions, Lee was consulted on the subject of naming a new commander for the Army of Tennessee.[6]

Lee's offering of advice continued in 1864. Throughout the early spring, he repeatedly made suggestions as to how Joseph E. Johnston should deal with Sherman in Georgia. He was consulted by Davis concerning the government's strategic plan for Johnston's army, even before Johnston himself learned of the plan. Too, Lee conferred closely with General James Longstreet, then maintaining an indepen-

---

[6] Lee to Davis, January 6, 1863, in Grady McWhiney (ed.), *Lee's Dispatches: Unpublished Letters of General Robert E. Lee, C.S.A., to Jefferson Davis and the War Department of the Confederate States of America 1862–65* (New York, 1957), 68–70; Jones, *Confederate Strategy*, 199–214; Lee to Seddon, April 9, 1863, and Lee to Cooper, April 16, 1863, in Jefferson Davis Papers, Louisiana Historical Association Collection, Howard-Tilton Library, Tulane University; Lee to Davis, May 28, 1863, in McWhiney (ed.), *Lee's Dispatches*, 96–98; Lee to Davis, July 8, 1863, in Dowdey and Manarin (eds.), *Wartime Papers*, 543–44; Douglas Southall Freeman, *Lee's Lieutenants: A Study in Command* (3 vols.; New York, 1942–44), III, 220–22; Lee to Davis, September 9, 11, 14, 18, 29, October 1, 1863, in *Official Records*, XIX, Pt. 2, pp. 706, 712, 720–21, 730–31, 756, 766; Lee to Davis, September 23, 1863, in Georgia Portfolio, Vol. II, Duke University Library; Lee to Longstreet, September 25, 1863, in Jackson-Dabney Papers, Southern Historical Collection, University of North Carolina Library; Lee to Davis, December 3, 7, 1863, in *Official Records*, XXI, Pt. 3, pp. 779, 792.

dent command in east Tennessee, about combined operations between Johnston and Longstreet. Lee continued to consult with Davis regarding the north Georgia campaign until Johnston was removed in July, and then was consulted about Johnston's replacement. In fact, prior to this removal, Davis even asked Lee who should be placed in command of General Leonidas Polk's corps in the Army of Tennessee after that general had been killed. Meanwhile, in May, 1864, Lee advised Davis to send all organized forces from the Department of South Carolina, Georgia, and Florida to Virginia.

In early 1865, before his appointment as commander in chief, Lee continued to advise the government on other war theaters. In January he suggested bringing General John B. Hood's Army of Tennessee to Virginia; that same month he also recommended bringing Kirby Smith's Trans-Mississippi army to Virginia, and offered counsel on how Beauregard should contest Sherman in the Carolinas.[7]

If Lee so often advised on overall matters, what did he propose? Although he never formulated a comprehensive plan of strategy, several factors were evident in his views and predominated his thinking. First, Lee possessed an apparent lack of knowledge as to the war situation in the western theater between the Appalachian Mountains and the Mississippi River. For example, he did not seem to appreciate that the Federals were maintaining a two-front war between the Appalachians and the Mississippi, a military effort manned by the Federal Departments of the Tennessee, Cumberland, and the Ohio. Too, Lee seemed inclined to consider that only the seizure of Richmond and the control of the Mississippi River were prime Federal objectives. The long-existing plan of advance upon Chattanooga, and eventually Atlanta, which was initiated in May,

[7] Lee to Longstreet, January 16, February 17, 1864, in James Longstreet Papers, Emory University Library; Lee to Davis, April 5, 1864, in Robert E. Lee Papers, Emory University Library; Lee to Davis, June 21, 1864, in McWhiney (ed.), *Lee's Dispatches*, 255–56; Lee to Davis, February 3, March 25, 30, April 8, June 15, July 12, 1864, Lee to Longstreet, March 28, 1864, Lee to Bragg, April 7, 16, 1864, all in Dowdey and Manarin (eds.), *Wartime Papers*, 682–83, 687–88, 693–94, 708–709, 783, 821, 684–85, 692, 701; Lee to Longstreet, March 8, 19, 28, 1864, Lee to Davis, April 2, 1864, all in *Official Records*, XXXII, Pt. 3, pp. 594, 656, 648, 736.

1862, received secondary attention in Lee's correspondence until 1864.

Too, Lee seemed not to fully appreciate the problems of Federal strength and Confederate weakness in the western theater. Here the Federals maintained three field armies from early 1862 until 1865, in the Departments of the Tennessee, Cumberland, and the Ohio. The only legitimate Confederate army in this vast territory between the Appalachians and the Mississippi River was the Army of Tennessee. There was an additional Confederate army in the Mississippi-Alabama department, but this satellite element sustained itself only by reinforcement from the Army of Tennessee. The only time the Mississippi army achieved any respectable strength was after it had been reinforced from the Army of Tennessee three times between December, 1862, and May, 1863.

Lee's response to the Federal threat in the West indicated that he perhaps failed to appreciate the disparity of forces there. For example, in September, 1862, he argued that the Federal concentration in Virginia necessitated bringing Bragg's Army of Tennessee to protect Richmond. At that time, the western Federals outnumbered Bragg's army and its satellite forces by a ratio of almost 3 to 1, and one Federal unit, the Army of the Ohio, was maneuvering to within twenty miles of the critical rail junction at Chattanooga. Again, in December, 1862, when he suggested that Bragg's army be sent to Virginia, Federal power on the Tennessee front consisted of at least 125,000 available troops. In June, 1863, after maintaining that "Virginia is to be the theater of action," Lee urged that Bragg's Army of Tennessee advance toward Ohio. Lee overlooked the fact that Federal strength in the West had been increased to well over 200,000 men, and that Bragg, after reinforcing Pemberton in Mississippi, possessed scarcely 50,000 men.

There are other instances when Lee seemed unappreciative of this western problem. Repeatedly in the spring of 1864 Lee suggested that Joseph E. Johnston take the offensive against Sherman because "the great effort of the enemy in this campaign will be made in Virginia." Thus, argued Lee, such a great force in Virginia must have come from the western Federal armies. To the end, Lee underestimated the western threat. In March, 1865, he naïvely reported that General Joseph E. Johnston's small army in North Carolina "is believed . . . to be inferior to that of the enemy." At that time Johnston could muster scarcely twenty thousand effectives arrayed against over one hundred thousand troops under Sherman and John M. Schofield, not to mention an additional eighty-seven thousand reserves in Kentucky and Tennessee.[8]

Lee's strategic views were also conditioned by a lack of understanding of the overall geography of the Confederacy. Lee admitted to Davis that he knew little of the West. Some of his misconceptions are well known, such as his statement that summer weather in Mississippi would force a withdrawal of Grant from the area in June, 1863, and his belief expressed in 1865 that Sherman could not march across the Carolinas.[9]

Other miscalculations run much deeper than these two misjudgments. Lee's correspondence indicates that he never fully grasped the importance of the South's munitions supply area of Georgia, Alabama, and Tennessee—at least not until 1864. Twice in 1862 he recommended an almost wholesale withdrawal from the area in order to protect Richmond. In the spring of 1863, when the Confederacy was threatened simultaneously on three fronts—Mississippi, Tennessee, and Virginia—Lee interpreted the problem to be merely which of two areas, the Mississippi River or Virginia, was more endangered. In late 1863, after Bragg had lost Chattanooga and

---

[8] Lee to Davis, September 3, December 6, 1862, May 11, 1863, April 5, July 5, 1864, Lee to John C. Breckinridge, March 9, 1865, in Dowdey and Manarin (eds.), *Wartime Papers,* 292–94, 352–53, 483, 690–91. 814–15, 913; *Official Records,* XXIII, Pt. 2, pp. 378–80, XXIV, Pt. 3, p. 249, XLVII, Pt. 3, pp. 73–74, 748, XLIX, Pt. 1, pp. 792, 798, 801, XXIII Pt. 2, p. 806. See also Lee to Davis, September 11, 1864, in *Official Records,* XXIX, Pt. 2, p. 712, XXXVII, Pt. 2, pp. 543, 547, 552–53, 555, XXVII, Pt. 3, pp. 806, 809, 811, 814, 815, 818, 1065, 1067, 1068, XIX, Pt. 2, pp. 374, 660, XVIII, Pt. 2, pp. 441, 750–51, XLVII, Pt. 3, pp. 73–74, 748–49, XLIX, Pt. 1, pp. 792, 798, 801, XLVI, Pt. 3, pp. 389–92, XXXVIII, Pt. 4, pp. 374, 376, XXXVI, Pt. 3, pp. 326–27, XXIII; Pt. 2, pp. 606–607, XXIV, Pt. 3, p. 568.

[9] Lee to Seddon, April 9, 1863, Lee to Cooper, April 16, 1863, in Davis Papers, Tulane; Jones, *Confederate Strategy,* 204; Lee to Seddon, May 10, 1863, Lee to Breckinridge, February 19, 1865, Lee to Davis, February 23, 1865, in Dowdey and Manarin (eds.), *Wartime Papers,* 482, 904–905, 909.

the Federals threatened to seize the Atlanta railroad, Lee bemoaned his decision to allow Longstreet to reinforce Bragg.[10]

Nor did Lee seem to appreciate fully the geographical problems of maneuvering in the vast western theater. By mid-1862, for example, the western Confederates had lost control of the Memphis and Charleston Railroad. Thereafter, rail communication between Mississippi, Alabama, and Georgia was thrown back along a circuitous route which dipped to Mobile, near the Gulf of Mexico. Too, Federal control of the three main western rivers, the Mississippi, Cumberland, and Tennessee, always interposed the threat of a flanking force. There was also the constant concern for the protection of the South's central area of iron production in Alabama, its chief munitions factories of Georgia and Alabama, its chief gunpowder production area in Georgia, and its main copper source in eastern Tennessee.

Various suggestions made by Lee would seem to indicate that he failed to appreciate the difficulties of the western logistical and transportation problems. Two strategic proposals by Lee in early 1864 indicated his lack of understanding of western matters. Although he admitted to Longstreet that "I am not sufficiently acquainted with the country to do more than indicate the general plan," he suggested in March an unrealistic joint offensive by Longstreet and Johnston. From his base at Dalton, Georgia, Johnston was to bypass Sherman at Chattanooga, and move northeast into the East Tennessee Valley. There he would join Longstreet, who would descend the same valley, bypassing the army of General Ambrose Burnside at Knoxville. Once united, the Confederates would then strike westward across the wide, barren Cumberland Plateau and invade middle Tennessee.

Such a move was geographically impossible. Sherman blocked the valley at Chattanooga, and a move into the East Tennessee Valley would totally expose Johnston's flank to the Federals. Too, Johnston simply could not move his army almost four hundred miles across

---

[10] Lee on May 10 told Seddon that the government must decide whether the line of Virginia was more in danger than the line of the Mississippi. Lee to Seddon, May 10, 1863, in Dowdey and Manarin (eds.), *Wartime Papers*, 482.

the well-foraged East Tennessee Valley and the barren Cumberland Plateau. Yet such a proposal was no less unrealistic than one made the previous month by Longstreet, in which Lee took great interest. At Longstreet's request, Lee inquired of Richmond whether enough transportation could be made available for Longstreet to mount his independent east Tennessee force on mules and raid Kentucky.[11]

Aside from his lack of comprehension of the western theater, Lee's strategic policies were colored by a second principle that may explain much of his attitude toward other theaters of operation. Lee, convinced that the main war zone was in Virginia, shaped his strategy accordingly. In the fall and winter of 1862 he seemed certain that the main Federal concentration was on his front. Even with Grant and Rosecrans massing for separate western operations, Lee in May, 1863, declared that "Virginia is to be the theatre of action." And although Sherman had amassed three departmental armies against Johnston in the spring of 1864, Lee contended in April that "the great effort of the enemy in this campaign will be made in Virginia." He proposed that such large reinforcements could come only from the western Federals; thus Johnston must take the offensive to relieve the Virginia front. Again in April, Lee urged that the approaching storm would "burst on Virginia," unless it could be diverted by Johnston's taking the offensive. On a third occasion, Lee argued that the main concentration was in Virginia, and that Johnston must take the offensive to halt it.[12]

Thus Lee's strategy was based on defending Virginia. From the summer of 1862 until the spring of 1864, he practiced his well-known policy to maneuver and to take the offensive in order to break up the enemy's campaigns, and keep him away from the heart of Virginia,

---

[11] Lee to Davis, January 6, 1863, in McWhiney (ed.), *Lee's Dispatches,* 68–70; Lee to Longstreet, February 17, 1864, in Longstreet Papers, Emory University; Lee to Longstreet, March 8, 1864, in J. William Jones, *Life and Letters of Robert E. Lee: Soldier and Man* (New York and Washington, 1906), 327–28; Lee to Davis, February 3, 1864, in Dowdey and Manarin (eds.), *Wartime Papers,* 666–67.

[12] Lee to Davis, May 11, 1863, Lee to Bragg, April 7, 1864, in Dowdey and Manarin (eds.), *Wartime Papers,* 483–84, 692; Lee to Davis, April 5, 1864, in Jefferson Davis Papers, Emory University Library; Lee to G. W. C. Lee, March 29, 1864, in Jones, *Life and Letters,* 303.

above all away from Richmond. When failing manpower and logistics made this impossible in 1864, Lee reverted to a defensive that was still designed to keep the Federals away from the capital.

This strategy was basic not only for Virginia but for the entire South. During both of these periods, Lee's interest in the West seemed limited to what that region could do to help Virginia. Either the West should contribute troops to the East or take the offensive to improve conditions in the East. In the fall and winter of 1862 his recommendations were for a wholesale reinforcement of Virginia. In the spring of 1863 the plea was for a strong Virginia reinforcement, and at best, a negation of any suggestion of sending reinforcements from his army to the western front. In the autumn of 1863 Lee maintained that a quick thrust should be made against Rosecrans so that Longstreet could be returned to Virginia. In the spring of 1864 Johnston was urged to take the offensive to curtail reinforcement of Virginia.

Did President Davis heed Lee's advice? All recommendations to strengthen Virginia at the expense of the West were rejected. Even if Davis did not regard some of Lee's advice as unrealistic, pressure from Lee was being opposed by a formidable lobby of western generals and politicians. Also, Lee's advice implied large western territorial sacrifices at a time when he was holding his own without western reinforcement. In this sense his successes undermined his own advice. On the other hand, Davis was very receptive to suggestions that Lee receive reinforcements from other areas of the Atlantic seaboard. Too, on only one occasion did Davis overrule Lee's objections to drawing reinforcements from his army in Virginia to aid the West.

The impact of these pressures on Davis created a strong tendency to stabilize the distribution of troops between Virginia and the western theaters. Davis refused to reinforce Virginia from the West; Lee resisted Virginia reinforcements for the West.

An example of such pressures at work was the Confederacy's crisis in the spring of 1863. With Grant poised for a final thrust against Vicksburg, and Rosecrans mobilizing for a push on Chattanooga, the government in April had toyed with the prospect of sending aid to the West from Lee's army. By early May, Davis and Secretary of War Seddon had decided against reinforcing the West from Virginia, though some troops were sent from South Carolina.

An important factor in this decision was General Lee's analysis of the war situation in Virginia and other theaters. His concern with reinforcement was usually a one-way matter. It sometimes led him into inconsistent reasoning, so much so that it seems his basic policy was either to reinforce Virginia or let each man shift for himself. In the crisis of April–May, 1863, Lee was initially hard pressed by Davis, Seddon, and Samuel Cooper to reinforce the West. He seemed to grope for practically any reason why he could not do so, and showed inconsistency. He argued that it was unwise to transfer troops between departments; that whenever shifts were made by the Federals, it did no good for the Confederates to make corresponding shifts. Yet his requests for having the western army sent to Virginia in September and December of 1862 had been based upon the reverse principle, that a heavy Federal concentration was occurring in Virginia and that a corresponding Confederate shift should be made. Later, in July, 1863, Lee requested a major shift of troops from Beauregard's command in South Carolina to offset a similar move by the Federals. In May, 1864, Lee argued again that, since two Federal corps had been removed from the Carolinas to Virginia, the Confederates should make a corresponding move. But, in April, 1864, Lee had completely reversed the reasoning by which he had opposed sending Johnston reinforcements in the spring of 1863. Noting a heavy Federal concentration in Virginia, he argued that troops from less threatened departments should be sent to Richmond.[13]

Only on one occasion did Lee consent to a reinforcement of the West, when two divisions of Longstreet's corps were sent in September, 1863, to reinforce Bragg below Chattanooga. This reinforcement has been magnified out of proportion as to both aim and extent.

[13] Lee to Seddon, April 9, 1863, Lee to Cooper, April 16, 1863, in Davis Papers, Tulane; Jones, *Confederate Strategy*, 203–204; Lee to Davis, May 11, 1863, July 8, 1863, May 4, 1864, Lee to Seddon, May 10, 1863, in Dowdey and Manarin (eds.), *Wartime Papers*, 482–84, 544, 719–20; Lee to Davis, April 5, 1864, in Davis Papers, Emory University Library.

As mentioned, Lee's purpose was not to bolster Bragg's strength against a Federal threat on Georgia, but to save Knoxville lest western Virginia be endangered. Too, Lee was unenthusiastic at the move. Even while conferring with Davis in late August and early September, he wished to keep his troops in order to take the offensive against Meade. As late as August 31 he instructed Longstreet to ready the army for an offensive and spoke of crushing Meade. The slowness in determining this reinforcement was a factor in the lateness of Longstreet's arrival in Georgia. Fewer than five thousand of Lee's troops were engaged at Chickamauga. Also, even before the last of Longstreet's men had arrived in Georgia, Lee had written Davis twice asking that they be returned. By September 25 Lee had already penned four suggestions for Longstreet's return to Virginia. [14]

Lee's apparent belief that the main Federal front was in the East indicated a third element in his strategic policy. Historians have speculated what he might have done had he held the powers of a generalissimo, or had he possessed even stronger powers in his positions of military adviser, army commander, and finally commander in chief in 1865. Usually the conclusion is somewhat rhetorical—that Lee possessed an overall strategic mind but no power. The consistent theme in his advice to Davis indicates his dominant concern, the element of localism in his thinking.

Keeping the enemy away from Richmond seemed to dominate Lee's strategy from the time of his emotional pleas in the May, 1862, Richmond meeting, when he declared that the city must not be given up. Pressed, in addition, by logistical problems and dedicated to the task of maneuvering in Virginia to keep the Federals out, Lee seemed to choose the short gain. When he proposed the Maryland campaign, and later in his report of that invasion, his emphasis was on what such a campaign would accomplish locally in Virginia. One biographer, Clifford Dowdey, notes that in his Sharpsburg planning, Lee was willing to settle for the short-range goal of clearing Virginia of Federals even if it meant defeat. Plans for the Pennsylvania

[14] Lee to Longstreet, August 31, 1863, September 25, 1863, Lee to Davis, August 24, 1863, September 9, 11, 14, 18, 23, 27, 1863, in Dowdey and Manarin (eds.), *Wartime Papers*, 593–94, 596–97, 599–607.

invasion also demonstrated Lee's short-range thinking. As noted, his decision to invade the North probably had little if anything to do with the western situation. His June 8 explanation for desiring such an invasion was based not on national considerations but on the fear that the Federals would soon advance upon Richmond. Lee added that "it is worth a trial" to prevent such a move.

One might also question whether Lee could have shed his preoccupation with Virginia sufficiently to give a dispassionate appraisal of war matters in other theaters. Theater commanders in all armies seemed naturally to overestimate the importance of their own commands, and this myopic concern for one's own army and region was certainly endemic in the Confederate high command. Yet Lee, in spite of his closeness to Davis and his opportunities to perceive the total Confederate situation, seemed to evince as localistic and provincial an outlook as every other major Confederate leader did, if not more so. In fact, one might infer that Lee was fighting for Virginia and not for the South. He said this, in effect, in the spring of 1861, when he confided to relatives that he had no desire to fight save for the defense of Virginia. To the Virginia convention in 1861 he declared his allegiance solely to the service of Virginia, although that state's placement in the Confederacy was certain. In fact, practically all Lee biographers have commented upon his paramount sense of obligation to Virginia, beginning with early postwar depictions by John Esten Cooke, J. William Jones, Emily Mason, and others. Lee's comrade at Washington College, J. William Jones, remarked that "Robert Edward Lee regarded his allegiance to the sovereign state of Virginia as paramount to all others."[15]

Too, the makeup of Lee's command organization in his Army of Northern Virginia could do little but reinforce its commander's intense concern with one area of the Confederacy. Whether by chance or otherwise, he was surrounded with Virginia-bred officers who led an army composed of troops from the entire South. In July, 1862, seven of Lee's twelve infantry corps and division commanders were Virginians. At Gettysburg, four of his five chief infantry, cavalry,

[15] Jones, *Life and Letters*, 126.

and artillery commanders were from Virginia. By the beginning of the May, 1864, campaign, he possessed fifteen corps and division commanders in his infantry and cavalry. Nine were Virginians, including one of Lee's sons and a nephew.

Perhaps it will never be clear to what degree Lee's advice was conditioned by his two roles, as commander in Virginia and as adviser on Confederate strategy. Lee himself may not have been able to differentiate his two roles. In recommending reinforcement from other lines of operations for either an offensive or defensive action on the Virginia line, he was making a quite Napoleonic and Jominian recommendation.

Clearly Lee was no exponent of the cordon system, and could see the possibility of coordination and concentration among several lines of operations. Yet, like every Confederate department and army commander, he had a proprietary feeling about "his" army and the units within it. For Confederate generals most transfers from one department or line of operations to another were always troops "loaned" or "borrowed."

In Lee's case, however, such proprietary feeling has special meaning. While such viewpoints were common to departmental and army commanders, he, by virtue of his position as adviser to the President and his prestige as a winner, thus was in a peculiar position to influence Confederate strategy. When there was a question of concentration on a line of operations other than Virginia and of taking troops from Virginia, Lee may unconsciously have reverted to his role as an army commander and resisted a dispersion or division of his force. He could clearly see that the enemy was concentrating on a single line in Virginia. He quite properly felt that he must do likewise or he would be making the same mistake his enemies had made in 1862. "His" army must remain concentrated on the Richmond-Washington line, and he implicitly removed it from the general Confederate strategic reserve. Given his peculiar position as adviser and his great prestige, he was able to accomplish such matters more successfully than other Confederate officers who were perhaps equally provincial.

Too, when Lee constantly insisted that the Union was concentrating in Virginia, he may have translated their concentration *within* Virginia to a concentration *on* Virginia, and in his thinking he may have seen all Union and Confederate operations as simple extensions of those in Virginia. Longstreet quotes Lee as objecting to sending troops west because this would "force him to divide his army."[16] Without realizing it, Lee may have assumed that a Union abandonment of serious efforts on all but one line of operations in Virginia meant an abandonment of serious efforts on all lines of operations outside Virginia. However tenuous such a hypothesis may be, there may be truth in it. People often have great capacity for imposing their own conceptions on the facts, and Lee had no opportunity or reason to change his perspective since his involvement with Virginia was uninterrupted.

If these conceptions were factors in Lee's ideas on strategy, they harmonize well with the other factors which apparently made it impossible for him to apply the Napoleonic-Jominian strategic grasp he displayed in Virginia, to Confederate strategy as a whole. His prescriptions were usually limited to recommending reinforcements for Virginia and to recommending advances by other armies which would operate as distractions; and, as a rule, distractions from the Union's effort on the Virginia line of operations. His prestige as a winner and his unusual opportunity to advise undoubtedly to some degree influenced the government to take a narrower view on strategy and to go for the short gain in Virginia where victory seemed more possible.

Jefferson Davis badly needed different strategic advice. He particularly needed advice that would have given to all Confederate operations the kind of unity Lee supplied in Virginia. A group of generals sought to fill this need and to supply Davis with a point of view that was so western-oriented as to be a counterweight to Lee's Virginia-oriented influence.

---

[16] James Longstreet, "Lee in Pennsylvania," in *Annals of the War* (Philadelphia, 1879), 416.

III
The Western
Concentration Bloc

Confederate military history, like other fields of research, often suffers from oversimplification. The casual observer thinks of the war in terms of Grant and Lee, Gettysburg and Appomattox Courthouse. On occasion, even trained historians have been guilty of applying stereotypes. This tendency seems particularly true in regard to the study of political, personal, and military factions within the Confederacy. Usually such groups are divided only into two divisions: those who agreed with Davis administration policy, and those who have been labeled as the "antiadministration bloc."

This rather simplistic view ignores two important questions: (1) Did President Davis and his advisers represent the traditional power and policies of the entire South? (2) Were the antiadministrationists powerless and ineffectual?

It cannot be doubted that General Robert E. Lee was in close contact with President Davis throughout the war, but it would be a mistake to assume that there were not others who were also urging Davis to follow particular courses of action. Generally, historians have cast Davis and his chief advisers, Lee, Judah P. Benjamin, and James A. Seddon, as the main power group within the South. Those who opposed these policies emanating from Richmond have been lumped together as a group of outsiders who lacked power and influence. This group of "outsiders," however, subdivided into various factions as they were, did in fact exert a great deal of pressure upon Davis to recognize their suggestions.

First, the policies of Davis' advisers were not easily accepted. Lee, with his great concern for the defense of Virginia at almost any cost, did not represent the entire South. It was not until at least the summer of 1862 that Lee became respected and well known in the South. In fact, when Lee first established a close relationship with the President in 1861, he was something of an object of derision because of the unsuccessful West Virginia campaign.

Others upon whom Davis leaned for advice and friendship were also unpopular and unacceptable leaders. General Albert Sidney Johnston was virtually unknown outside of the regular army when his old friend Davis gave him the western theater command in September of 1861. By March of 1862 Johnston's failures in Tennessee and Kentucky had incited a widespread outcry for his removal. General Braxton Bragg, by the autumn of 1862, was even more unpopular. Bragg was so disliked that as early as September of that year, a petition of fifty-nine members of the Confederate House and Senate asked Davis for his removal. Bragg's own generals repeated this request frequently in 1862 and 1863, and almost mutinied against Bragg after the Chickamauga campaign. General John C. Pemberton, also strongly supported by Davis, was so unpopular after Vicksburg's surrender that Mississippi troops threatened to mutiny if they were placed under his command again. Davis' chief adviser in foreign policy matters, Judah P. Benjamin, was frequently criticized for a number of sins ranging from his Jewish origins to his conduct as Secretary of War.

Davis himself seemed to feel estranged and unjustly criticized as did the friends who served him. By late 1862 the comparative freedom from criticism enjoyed by President Davis in 1861 had vanished. Losses at Mill Springs, Roanoke Island, Forts Henry and Donelson, Shiloh, Perryville, and elsewhere had produced a rising hostility to the administration. This hostility was vented in the newspapers, the Congress, and the army. Some older supporters of Davis, such as Senator Louis T. Wigfall of Texas and James L. Orr of South Carolina, had abandoned the administration's camp by late 1862. By 1863 it was no disgrace to campaign for a seat in the Second Confederate Congress as an antiadministration man.

Davis' correspondence in 1862 and 1863, particularly that written to friends under attack, has a tone of alienation. Part of this sense of alienation may have been derived from an awareness that he was a southwesterner who was conducting a war amidst the Tidewater society, which occupied itself in a silly and frantic social whirl and still thought of the western theater as "the frontier." There also may have been a sense of loneliness that intensified as Davis' enemies increased. At times he was berated for maintaining Bragg in Tennessee, Benjamin in Richmond, Lucius B. Northrop in the Commissary Bureau, Pemberton in Mississippi, and Sidney Johnston in the West. To Davis, these men represented bonds of friendship amidst turmoil. Perhaps Davis saw that they were bearing the President's own cross, and were maligned for their close association with the government.

A feeling of smugness might also have caused Davis to consider himself an outsider rather than the commander in chief he was supposed to be. He was often inflexible in his military views, and possessed an irritating characteristic of rarely admitting a mistake. It would have been relatively easy for the President to view himself as a long-suffering war leader, berated by the foolish or the ignorant, and waiting for his policies to be vindicated by success. Thus, when Albert Sidney Johnston was under attack for disasters in Tennessee, Davis hoped that "the public will soon give me credit for judgment rather than continue to arraign me for obstinacy." The President could perceive that some of his most important judgments about people had been vindicated. He had been right about Lee and thought he had been just as perceptive about Sidney Johnston. Thus, after the loss of Vicksburg, Davis could tell Pemberton: "To some men it is given to be commended for what they are expected to do, and to be sheltered when they fail by a transfer of the blame which may attach; to others it is decreed that their success shall be denied or treated as a necessary result; and their failures imputed to incapacity or crime." To Davis the matter was simple. Pemberton, who was accused of disloyalty as well as incompetence, was being castigated because the public had been deluded "by unscrupulous men who resort to the newspapers to disseminate falsehood and forestall the public judgment."[1]

In other instances Davis' correspondence smacked of a conde-

[1] Davis to Albert Sidney Johnston, March 26, 1862, in William Preston Johnston, *Life of Gen. Albert Sidney Johnston* (New York, 1878), 522; Davis to Pemberton, August 9, 1863, in Jefferson Davis Papers, Louisiana Historical Association Collection, Howard-Tilton Memorial Library, Tulane University.

scension, and a belief that he was one of a minority of right-thinking men whose views were yet to be vindicated publicly. In August, 1863, when Lee offered to resign amid criticism over Gettysburg, Davis spoke of Sidney Johnston's also being "overwhelmed by a senseless clamor." Davis told Lee that "there has been nothing which I have found to require a greater effort of patience than to bear the criticisms of the ignorant."[2] Bragg also received such counsel. Davis' upholding of Bragg was no mere stubbornness. The President was convinced that the public's opinion of Bragg was due to ignorance. Davis thought the public was misled about Bragg by three factors: ignorance of what Bragg was doing, an acceptance of the views of Bragg's enemies within the army and the press, and a failure to understand Bragg's personality. Of Bragg, Davis wrote, "It is not given to all men of ability to excite enthusiasm."[3]

Even with these factors working against the President and his friends and advisers, one may still have to concede that they constituted the strongest single military and political force. But this is not to say that the Richmond policies reflected the established power and policies of the entire Confederacy. It may well be that the Confederate "establishment" rested rather in a group, which, for convenience, are here called the western concentration bloc.

Some of the members of this informal association, the western concentration bloc, were closely linked by family ties and by long-lasting friendships. For example, Generals Joseph E. Johnston, Wade Hampton, John B. Floyd, William Preston, and John C. Breckinridge were all related. On the other hand, bitter personal enemies coexisted within the bloc. During the war there was great antipathy between Generals P. G. T. Beauregard and Leonidas Polk, between Polk and Braxton Bragg, between Bragg and James Longstreet, and eventually between Bragg and Joseph E. Johnston.

The motivations for being a member of the western bloc were as varied as its membership. Longstreet's peculiar interest in a western

---

[2] *Official Records*, XXIX, Pt. 2, p. 640.

[3] Davis to Johnston, February 19, 1863, in Dunbar Rowland (ed.), *Jefferson Davis, Constitutionalist, His Letters, Papers, and Speeches* (10 vols.; Jackson, Miss.), V, 434, 507, 539.

concentration seemed to be based on selfish ambitions—he hoped to obtain command of the Army of Tennessee. Beauregard's interest seemed to be dominated by a desire to apply textbook principles of the Napoleonic style of concentration. Senator Louis T. Wigfall, another member of the faction, seemed to evoke concern for the West as a convenient device for attacking administration policy.

Whatever the personal motives, the western concentration bloc functioned as one of the most important informal organizations in the South.[4] Although individual plans often varied, the group which appeared in 1862 was dominated by two ideas. First, its members rejected what appeared to be a governmental policy of a cordon defense of the West, and they advocated risking the loss of territory in order to secure an offensive concentration of western manpower. This type of concentration was not the same as the type often practiced by Richmond—responding to an enemy buildup on one line of

---

[4]The concept of the informal organization is drawn from social psychology. All "organizations whether legislatures, political parties, labor unions, business enterprises, universities, churches, armies, or professional associations—respond in fact to a variety of informal patterns of influence among their membership." These informal organizations, are defined as the "interpersonal relations in the organization that affect decisions within it but either are ommitted from the formal scheme or are not consistent with that scheme." These informal relationships, which seem to abound in all organizations, almost invariably create "ties of allegiance, external and internal, that cut across the lines of command and bind together groups of officials and employees on some basis other than that of loyalty to their formal superiors." These ties of allegiance may be to a leader around whom an informal personal organization develops. The members of this organization feel a "substantial degree of personal compatibility with the intellectual approach and the outlook" of the leader.

Another of the many bases of informal organization is the ideological. The policy, purposes, or spirit of the organization become the subject of ideological divisions within the organization and "ideological factions—here the 'liberals,' there the 'conservatives,' " struggle to affect the policy of the organization. Informal organizations with a personal or ideological base, like those with other roots, often may create a conflict between the "actual leadership sensed within the organization" and the "formal location of authority." Thus in the Confederate Army and government, as in other organizations, "the actual pattern of human relationships and allegiances within the formal organization is distinguished by complexity. . . . Uncrowned leaders compete with crowned ones. Informal and often unaccountable groupings brought to life for various purposes press against one another." There is an extensive literature on this subject. The quotations are drawn from Harvey C. Mansfield and Fritz Morstein Marx, "Informal Organization," in Fritz Morstein Marx (ed.), *Elements of Public Administration* (Englewood Cliffs, N.J., 1959), 274, 278, 283, 286; and Herbert A. Simon, *Administrative Behavior* (New York, 1959), 148.

advance by a Rebel concentration on that same front—instead, the western bloc embraced a Napoleonic concept. Concentration was to be effected upon one of the weakest of the multiple lines of advance used by the western Federals, followed by a rapid concentration for an offensive. Then, a diagonal move against the communications of the alternate line of Union advance would be effected. For example, in 1863 members of the group suggested a rapid concentration against General William S. Rosecrans' line of advance in middle Tennessee. Then the Confederates would take the offensive against Rosecrans. If victorious, the Confederates would make a diagonal move against the communications of General U. S. Grant's army in Mississippi.

Second, the western concentration bloc was also motivated by a strong concern for the fate of the central South. They were preoccupied with the central corridor via Nashville, Chattanooga, and Atlanta into the lower South. Gradually, many of the group's strategic proposals centered on the need to thwart a Federal advance on the Chattanooga–Atlanta route into the lower South's munitions complex of Macon, Augusta, Selma, and Columbus.

Although there was some agreement in the goals of the western concentration bloc, the motives and relationships of its members were very diverse. There has been some attempt to analyze the group often referred to as the "antiadministration" bloc. A pioneer article on this second Confederate power group was published by Alfred P. James almost fifty years ago in the *Mississippi Valley Historical Review*. This article, "General Joseph E. Johnston: Storm Center of the Confederate Army," was an early attempt to ferret out some factions within the Confederacy. However, Professor James's subject needs further study. James depicted the opposition bloc as being led by General Joseph E. Johnston. He described Johnston as the symbol of opposition to governmental policy, an opposition based upon family ties. Yet Johnston was not the leader of any group, though he was a key member of one of these factions which supported the western concentration viewpoint on strategy.

The extensive influence of the western concentration bloc in Confederate history was probably the result of its relationship to other factions within the Confederate military system. Historians not only have underrated the western concentration bloc's contributions to strategic thought and action, but also have failed to examine the informal organizations which constituted it. These interrelated organizations, for the sake of identification, might be termed (1) the Abingdon-Columbia bloc (2) the anti-Bragg bloc (3) the Kentucky bloc, and (4) the Beauregard bloc. The size and power of these four factions were impressive. They were interconnected by a variety of factors, among them family ties, personal friendships, common strategic views, and political rivalries. Thus they not only combined to form the western concentration bloc, but they independently wielded substantial influence in Confederate affairs.

The keystone of the Abingdon-Columbia bloc was an intricate set of family relationships embracing many well-known Confederate names, such as Johnston, Floyd, Preston, Breckinridge, and Hampton. Many of these families, such as the parents of General Joseph E. Johnston, had dominated the society of the lower Appalachian Valley of Virginia. They had been the prominent families of southwestern Virginia, and had centered their living at the town of Abingdon. There Johnston's own father was a judge of the Virginia state circuit court, and there the future general spent his boyhood.

Johnston was kin to many powerful families which at one time had flourished in the Abingdon vicinity, and then had gradually migrated either to South Carolina or to Kentucky. Johnston's grandmother was a sister of Patrick Henry. Another Henry sister had married General William Campbell, a hero of King's Mountain. From this relationship Johnston was kin to the powerful Preston family. General William Campbell's daughter married Francis Preston of Abingdon. One son, John Smith Preston, practiced law in Abingdon before becoming prominent in prewar South Carolina politics. Preston, a South Carolina commissioner to Virginia in 1861, also had ties with Beauregard. In 1861 he had served with Beauregard as an aide, at both Charleston and Manassas; eventually the Creole recommended Preston for a brigadier generalship. Later Preston headed the Bureau of Conscription.

Another son of the Campbell-Preston marriage was Senator William

Campbell Preston of South Carolina. This Preston, who died in 1860, was a graduate and later president of South Carolina College. Many of those within this faction were graduates of this college, now the University of South Carolina. A third son of the Campbell-Preston marriage, Thomas Preston, served on Johnston's staff during the war.

These Preston kinships were even more embracing. General William Preston, an avowed member of the anti-Bragg faction in the Army of Tennessee, was a son of William Campbell Preston. Another relative, William Ballard Preston, was an influential Virginia lawyer, congressman, and cabinet member prior to the war. This Preston's grandparents also hailed from Abingdon, and during the war, William Ballard Preston was both a Confederate senator from Virginia and a strong supporter of Joseph E. Johnston.

Gradually the ties became more intermingled. General Wade Hampton, a wartime supporter of Johnston, was a distant relative of the general's. Hampton, also a South Carolina College alumnus, had married Margaret Preston. Margaret Preston was the sister of Johnston's relative and Beauregard's aide, the future head of the Conscription Bureau, John S. Preston.

The Floyd family of Kentucky and Virginia also was interconnected to this group. General John B. Floyd was tied by geography, sentiment, and kinship to the Abingdon-Columbia bloc. He also had been raised in the Abingdon vicinity, and had attended South Carolina College. Floyd's mother was the daughter of William Preston of Abingdon. This William Preston was also the grandfather of the Confederate General William Preston. Later, Floyd married his cousin Sally Buchanan Preston, a granddaughter of General William Campbell. By these ties, Floyd was kin to Joseph E. Johnston, Wade Hampton, William Preston of Bragg's army, and the pro-Johnston Senator William Ballard Preston of Virginia.

Floyd was also tied to the group by sentiment. A cousin by marriage to Joseph E. Johnston, Floyd as Secretary of War in the 1850's was accused by some, including Robert E. Lee, of favoritism to his relative. The climax to this matter occurred in 1860, when Quartermaster General Thomas Jesup died. General Winfield Scott recommended to Floyd four possible successors: Albert Sidney Johnston, Charles Smith, Joseph E. Johnston, and Robert E. Lee. Although some of these officers outranked Joseph E. Johnston, he was supported successfully by Floyd. Senator Jefferson Davis, chairman of the Senate Military Affairs Committee, evidently supported a long-time friend, Albert Sidney Johnston.

Later, Joseph E. Johnston's supporters maintained, though probably with much exaggeration, that part of the President's hostility to the general came from this 1860 defeat. There may have been some strain between Davis and the Johnston-Floyd families in 1862. After his poor performance at Fort Donelson, Floyd was, without any formal inquiry, relieved from command by Davis.

Other Rebel families were tied to this network of in-laws. General John C. Breckinridge of Kentucky, former United States Senator and Vice-President, was a powerful member of the anti-Bragg faction in the Army of Tennessee. Breckinridge was related, at least by marriage, to Joseph E. Johnston, John B. Floyd, Wade Hampton, and William Preston. Breckinridge's grandmother, Letitia Breckinridge, had been the daughter of John Preston of Abingdon. The interrelationship of the Breckinridge family with other bloc members was best expressed by the name given to General John C. Breckinridge's first cousin, who was a nephew of John Smith Preston of the Conscription Bureau. This Breckinridge, a colonel in General John Morgan's cavalry, was named William Campbell Preston Breckinridge. Breckinridge had been Vice-President when Floyd served as Secretary of War and Howell Cobb Secretary of the Treasury.

The family of General Albert Sidney Johnston was also related to this group. Johnston's first wife, Henrietta Preston, was the sister of the anti-Bragg officer General William Preston. Johnston's wife did not survive to see her son, William Preston Johnston, enter Confederate service. After her death, while Albert Sidney Johnston was absent in the service of the Republic of Texas, William Preston Johnston was raised by relatives. One responsible for his upbringing was General William Preston.

The interweaving of this group embraced far more than family ties. Friendships, common strategic views, or even particular antagonisms toward the Richmond government connected a loose network of individuals, many associated with South Carolina. One such was General P. G. T. Beauregard, a leader of the Abingdon-Columbia faction. Beauregard had no kinship to others in this group, but he possessed their affection. Two thirds of Beauregard's Civil War career was spent in South Carolina: first as commander of the original Charleston defenses, and later as commander of the Department of South Carolina, Georgia, and Florida.

Another member of the faction, who also supported Beauregard heartily, was Senator Louis T. Wigfall of Texas. In May of 1863, it was to Wigfall that Beauregard sent his plan for the summer campaign, urging its presentation to the War Department. It was also Wigfall who from late 1862 until 1865 was both a warm friend and a military supporter of Johnston.

Wigfall had two ties with the Abingdon-Columbia bloc. He was a South Carolinian, born in the Edgefield District, and an alumnus of South Carolina College. Wigfall's wife was a native of Charleston, and her family lived in Columbia. His army service had been in Virginia under Johnston and Beauregard.

Also, like many members of the Abingdon-Columbia bloc, Wigfall was, after the autumn of 1862, an administration critic. This aligned him with both Johnston and Beauregard. Wigfall in 1862 had first championed Beauregard, and had supported the September petition to have the Creole reinstated in command of the Army of Tennessee. When Davis made it clear this would never come to pass, Wigfall, by November of 1862, had shifted his efforts to promoting Johnston as a Bragg successor.

It is also true that Johnston and Wigfall were good friends and their wives also corresponded regularly. Johnston had recuperated from his wound suffered at Seven Pines in Wigfall's Richmond home. Later, after his removal from command in the Atlanta campaign, Johnston took up residence in Columbia, the home of Mrs. Johnston's sister. There Wigfall's two daughters lived with the Johnstons. They had been left with the general since June, 1864, when their parents had departed on a trip for Texas. Through the war, Wigfall and Johnston also maintained a warm personal correspondence.

Yet Wigfall probably also used Johnston to advance his anti-Davis position. As mentioned, Wigfall had first been a strong backer of Beauregard until he saw such a policy was not feasible. Wigfall often seemed more interested in how Johnston could promote the antiadministration position in Congress rather than evincing interest in the general himself. In 1863, while promoting Johnston as a successor to Bragg, Wigfall evidently was also pushing Longstreet as a successor.

Other members of the Abingdon bloc had close ties with its two leaders, Johnston and Beauregard. Both generals seemed to possess power bases within South Carolina, due to either kinship, admirers, or mutual dislike of Davis, Bragg, or general governmental policy. Young Wade Hampton IV, son of the Confederate general, was an early member of Johnston's staff. It was to Johnston that General Wade Hampton owed his appointment in the spring of 1862 as brigadier general. The Manning family was also within the Johnston circle. Governor John Manning occupied the South Carolina statehouse until 1862. Before the war, he had been a political rival of Colonel James Chesnut, a strong Carolina Davis supporter. Manning's son Richard also served on Johnston's staff.

Beauregard's long tenure in South Carolina, coupled with his admirable defense of Charleston in the 1863 siege, endeared him to many in the state. Beauregard's seat of power within South Carolina appeared to be in Charleston, while Johnston's was in Columbia. One such Beauregard supporter was William Porcher Miles, who represented the Charleston district in the Confederate Congress. Miles had been one of the three commissioners selected by the general to arrange the terms of Fort Sumter's surrender. By August of 1861 Beauregard was already using Miles to further his cause in the Confederate Congress. Miles, chairman of the House Committee on Military Affairs, was a frequent Beauregard correspondent. He, too, supported the petition for Bragg's replacement by Beauregard in September, 1862.

The Abingdon-Columbia faction maintained close ties with the members of other Confederate pressure blocs who also were generally antagonistic to administration policy. One such was the anti-Bragg faction, a powerful bloc within the Army of Tennessee. Like the anti-Bragg group, the Abingdon-Columbia bloc generally favored Bragg's replacement. Not all members of the Abingdon group were, however, hostile to Bragg. Both Johnston and Beauregard maintained fairly good relationships with Bragg until 1864.

Yet Bragg seemed the vulnerable spot in Richmond's war policy. To Davis' opponents in Congress, this unfortunate general was a useful tool with which to criticize the government. By the summer of 1863 Bragg had a long record of defeats—Perryville, Murfreesboro, and the Duck River line. To demand a reinstatement of Johnston or Beauregard in Virginia, or to attack Lee at all seemed foolish. Lee had turned back McClellan at the Seven Days' campaign, had destroyed General John Pope's reputation at Second Manassas, and had slaughtered General Ambrose E. Burnside's men at Fredericksburg. But Bragg was a loser, and by 1863 was extremely vulnerable.

The sentiment against Bragg within the Abingdon bloc went deeper than merely being a political device to attack Davis. Johnston and Beauregard exemplified a certain frustration. Both men had commanded the South's two main field armies, and the Western Department as well. Yet in 1862, both had apparently been shuffled by Richmond to less important positions. Beauregard had been removed from the command of the Army of Tennessee in June. Johnston had been replaced by Lee after his severe wound at Seven Pines, and, after recuperating, was simply not reassigned to his old command. Instead, Johnston was given command of the vague Western Department. In fact, from June of 1862 until the end of the war, Beauregard never again independently commanded a large field army.

From their base within the Abingdon-Columbia group, both Johnston and Beauregard felt, for a large part of the war, a sense of exile. They and their admirers could speculate freely on the government's military errors, and could peruse metahistorical questions of what might have been done. They had left the two chief field commands in June, 1862, when Confederate strength seemed to be rising. By the autumn of 1862, Confederate power, at least in the West, already seemed to be declining. The obvious conclusion drawn by these generals and their supporters was that had they and not Bragg commanded, matters would have been different.

Instead, because of either stubbornness or hatred, Davis had been willing to sacrifice the Confederate West by supporting Bragg. Although many disliked Bragg, this was not the issue. It was he who held commmand of the Army of Tennessee, at the expense of Johnston, Beauregard—and perhaps success.

This was a convenient argument, and a difficult one to combat. The Abingdon bloc and its two leaders dealt with questions of what might have been, and Beauregard's admirers in the autumn of 1862 argued that if he had led the Kentucky invasion, the Rebel flag would now be implanted in Cincinnati. Johnston had similar opportunities. From late 1862 until well into 1864, Johnston's admirers preached that the general bore the cross of Richmond's dislike. Johnston was always pictured conveniently as the general who was there, or who was not there. He commanded the West during the disastrous Murfreesboro campaign, but his admirers maintained that the government was responsible for the defeat because it had given Johnston no real power as theater commander. He commanded the Mississippi defenses as well in the spring of 1863, but the same argument attempted to exonerate Johnston of responsibility for Grant's success in maneuvering against Vicksburg. Johnston commanded the field army assigned to relieve the Vicksburg garrison in May–June, 1863. Again he failed because the government would not support him. Johnston commanded the Western Department in June–July, 1863, when General William S. Rosecrans won middle Tennessee from Bragg. Again, the government was to blame for not telling Johnston that he still had authority over Bragg. In late 1863 Johnston commanded the almost defunct Mississippi department after Vicksburg's surrender. This, too, was a government plot to keep him in obscurity. But in December, 1863, the government appointed him to command the Army of Tennessee. Within two months, Johnston's correspondence to friends such as Wigfall had set the tone. He would fail in Georgia because the government, either from malice or stubbornness, would not support him.

These ideas, advanced by the Abingdon-Columbia faction, were closely related to their dislike of Bragg's generalship. Clearly, Davis was playing favorites, and the Confederacy was suffering while

Johnston and Beauregard languished in storage. This resentment against Bragg bound the Abingdon bloc to a second faction, the anti-Bragg bloc.

The anti-Bragg bloc was one of the most militant of the informal groups in the Confederacy. It possessed immense power within the Army of Tennessee, strong support in the Congress, and broad sympathy from factions such as the Abingdon bloc. The anti-Bragg bloc, centered within the Army of Tennessee, also exemplified the overlapping of partisan groups. Several key members, such as Generals James Longstreet and Leonidas Polk were also in the western concentration bloc. Others, such as Generals John C. Breckinridge and William Preston, were among the interconnecting family groups of the Abingdon bloc.

The anti-Bragg bloc must be defined with caution. Not all who disliked Bragg were members. The term does not apply to general resentment throughout the Confederacy against Bragg's generalship. Instead, the true anti-Bragg faction was a combination of dissident generals within the Army of Tennessee who in late 1862 began to form a coalition to oust Bragg. By September of 1863 the coalition was so strong—embracing all four army corps leaders—that the group rose to challenge Bragg in an exhibition of near mutiny.

The anti-Bragg bloc was also an intriguing example of the workings of several minute groups, or subfactions, within a larger faction. In its early stages, until the summer of 1863, the movement was composed of members of three power groups within the Army of Tennessee. Two of these groups were led by the Army of Tennessee's only two corps leaders, Generals Leonidas Polk and William J. Hardee. A third faction was composed of Kentucky generals. It was led by General John C. Breckinridge until the summer of 1863, when General Simon Buckner assumed the leadership.

Each of these groups developed from a dual cause—disgust with Bragg's generalship and anger at Bragg's penchant for blaming failures on subordinate officers. Polk, never a Bragg admirer, began campaigning for his removal after the retreat from Kentucky in October of 1862. Polk, then as he did later, took advantage of his warm prewar friendship with President Davis. He frequently sent private letters to Davis, arguing that Bragg had lost the army's confidence and urging his replacement by Johnston.

By October, General William J. Hardee had aligned himself with Polk. Like Polk, Hardee showed that anti-Bragg men were not necessarily also anti-Davis men. If Polk possessed Davis' friendship, Hardee commanded the President's respect because of his long reputation as a scholar-soldier. Beginning with the Kentucky retreat, Hardee had become so disgusted with Bragg that he openly criticized him in conversations with his own adoring staff and division officers, among them General Patrick Cleburne. Hardee maintained that only Polk's conduct in Kentucky had saved the army from disaster. In November, Hardee wrote Davis' aide, Colonel William Preston Johnston, that Bragg was a failure and should be removed. Hardee's December report of the Kentucky operations took the same line as Polk's November report. Both generals contended that in Kentucky, Bragg had been fooled completely by General Don Carlos Buell's clever maneuvering. Both insisted that at Perryville they had known that Buell's main army was on the field, but they were unable to convince Bragg.

The Kentucky generals also began to join the critics of Bragg that autumn. The Kentucky officers were infuriated at Bragg's charges that the campaign had failed because Kentucky people were too cowardly to enlist in the army. The Kentucky officers were also frustrated that the campaign to redeem their home state had failed. For this failure they blamed Bragg's generalship.

After the battle of Murfreesboro, the anti-Bragg movement began to grow even stronger. During the spring of 1863, Bragg became involved in quarrels with the three leaders of the subfactions, Polk, Hardee, and Breckinridge. The basic cause of these new disputes was a change in Bragg's personality. He had always been suspicious, sour, and quick to use subordinates as scapegoats for his own failures. But by January of 1863, he became even more aggressive and he relished clashes with army opponents. Bragg was nearing the mental collapse that became obvious in the early summer. Much of his time in the spring was consumed not with concern over Rosecrans but in preparing briefs against his own generals. One observer noted sagely that Bragg would rather win one battle in Richmond than two in the field.

Probably the key cause of his new aggressiveness occurred in January. Bragg was besieged by newspaper criticism over the Kentucky and Murfreesboro operations. One such newspaper, the Chattanooga *Rebel,* speculated that Bragg would soon be replaced. From other sources, Bragg heard that either Beauregard or Kirby Smith might soon replace him.

Since most criticism indicated that he had lost the army's confidence, Bragg determined to squelch this. Unfortunately his efforts strengthened the opposition bloc. On January 10 Bragg assembled his staff and announced that he would resign if he had lost the army's confidence. Bragg, obviously selecting a favorable audience, asked his staff if such rumors were true. To his surprise, his own staff caucused and returned a verdict that the general should step down.

The following day, Bragg refused to drop the matter. Rebuffed by his own staff, he turned to his enemies for support. Bragg composed a circular letter to all corps and division commanders. While most of the note concerned the question of who had favored a retreat from Murfreesboro, Bragg dangled a tempting morsel. He declared that he would resign if he had lost the army's confidence.

The replies were humiliating. Polk was away on a visit, so his division commanders shrewdly decided to await his return before committing themselves. But Hardee's officers did not hesitate. Hardee informed Bragg that he had consulted his two division heads, Cleburne and Breckinridge. All three, Hardee asserted, thought that Bragg should resign. Cleburne and Breckinridge sent their own notes. Each stated that the vote among their brigade commanders was unanimous: Bragg should resign.

Although Bragg had promised to quit if his generals did not support him, he now rationalized that dissent was not widespread, but was only the handiwork of a few dissident generals who desired to cloak their own failures. This face-saving rationale dominated Bragg's thinking during the spring. To justify not resigning, he reasoned, he must shift the blame to others, and root out the malcontents. Thus he explained his new policy to President Davis as "assailed, myself, for the blunders of others, and by them and their friends, my mind is made up to bear no sins in the future but my own."[5]

In February, Bragg went on the offensive against his generals. He was encouraged by a visit from the theater commander, General Joseph E. Johnston. Davis on January 22 had sent Johnston to probe the extent of the anti-Bragg sentiment which the President admitted did exist, and to "decide what the best interests of the service require."[6]

Johnston dodged the issue. He was aware that congressional friends were pushing to have Seddon give him Bragg's command, and his two February reports seemed to lean over backwards in praise of Bragg, and did not recommend his replacement. Johnston did admit that "some or all" of the general officers lacked confidence in Bragg. He could hardly have escaped noticing this. While at Tullahoma, Johnston was told by both Hardee and Polk that the army distrusted Bragg. Polk on February 4 had sent another secret letter to Davis urging Bragg's dismissal.

But Johnston's visit only encouraged Bragg. He gloated over Johnston's praise, praise which was used later by Davis against Bragg's opponents in the Congress. Elated, Bragg first attacked Breckinridge. There were several threads of dislike between them. Bragg had criticized Breckinridge for failing to arrive in October for propaganda needs in the Kentucky campaign, and was angered by Breckinridge's conduct at Murfreesboro. Bragg also disliked Breckinridge's brigade commanders, especially General William Preston and Colonel Randall Gibson, and Breckinridge's adjutant-general, the Kentucky poet Theodore O'Hara. In 1861 Bragg had discharged O'Hara at Pensacola as "a disgrace to the service."[7] By 1863 O'Hara had taken a position on Breckinridge's staff. Bragg learned that he was furnishing an anti-Bragg newspaper correspondent with official correspondence of the Murfreesboro campaign. Finally, the Kentucky officers had

---

[5] *Official Records*, LII, Pt. 2, p. 426.

[6] Davis to Johnston, January 22, 1863, in Joseph E. Johnston Papers, William and Mary Library.

[7] Bragg to W. W. Mackall, February 14, 1863, in W. W. Mackall Papers, Southern Historical Collection, University of North Carolina.

given a vote of no confidence in reply to Bragg's January round-robin letter.

A long quarrel ensued which strengthened the Kentucky resentment against Bragg. Bragg's February report of Murfreesboro placed heavy blame on Breckinridge. The Kentucky brigadiers urged Breckinridge to resign and challenge Bragg to a duel. Instead, he fought back with his own official report. A tiresome three-month war ensued, with each officer bombarding the government and the press with countercharges. Only in May when Breckinridge was transferred to Mississippi did the argument cool.

Bragg in February also solidified the opposition by attacking the popular General Frank Cheatham, commander of the Tennessee division in Polk's corps. The rough, unprofessional Cheatham was immensely popular among both Tennessee soldiers and congressmen. In January, Bragg had charged that Cheatham was drunk during the Murfreesboro operations and in February, Bragg's official report conspicuously left Cheatham's name off a long list of corps and division officers who were commended. Another uproar arose in Polk's corps when the report was released.

This uproar led President Davis to order two visitors to Bragg's army. Faced with widespread accounts of army discontent, Davis, on March 9, ordered Johnston to take command of the Army in Tennessee and to order Bragg to Richmond. But a series of incidents, including a serious illness of Bragg's wife and a recurrence of difficulties from Johnston's old wound, prevented any real change in command. By April the government was willing to let the matter drop and Bragg remained in command. Another visitor also sustained Bragg. On March 12 Davis had sent his aide, Colonel William Preston Johnston, to examine the army.

Davis probably hoped for an impartial view, since young Johnston had ties with both pro- and anti-Bragg elements. Bragg and Johnston were friends, and the Kentuckian's cousin, Stoddard Johnston, was on Bragg's staff. On the opposite side, two of Albert Sidney Johnston's staff officers commanded brigades in Breckinridge's division. One, General William Preston, was young Johnston's uncle. Polk had been a warm friend of Albert Sidney Johnston. The result was a lukewarm report by the obviously embarrassed Davis aide. Johnston completely avoided mention of the army's internal problems, and concentrated on ordnance and logistical matters.

Again encouraged, Bragg moved against Hardee and Polk. Angered by their reports of Kentucky operations, Bragg issued another circular letter in April to his generals. He asked them to what extent they had supported Polk's disobedience of orders in calling two councils of war at Bardstown and Perryville, during Bragg's absence. Also, Bragg's official report severely attacked Polk's Kentucky conduct. In fact, the attack was so severe that Polk expected to be arrested. This final quarrel made complete the breach between Bragg and his generals. In late May, Bragg admitted to Davis that "it will not be possible for the cordial official confidence to exist again."[8]

The importance of these attacks by Bragg was that they solidified the opposition. Several bold anti-Bragg strokes were taken. Polk continued to write letters to Davis urging Bragg's removal. Also Polk, Hardee, Preston, and Buckner combined to publish a pamphlet attacking Bragg's Perryville and Murfreesboro operations. The pamphlet, evidently composed by one of Preston's staff members, was so strongly worded that its backers decided not to have it published.

Both Bragg and the opposition maintained strong lobbies in Richmond. Bragg's chief agent was Colonel John Sale, who was sent by Bragg to furnish aid to pro-Bragg congressmen, such as Senator James Phelan of Mississippi and Congressman James Pugh of Alabama. Sale also conferred with Davis, who furnished private correspondence with Joseph E. Johnston and official documents to Bragg's congressional friends.

The opposition did not do badly. Wigfall continued his dual fight to oust Bragg and have Johnston appointed. Congressman Henry Foote and Senator Gustavus Henry of Tennessee supported Polk strongly. In March the Tennessee congressional delegation even asked Davis to remove Bragg from their state because he depressed the people. Meanwhile, Kentucky congressmen such as Senator H. C.

---

[8] Bragg to Davis, May 22, 1863, in Braxton Bragg Papers, Duke University Library.

Burnet, assaulted Bragg for his attacks on General Breckinridge.

For two key reasons the anti-Bragg move dwindled during the summer. First, the loss of middle Tennessee to Rosecrans in July and the threat of a Federal advance on Chattanooga in August preoccupied the generals. Second, many of the bloc's leaders were transferred. In July, Hardee had been sent to Johnston's command in Mississippi. Breckinridge had already been sent to Mississippi and Preston to southwestern Virginia.

By September, however, the anti-Bragg faction had been rejuvenated, and was nearing its zenith. New blood had strengthened the opposition as the army acquired three new corps commanders, all hostile to Bragg. In late July, General Harvey Hill replaced Hardee. Hill, a classmate of Bragg's at West Point, was much like Bragg. He was nervous, easily affronted, and quick to criticize. By mid-September, Hill had become convinced that Bragg should be replaced.

His opinion was shared by General Simon Buckner. Buckner in September came to the army as commander of a new 3rd Corps. He also came with two old resentments. Like other Kentuckians, Buckner had been angered by Bragg's attacks against his state the previous autumn. Even worse, a morass of administrative confusion between Bragg's Second Department and Buckner's Department of East Tennessee during the summer had produced ill feeling. Buckner's department was to exist "for administrative duties" but was also to be part of Bragg's department. Thus in early September Bragg ordered Buckner's small east Tennessee army, now designated the 3rd Corps, to join the concentration below Chattanooga at Chickamauga. A serious argument promptly erupted. Buckner believed that he still held authority to decide upon the organization of his troops, Bragg believed that since Buckner was out of his old department he had surrendered both administrative and strategic control. Thus Bragg proceeded to reorganize Buckner's command, and the Kentuckian protested violently.

A third corps leader who joined the concentration below Chattanooga also united with the anti-Bragg camp. Twice before in 1863 General James Longstreet had sought independence from Lee's command. In January and again in May, Longstreet had suggested that his corps be sent to reinforce Bragg. Evidently Longstreet had in mind that he would also replace Bragg, for he was corresponding with Wigfall on this matter in early 1863. In August he again proposed to Lee and Seddon that his corps be sent to reinforce Bragg. He admitted tht he would take Bragg's position if it were offered. Then, on September 5, as Davis and Lee approached a favorable decision to reinforce Bragg, Longstreet became more direct. To Lee, Longstreet gave a low estimate of Bragg, and proposed that he be given the command. Longstreet said the western army lacked confidence in Bragg, and that therefore the general was not likely "to do a great deal for us."[9]

Longstreet was not happy with the outcome of the Davis-Lee deliberations. He was not given command of Bragg's army, but was ordered only to reinforce Bragg with two divisions. A disgruntled Longstreet confided to Wigfall that he did not think he should have to serve under Bragg. Thus Longstreet had, from afar, fully absorbed the anti-Bragg point of view, and he gave the anti-Bragg group his full allegiance immediately upon his arrival in Georgia.

By the time of the battle of Chickamauga, September 19–20, the anti-Bragg membership was at its peak. Of the original group, only Hardee was now absent. Buckner had returned as a corps commander. Preston was now back, commanding a division in Buckner's corps. In late August, Johnston had sent two divisions from Mississippi to reinforce Bragg. One was led by Breckinridge, and was reincorporated into Hardee's old corps. Together with Polk, Hill, and Longstreet, this display of anti-Bragg power was awesome.

Five days after the battle of Chickamauga, the anti-Bragg faction moved against the army's commander. On September 26 the four corps leaders—Hill, Buckner, Longstreet, and Polk—held a secret meeting. Probably there were two motivations: First of all, they were disgusted by Bragg's apparent failure to capitalize on the Chickamauga victory and pursue Rosecrans, nor could they understand Bragg's defensive posture; and second, these generals probably smelled trouble and sought to strike the first blow. Bragg's record of blaming

[9] *Official Records*, XXIX, Pt. 2, p. 699.

subordinates was well known. Many times during the campaign the Confederates had lost good opportunities due to mixups within the high command. On September 22 and again on September 25, Bragg had sent stiff, foreboding notes to Polk, demanding an explanation for Polk's failure to attack promptly on the morning of the twentieth. Unknown to the group, Bragg had gone even further. He had also sent two letters to Davis and a staff officer with a verbal report as well. Polk's failures were basic in the reports.

Then the anti-Bragg men struck. On September 26 the corps leaders agreed to instigate a letter-writing campaign against Bragg. Longstreet agreed to write Lee and Seddon, while Polk wrote his old friend the President, and Lee as well. All the letters were similar. A glorious opportunity, they said, had been lost after Chickamauga, and Bragg should be removed.

The near mutiny was brought into the open by Bragg's own actions. On September 29 he suspended Polk and one of his division commanders, General Thomas C. Hindman. Polk was ordered to Atlanta. The outcry against Polk's removal created such an uproar that on October 9 Davis himself hurried to the army. He had come to Georgia in answer to frantic telegrams from his aide, Colonel James Chesnut. Chesnut, sent the previous week to ascertain the situation, telegraphed Davis on October 5 to hurry to Georgia. He arrived too late. On the previous night, the anti-Bragg men had taken a further step.

On the night of October 4 Buckner, Longstreet, and Hill held another secret meeting. A petition was drafted to Davis, and was signed by the three corps commanders and nine other generals, including Cleburne and Preston. The long document carefully avoided any criticism of Bragg's military ability. Instead, it concentrated on one issue, that "the condition of his health unfits him for the command of an army in the field."[10]

Although the petition was actually never delivered to Davis, the President had opportunity to hear the anti-Bragg bloc in action after his October 9 arrival. Both Buckner and Longstreet privately urged

[10] Buckner, Hill, Longstreet, *et al.*, to Davis, October 4, 1863, in Simon Buckner Papers, Henry E. Huntington Library.

Davis to remove Bragg. Polk had already urged the same in a conference with the President at Atlanta. Then, probably on October 10, Davis called a meeting of the corps commanders at Bragg's headquarters. There, in Bragg's presence, all four corps commanders, Longstreet, Hill, Buckner, and Cheatham (temporarily commanding Polk's corps) stated that the commander should be replaced.

The rebellion was a complete failure, and in the end, the anti-Bragg faction destroyed itself. It was not merely that Davis chose to sustain Bragg. Whether deliberate or not, Davis and Bragg arranged for a dispersal of the opposition. On October 23 Polk was transferred to Johnston's Mississippi department. On October 15 Davis authorized Bragg to remove Hill from his corps command on the flimsy grounds that he "weakens the morale and military tone of his command." General Nathan Bedford Forrest, another violent Bragg critic, was transferred by Davis to the Mississippi command. In late October, Davis formally abolished the east Tennessee department. Buckner also lost his status as corps commander and was reduced to the rank of division commander. General William Preston, another petition signer, was reduced to the rank of brigade commander. Davis in October also authorized Bragg to reorganize the army. His later explanation was that there were too many brigades in a single division from the same state. Actually, Bragg had for a long time nourished the idea of breaking up the powerful Tennessee and Kentucky cliques. The new November organization seemed an attempt at realizing this concept. Cheatham's division had formerly boasted twenty-two Tennessee regiments, a hard core of Polk support. By November 13 Cheatham possessed only six. Breckinridge's Kentucky division was also decimated. Not a single brigade which had served under Breckinridge during the previous spring was retained under his command.

The only corps commander to escape immediate censure, transfer, or demotion was Longstreet. By November 5 this, too, had been accomplished. The previous day, Bragg had ordered the detachment of Longstreet with seventeen thousand troops in the famous independent campaign against Burnside's corps in east Tennessee. Why did Bragg allow such a detachment which would leave only thirty-six thousand at Chattanooga to oppose an estimated eighty thousand Federals when Longstreet's seventeen thousand men would scarcely be adequate to insure quick success against Burnside's reported twenty-five thousand men?

Probably Bragg authorized the detachment—and Longstreet desired it—as a final move in the anti-Bragg war of 1863. By early November, relations between Bragg and Longstreet had broken down almost completely. Longstreet, who commanded Bragg's left wing in the vicinity of Lookout Mountain, rarely communicated with his superior. Longstreet, who doubtless still desired an independent command in the West, was anxious to be free of Bragg's authority, and Bragg seemed equally desirous of being rid of Longstreet. On October 31, Bragg had labeled Longstreet to Davis as "disrespectful and insubordinate." According to General St. John Liddell, Bragg admitted that he sent Longstreet to Knoxville "to get rid of him and see what he could do on his own resources."[11]

By December of 1863 Bragg's resignation after the battle of Missionary Ridge, coupled with the reorganization and shuffling of the previous two months, ended the organization of anti-Bragg men by removing their cause. Although it had existed as a united front for less than a year and a half, the anti-Bragg faction had possessed broad influence. The power of the faction within the Army of Tennessee was obvious. Beyond the army, it was linked to the Abingdon bloc by family ties and a common resentment of Bragg. Like the Abingdon bloc, the anti-Bragg people were a component of the western concentration bloc. The uproar created by Bragg's opponents in itself focused attention on western matters. The correspondence of its members with Davis, Seddon, Wigfall, and others stressed the need for more attention to the West. Such correspondence also often urged the strategic policies of the western bloc.

The anti-Bragg faction was also influential because of its ties with another Confederate informal organization—the Kentucky bloc. This geographic faction was composed of a number of prominent Kentucky generals and politicians who maintained a close relationship through-

[11] General St. John Liddell reminiscences, in Daniel Govan Papers, Southern Historical Collection, University of North Carolina.

out the war. Its military adherents included Generals John Morgan, William Preston, Joseph Lewis, Humphrey Marshall, Simon Buckner, and John C. Breckinridge. Its political members included the Confederate "governor" of Kentucky, Richard C. Hawes, and Senator H. C. Burnet.

The group was bound by a single ideal—to pressure the Confederates to attempt to regain Kentucky. This desire led to rapport with other factions. The Kentuckians' goals made them natural members of the western concentration bloc with its stress on the need for a concentrated offensive in the West. They were far less interested than other members of the western concentration bloc were in the fine points of Napoleonic strategy or in the threat to the Chattanooga-Atlanta front. An offensive meant a promise of redeeming their native state. Like the Abingdon-Columbia and the anti-Bragg factions, the Kentucky bloc, generally was strongly opposed to Bragg because of that general's two sins—questioning Kentucky's courage and failure to recapture the state.

This desire to retake Kentucky was also a connecting bond between the ideas of the western concentration bloc and official Richmond policy. It had been a blow to Davis' hopes when Kentucky in 1861 refused to secede. Then, in early 1862, Sidney Johnston's loss of southern Kentucky and most of Tennessee wrecked Rebel hopes of a defensive line on the Ohio River.

For the remainder of the war, Davis, the Kentucky generals, and several members of the western concentration bloc shared a common ideal—the pervasive "Kentucky dream." This ambition to push the southern frontier to the Ohio River was a slow-dying dream. Regaining Kentucky was attempted by Bragg and Kirby Smith in mid-1862. It was spoken of frequently in 1863 and early 1864. Late in 1864 it was again attempted by General John B. Hood's pitiful Army of Tennessee.

The ambition was intensified because many southerners, including Davis, believed that Kentucky was a captive state. They believed, at least before the 1862 Kentucky campaign, that Kentucky was being held in the Union against her will, and that a Confederate invasion would produce a mass uprising.

In accepting this view, Davis and others ignored past signs of lethargy in Kentucky. In the autumn of 1861 General Simon Buckner, popular commander of the Kentucky state militia, fled to Bowling Green and joined Albert Sidney Johnston's command. Buckner issued two proclamations from Bowling Green, calling for Kentuckians to rise in numbers to aid Johnston. Johnston also issued a similar proclamation. In October, General John C. Breckinridge, who had also joined Johnston, issued another appeal. In December a plea for mass volunteers was repeated in eastern Kentucky by General Felix Zollicoffer. Finally, in January of 1862, Zollicoffer's successor, General George Crittenden, issued yet another similar proclamation. Crittenden, a member of a prominent Kentucky family, was as unsuccessful in gaining support as had been Buckner, Breckinridge, and the others.

Still the Confederates believed that Kentucky was held in bondage, and in November of 1861 a provisional government was established at Russellville. A Confederate governor of Kentucky was elected, congressmen were received in Richmond, and another star was placed on the flag.

By the summer of 1862 the government was under pressure to invade Kentucky. Reports from Kentucky officers indicated that there was wholesale discontent with Federal rule in the state. Probably the Confederates misread such reports. There was widespread discontent with the repressive and inept administration of the state's commander, General Jeremiah Boyle. This discontent was not necessarily synonymous with pro-Confederate sentiment, however, since Kentucky, as a border state, had a long record of neutrality.

It is also probable that Richmond misread the results of General John Hunt Morgan's June cavalry raid into Kentucky. Morgan's colorful band excited widespread interest among Kentucky civilians, and what Abraham Lincoln termed a "stampede" among the Federals. But the vain, flamboyant Morgan totally misled the government. In July he sent his departmental commander, General Kirby Smith, a famous dispatch which was rushed that same day to Richmond. Morgan boasted that the whole country was rising. He promised that if a Confederate army invaded the state, between twenty thousand

and thirty thousand volunteers would join "at once." Morgan also boasted that he had procured enough recruits to hold most of the Bluegrass region.

Such boasts proved inflated. Morgan himself had received only three hundred volunteers. He was unable to hold the Bluegrass even on the day after his dispatch was written. Although he was cheered by many (who did not volunteer), Morgan probably misinterpreted his own popularity and the romantic sentiment for his colorful raiders as sentiment for the Confederacy.

Confederates, generally, never saw that popularity of Kentucky officers did not necessarily imply Confederate sympathy among Kentuckians. Men such as Breckinridge, Buckner, and Morgan were immensely popular in Kentucky. This, however, was not synonymous with sympathy for the Rebels among Kentuckians. Twenty-three of the most staunch Union counties had voted for Breckinridge in 1860, but only one had elected a pro-secession congressional candidate. Breckinridge had also carried fourteen Bluegrass counties, but the secessionists had carried only four.

Bragg had problems with Kentucky generals because he did not comprehend their great pride and their widespread support. To the Kentucky bloc, the war was a personal matter. Breckinridge and Humphrey Marshall, another of the powerful political figures in the state, had fled as fugitives to the Confederacy. Buckner had been a prominent military figure and Morgan a wealthy Lexington merchant. All of their prestige had been swept away, and these men had been cast as refugees. Thus the group was also bound together psychologically.

Unable to see this important difference between individual popularity and loyalty to the Confederacy, many Confederates were elated by Morgan's report. Kirby Smith and Bragg were also convinced that an invasion would produce great results. General Robert E. Lee urged Davis to attempt such an invasion because "it would produce a great effect."[12] Davis himself accepted this viewpoint. In August

---

[12] Lee to Davis, July 26, 1862, in Dowdey and Manarin (eds.), *Wartime Papers*, 238.

of 1862 he authorized a joint invasion of Kentucky by Bragg and Kirby Smith. Davis' motivation was as much political as military. He later admitted that the campaign had been inaugurated because it was believed that the Kentuckians would rise en masse. To encourage this, the President had furnished his generals with copies of a proclamation inviting Kentucky to throw off the Federal yoke.

The campaign's results should have convinced the Confederates that they had misjudged Kentucky sentiment. Neither Bragg nor Kirby Smith, marching on widely separate fronts, met with any sympathy until they reached north-central Kentucky. By late September, Bragg and Kirby Smith desperately needed reinforcements which did not come. Thousands of small arms had been carried along to arm the expected volunteers. In early October, Bragg even suspended military operations long enough to inaugurate Richard Hawes at Frankfort as the Kentucky governor. Some have belittled this ceremony as a farce. Actually Bragg exhibited some political savvy. Kentuckians had advised him that many wanted to volunteer, but that they feared Federal reprisals on their families. Thus Bragg was encouraged to establish a civil government so that conscription would be absolutely legal. Then, Bragg was told, those afraid to volunteer would not mind being conscripted, since it would appear they had been forced to join the Confederates.

But Bragg's efforts failed to gain men. General Don Carlos Buell moved against Bragg at Perryville before the conscript law could be used. By October 9 Bragg's losses in Kentucky had reached forty-five hundred men. Yet, from mid-August until mid-October, the Confederates netted only twenty-five hundred volunteers in Kentucky instead of Morgan's promised twenty thousand. The lack of any visible sign of support was a key factor in the decision made by Bragg and Kirby Smith on October 12 to leave Kentucky.

But the Kentucky dream did not diminish. It remained a strong motivation until it was attempted again by Hood in late 1864. There were two reasons for this renewal of effort. One was that many Confederates simply did not accept Bragg's explanation that the Kentucky people had not supported him, and they believed instead that his failure resulted from poor generalship. His October explanation to the government was countered by a flood of explanations by Kirby Smith, Hardee, Polk, and the Kentucky generals. Each, with his own personal motivation, contended that the campaign had failed not because of a lack of support but because Bragg had bungled it. One Bragg supporter, the newspaper editor John Forsyth, attempted to defend Bragg in the Mobile *Tribune.* Forsyth, who had accompanied Bragg, echoed the general's charge that the Kentucky people had behaved in a cowardly manner, even to the point of fearing to invite Rebel officers into their homes for a night's lodging. But Forsyth's detailed analysis was countered by Governor Richard Hawes, who, in the Richmond *Enquirer,* argued that Bragg's poor generalship had caused the defeat.

Most of the Confederate press agreed with Bragg's critics. Exaggerated newspaper accounts told of how Bragg had routed Buell's army at the battle of Perryville. Also, tales that Bragg brought from Kentucky vast wagon trains filled with food, clothing, and other supplies filled the Rebel press. By the end of October, even the War Department believed that Bragg's wagon train was forty miles long, and many people wondered why Bragg retreated when he possessed such logistical support. Actually, the Confederates were on the verge of starvation and were almost threadbare when they reached the Tennessee border in late October. Bragg's famous wagon train was mostly myth. He did possess many wagons, but most contained the thousands of small arms carried into Kentucky to arm new recruits. In fact, on the retreat, General Kirby Smith had scattered ten thousand of his men, whom he described as "famished, to search for food."

A second reason the Kentucky myth persisted was that not only was Bragg's explanation disbelieved by many, but it served to cement the powerful opposition bloc of Kentucky officers who continued to propagate the myth. During 1862 and 1863 much of the activity of Buckner, Breckinridge, and Preston within the anti-Bragg faction was due to resentment at Bragg's retreat and his charges of Kentucky cowardice. Together with generals outside Bragg's army, such as Humphrey Marshall, and politicians such as Burnet, these Kentuckians maintained a strong lobby for another invasion. By the winter of 1863–1864, such propaganda appeared to be working. Already in 1863 many of the strategic proposals offered by Beauregard, Polk, and others spoke of a forward move which would eventually clear Kentucky of the Federals. By the winter of 1863–1864, a large number of Kentucky generals had congregated in Richmond, to lobby for another invasion.

Some of these officers were probably motivated by a loss of status. General John Morgan, once a favorite of the President's, was by 1864 in extremely bad favor. Already by the spring of 1863 Morgan's status in the western army was declining. Both Bragg and Hardee had expressed a lack of confidence in his generalship, and friends warned Morgan that his old admirer Bragg now disliked him. In 1863 Morgan led an unauthorized raid into Ohio and Indiana probably in an attempt to regain lost status. Instead, he lost his command and was imprisoned in the Ohio state prison. In the fall of 1863 Morgan and several other officers made a daring escape, and by January, he was in Richmond searching for a new command.

Breckinridge, too, probably sought to regain status. The October, 1863, mutiny against Bragg's generalship apparently had not hurt Breckinridge personally. He had refused to sign the petition written by Buckner, Longstreet, and Hill. This refusal probably produced a short period of respite in his quarrel with Bragg. By November, Breckinridge had been assigned to command an army corps at Chattanooga. But this respite was short-lived. Breckinridge's corps behaved badly in the battle of Missionary Ridge, and the general was blamed by Bragg for the defeat. After the battle, Bragg immediately relieved Breckinridge of his command, contending that the Kentuckian was so drunk during the battle, that he collapsed on the floor of a railroad station during the retreat. Regardless of whether Bragg exaggerated the matter, the shameful panic of his corps at Missionary Ridge probably doomed Breckinridge's hopes of future service in the Army of Tennessee.

There were other Kentuckians in Richmond with varied motives. Buckner, who had been allowed to retain command of the East Tennessee department, evidently sought a new position. General George B. Hodge was seeking approval of a bold plan to invade

Kentucky with a cavalry brigade, and also of a plot to destroy Federal supplies accumulated at Nashville. General Joseph Lewis, another Kentucky cavalryman, was seeking approval of a raid by his brigade into Kentucky. That magnificent English fraud, Colonel St. Leger Grenfell, came to Richmond as a special lobbyist for Morgan's interests. Captain Thomas Hines, who had escaped with Morgan in Ohio, had come to secure the War Department's authority for espionage activities in the Northwest, including the freeing of Confederate prisoners at Chicago.

Although the sum total of such plans was much bluster and little common sense, the Kentuckians were the lions of Richmond society during the winter. On Christmas Eve, President Davis, Buckner, Breckinridge, and Preston were special guests at a dinner given by John Smith Preston of the Conscription Bureau. Morgan's arrival in Richmond on January 7 created wild enthusiasm, with some seeking his autograph, others locks of his hair, while still others felt impelled to write poetry, and the city gave him a welcoming parade. A special reception for the Kentuckians was held at the city hall, and another ball was given in Morgan's honor in February. The Chesnuts also entertained the Kentuckians twice in January. Mrs. Chesnut commented that they "fill the town," that they came to her reception *"en masse"* and that they "move as one body." They were also feted at other balls, dinners, and theatricals.

By January 15 the mixed sentiments of the Kentucky bloc had coalesced into a formal proposal to the government. It came at an opportune time, when the government was deliberating what strategy General Joseph E. Johnston's Army of Tennessee should pursue in the spring. Of the five strategic proposals offered in the winter of 1863–1864 for Johnston's army, including that of the Kentuckians, all indicated some interest in Kentucky. This is not to say, of course, that the Kentucky bloc influenced all of these proposals. But their constant presence in Richmond, their appeals for an offensive, and their January plan could only whet the government's desire for the old Kentucky dream.

The plan of the Kentucky officers called for a two-front western offensive. It was presented to Davis on January 15 by Morgan,

Buckner, Breckinridge, and Lewis. It called for the concentration in east Tennessee of Kentucky regiments scattered throughout southern armies. These were to be converted into cavalry, and the Kentuckians expected to concentrate eight thousand men. When Johnston advanced from Dalton against the Federals at Chattanooga, the Kentucky corps would invade their native state via Cumberland Gap. Great results were promised to Davis. Federal communications in Tennessee would be cut, troops would be diverted from Johnston's front to Kentucky, and the Kentucky people would rise up to join their state's Confederate regiments.

Although this may have been a utopian scheme concocted by a body of generals of declining status, it was not treated so by the government. Seddon held several conferences with the Kentuckians in January. Although Seddon did not think it feasible to convert all the troops into cavalry, he did like the idea of a Kentucky corps to be assembled in east Tennessee. The matter was passed to Davis, who ordered his aide, G. W. C. Lee, to write Johnston for his opinion. When Lee approached Johnston on the matter in late January, Davis' office seemed excited over the possibilities. Lee stated that it was believed such a corps would bolster morale and would incite the Kentucky people to support the Confederacy. Also, Richmond seemed interested in the idea of a double offensive. Lee suggested that if eight thousand Kentuckians invaded the state from east Tennessee, combined with Johnston's advance, "they could enter Kentucky . . . occupy the center of the State, collect supplies and gather strength, and interrupt the enemy's communications." Lee stated that it was also believed they might "prove a legitimate military diversion" by drawing Federals from Johnston's front.

Johnston stifled the plan's chances by contending that "converting good infantry into bad cavalry" would accomplish little. Still the government's appetite for a Kentucky offensive was stimulated. Other proposals may have produced a similar effect. In December of 1863 Beauregard had forwarded another plan of strategy to his supporters in Richmond. The previous month he had already corresponded with Breckinridge on the government's past strategic errors. To the Kentuckian, Beauregard insisted that had his spring proposal been adopted, "Tennessee and Kentucky would then have been left open to us" and Kentucky placed in position "to show on which side she would cast her lot."[13]

Beauregard's new plan, sent both to Richmond friends and to Johnston at Dalton, still gave Kentucky this opportunity. Beauregard called for massing a strong force either at Knoxville or at Dalton, Georgia. This force would crush Grant's army at Chattanooga. Then perhaps Johnston could "pursue the routed enemy with vigor to the banks of the Ohio and Mississippi."[14]

During the winter of 1864 other plans for an offensive were proposed by James Longstreet, Leonidas Polk, and by the President and his military advisers. These, like those of Beauregard and the Kentuckians, all had some bearing on Kentucky. This is not to say that the Kentucky bloc wrote the government's strategy for the West in 1864. Yet they were in Richmond in great force and conferred extensively with Davis, Seddon, and others. If they did nothing else, the Kentucky generals did keep alive the old dream of the defensive line on the Ohio. There were similarities between their January proposal and the March plan sent to Johnston and Longstreet. Both entailed a forward move from east Tennessee. While the Kentucky bloc's plan called for an outright invasion of the state, the Davis plan gave Johnston the alternatives of either fighting in middle Tennessee or invading Kentucky. Still, the President made it clear that Kentucky's eventual occupation was of prime importance. Longstreet's plans were also similar to the Kentucky bloc's proposal. Both called for an invasion of Kentucky by widely separated columns.

The spring of 1864 saw the last activity of the Kentucky faction. A general desire to reconquer Kentucky remained until late 1864, when General John B. Hood attempted to reach the Ohio River in his disastrous Tennessee campaign. But as a group, the Kentucky bloc dissolved much earlier in the year, as the individuals scattered to different areas. Morgan was given command of the Department of Southwestern Virginia, and soon after was killed in east Tennessee.

[13] *Official Records*, XXVIII, Pt. 2, pp. 523–24.
[14] Beauregard to Pierre Soulé, December 8, 1863, in Beauregard Papers, National Archives.

Preston was appointed by Davis as minister to the Imperial Mexican government. Breckinridge in 1864 served first with General Jubal Early, later with Lee, and in 1865 became Secretary of War. Buckner was sent to the Trans-Mississippi Department to command the district of West Louisiana. Hodge also was ordered to the Trans-Mississippi Department in 1864. Lewis was sent to Georgia, where his brigade was merged into Wheeler's cavalry corps.

These three factions, the Abingdon-Columbia, anti-Bragg, and Kentucky blocs, formed a broad network of informal associations which largely composed the western concentration bloc. Yet the ties between all of these groups were based on family connections, friendships, state loyalty, or mutual hatreds. The final thread which connected these men was another informal but more embracing association, one that revolved around the personality and ideas of General P. G. T. Beauregard.

Beauregard's importance as a nucleus of several such factions goes beyond his membership in them. True, he shared the views of the western concentration bloc and, by virtue of his Carolina service, became a leader in the Abingdon-Columbia faction. Beyond that, however, Beauregard, like Bragg and others, benefited from an informal association composed of admirers.

There was a mystique surrounding Beauregard which in many respects seems unjustified. His vain, showy personality tended to alienate people. Quick to claim credit for any success and fearful of a lack of recognition, he could appear pompous. He repeatedly became enmeshed in quarrels with the government because of his great vanity.

When one considers his actual field service, Beauregard's reputation and self-esteem appears ill founded. Although his multitudinous plans were based on the movement of vast blocs of Rebel manpower, Beauregard had rarely directed any large operations himself. Prior to the arrival of General Joseph Johnston at Manassas in July, 1861, when Beauregard was superseded in command by the senior officer—the Creole had commanded only fifteen thousand field troops at Manassas Junction. In fact, for only two months during the war did Beauregard actually command the type of large, independent field force for which he so often plotted grandiose movements. His service as commander of the Army of Tennessee in April and May of 1862 was a dismal failure. True, much of the fault was not Beauregard's. He had, late on April 6 at Shiloh, inherited an impossible situation. The battle was already lost, as much by the army's own disorganization as by the enemy's action. Yet it was Beauregard's elaborate planning at Corinth prior to the battle which had contributed to the army's disorganization. His plans had been too complex, too optimistic for green troops to carry out.

These grandiose plans were another phase of the Beauregard image that did not quite jibe with his prestige and popularity. Many of Beauregard's plans were unrealistic, and some were even ridiculous. Perhaps his actual lack of experience commanding large field armies made him blind to the hard problems of logistics and distance. Perhaps his yearning for the Napoleonic in battle plans and field orders made him impatient with less glamorous matters such as wagon transportation.

Regardless of the cause, Beauregard's plans often seemed untenable—and sometimes humorous. For example, his plan of September, 1862, which he sent to Bragg, contained almost impossible features. This plan demonstrated a serious fault in his designs. Beauregard started with a sound concept—the junction of Bragg and Kirby Smith against a weak Union front—but then he carried the matter too far. He never knew when to stop talking, and the result was that basically sound plans were hooted at because he tried to envision, to promise, too much. In this case, after the hypothetical concentration had been effected and battle given to Buell, Bragg and Kirby Smith were to build fortifications on the Tennessee and Cumberland rivers, capture Louisville, build water batteries on the Ohio at Louisville, march to Cincinnati, erect more fortifications on the Ohio opposite Cincinnati, capture Fort Pillow, detach troops into Missouri, and accomplish yet other ambitious projects. His May, 1863, plan, sent to the government and to Johnston and Bragg also contained this same fatal error. The idea was sound—to mass troops against a single line of the Rosecrans western advance, but Beauregard again allowed his imagination to take over. Not only would Rosecrans be crushed, he claimed, but the Confederates would also build forts on the Tennessee and Cumberland rivers, seize control of the Mississippi River north of Memphis, crush Grant, and detach troops to aid General Sterling Price in Missouri and General Edmund Kirby Smith in Louisiana.

Despite all of his shortcomings, Beauregard possessed widespread influence, even though his personality inspired a number of enmities with such powerful men as President Davis and Secretary of State Judah Benjamin. Perhaps because he had never really commanded the type of army for which he freely offered advice, his grandiose plans were often merely pipe dreams. Yet he was influential in spite of and, in part perhaps, because he was something of a fraud, a cocky, bombastic, foppish officer who was more powerful with pen than with sword, and who delighted in signing orders "within hearing of the enemy's guns" and in appealing for plantation bells to cast artillery.

If Beauregard was a nonstop talker, he was also a frantic correspondent with generals, governors, authors, and congressmen. The government, in Beauregard's version, had exiled him to commands far from the eyes of Richmond. Even so, the Creole was determined that no one should forget his name.

His ensuing correspondence is amazing for its breadth. He conferred in detail on western strategy with Johnston, Bragg, Longstreet, Wigfall, and Breckinridge. He discussed diplomatic problems and blockade running with John Slidell. He outlined plans for a northwestern Confederacy with Governors Joseph Brown of Georgia and F. W. Pickens of South Carolina. He discussed the defense of the Gulf with General Dabney Maury. Beauregard talked of the loss of New Orleans with General Mansfield Lovell. He advised General Chase Whiting on the defense of the North Carolina coast and Governor Isham Harris on the defense of the Mississippi River fortifications in Tennessee. To Congressman William Porcher Miles he sent advice on grand strategy and on the matter of a northwestern Confederacy.

Beauregard resembled a candidate for public office. He took pains to lecture on the Napoleonic principles of concentration—to Bragg and Johnston, to novelist Augusta Jane Evans, to Congressman Charles Villeré, and to Governor Joseph Brown. He had a sympathetic word for the dissidents—for Lovell after his loss of New Orleans, for the troubled Whiting on the North Carolina coast, and for a miserable Johnston on the Tennessee front in the spring of 1863. He never let the South forget him. Even General John B. Hood would, in the spring of 1864, receive a cane carved from a Fort Sumter flagstaff that had been shot down during the 1863 siege. It was Beauregard to whom General G. W. Smith sent his "kind regards" when the disgusted anti-Davis officer resigned from the army. It was also Beauregard whom General Mansfield Lovell desired to have preside over a court of inquiry relative to New Orleans' surrender.

Probably no other Confederate moved as freely among so many varied factions as Beauregard did. His network of connections, expanded and reinforced through his voluminous correspondence, was the base of his influence. Beauregard appealed to frustrated Confederates—officers such as Lovell and G. W. Smith who believed they had been wronged by Davis, and anti-Davis politicians such as Wigfall and Henry Foote of Tennessee.

Because of his strategic views, he fit well into the western concentration bloc. His belief that concentration was needed in the West not only complimented the ideas of such officers as Bragg and Johnston, but also gained the appreciation of Senator Gustavus Henry of Tennessee, Governor Isham Harris of Tennessee, Vice-President Alexander Stephens, Governor Joseph Brown, and others. Beauregard also moved within the antiadministration bloc in Congress. Three of his former aides were in the Congress. Two of them, William Porcher Miles and Roger Pryor, were anti-Davis men, as was his brother-in-law by his first marriage, Charles Villeré of Louisiana. These, together with his supporter Wigfall, gave the Creole a base in Richmond.

Beauregard could identify with the anti-Bragg faction, and even be supported to replace Bragg by his old enemy General Leonidas Polk. The Kentucky bloc supported him warmly, for it was Beauregard who, in 1862, had drawn up two grand designs for the eventual reoccupation of their state. He maintained a correspondence with the bloc's leader, Breckinridge. In September of 1862 it was not a coincidence that one Kentucky senator and seven congressmen asked President Davis for Beauregard's replacement of Bragg. Beauregard also appealed to dissidents who transcended any particular faction. He seemed to share a common persecution by Richmond with Johnston, G. W. Smith, Whiting, Lovell, and others.

When one considers Beauregard a symbol of many varied Confederate frustrations, together with the Abingdon-Columbia, the anti-Bragg, and the Kentucky blocs, a powerful undercurrent appears. These four informal groups composed the western concentration bloc when they coalesced to advocate an opposition strategy. They had a broad power base and influence sufficient to counteract Lee's Virginia-oriented strategic recommendations.

When one views the western concentration bloc and its constituent factions, the placement of "established" power takes on a new importance. Some have accepted the idea that President Davis and his advisers, official and unofficial, represented the most powerful single bloc within the South. Yet this opposition element, containing such notables as Johnston, Beauregard, Longstreet, Hardee, Hampton, Buckner, Breckinridge—and even Bragg—questions this idea. Was it possible that the real power base of the Confederacy did not lie in Richmond? Did it instead rest on some intangible line stretching from the Bluegrass through the lower Virginia valley to Columbia and Charleston?

Even if one rejects the concept that the western bloc represented the Confederate "establishment," this informal association still must be considered a vital element in Confederate strategic thought. To a considerable degree, Jefferson Davis' conduct of military operations, and particularly his strategic decisions, were a product of conflicting pressures exerted by Robert E. Lee on one hand, and the western concentration bloc on the other.

IV
Davis as Generalissimo: The Confederate Departmental System

Several influences seem paramount in determining Confederate strategy. The Jominian and Napoleonic ideas which Davis and many of his generals may have learned either at West Point or through their reading could well have significantly influenced their thinking. The influence of General Robert E. Lee, who emphasized to Davis the importance of Virginia, was also important. Equally strong was the pressure produced by the interlocking informal organizations of generals and politicians, most importantly the western concentration bloc. Most of the generals in this group were strongly influenced by the ideas of Jomini and Napoleon as interpreted by General Beauregard. For the most part, the actions suggested by these Jominian-Napoleonic principles coincided with the western bloc's desire to give greater emphasis to the West. Thus both the western bloc's strategic theories and their concern for the West competed with the ideas of Lee, and strongly influenced Davis' conduct of the war.

Much of this strategic debate occurred within the confines of another important influence upon Confederate strategy, Jefferson Davis' concept of the military department. The evolution of Davis' strategy can be traced by looking at the proposals of his generals and at the structure of Rebel departmental command. Although Davis' ideas changed and his methods of control evolved, the departmental system was always the lens through which he perceived strategy. It was also the vehicle by which he almost invariably sought to implement any new strategic ideas or any development in his plan of control.

Yet the departmental system had another important role in Confederate strategy. Departmental command was inaugurated by Davis as an instrument to carry out policy. As the war progressed, the system became a policy in itself. Apparently Davis sometimes shaped his strategy around the maintenance of the departmental system, rather than the reverse. Thus for many reasons an examination of the evolution of the departmental command system may provide the key to Davis' thinking.

On April 9, 1865, General Robert E. Lee surrendered the remains of the Army of Northern Virginia. In this act, some 27,800 Confederate troops received their paroles. Two weeks later, General Joseph E. Johnston surrendered approximately 31,200 men of the Army of Tennessee. This deterioration of numbers in the South's two main field armies in 1865 has sometimes been cited as an example of the Confederacy's total defeat.

Yet there had been many other surrenders. Beyond the Mississippi River, General E. Kirby Smith's Trans-Mississippi Department possessed 60,000 troops in March, 1865. In May, General Richard Taylor of the Department of Alabama, Mississippi, and East Louisiana surrendered his department at Mobile. In Taylor's force alone, 42,293 men were paroled. This does not even include several thousand additional men surrendered in the mid-South that same month. By November, 1865, the War Department had reported that 174,233 Confederate troops had been surrendered and paroled. Of this number, only 59,048 belonged to the main war effort in 1865, the armies of Lee and Johnston.

Where were the Confederacy's field troops in April, 1865? The figure 174,233 itself is conservative, for it did not include many who deserted prior to official surrender. For example, even though Kirby Smith's muster rolls in March reported 60,000 men, he actually surrendered fewer than half this number. In short, there were probably well over 200,000 southerners under arms in April, 1865, and fewer than one third of these were engaged against Sherman and Grant.

The answer to this problem may be found in that administrative system known as Confederate departmental command. The departmental system was created by the Confederate government in 1861 as a means to organize and to administer military forces within every inch of southern terrain. However, the system became more than an instrument of organization: the idea of departmental command soon dominated the thinking in Richmond, resisted efforts at change, and became a controlling instrument of Confederate strategy.

The idea of departmental command was a product both of obvious needs and of the government's views on strategy. In theory, each military department was to be commanded by a general officer, and was to possess what was sometimes optimistically labeled an army. Departments were charged with the responsibility of defense of a specific, designated war zone. Also, in some cases, departments were delegated additional specific tasks which were often delegated in turn to subdivisions of departments known as districts or subdistricts. For example, in October, 1861, the District of Alabama, a unit of the Department of Alabama and West Florida, was chiefly responsible for the defense of Mobile. Another loosely organized district within that department, known only as the Army of Pensacola, defended Pensacola harbor. Likewise, the Department of Southwestern Virginia was created in the spring of 1862 chiefly to safeguard the Virginia and Tennessee Railroad and the salt and lead production areas north of Abingdon.

President Jefferson Davis' theory of departmental organization granted considerable autonomy to each commander. In theory, though often not in practice, Davis delegated a dual authority. The department commander was responsible for offensive and defensive planning within his jurisdiction. He was usually the final voice in any prospective reinforcement of another department, or in any cooperative effort with another department. Thus did Davis describe his policy in early 1863: "In the conduct of military operations in the various districts occupied by our forces a large discretionary power is necessarily vested in the several Departmental commanders."[1]

A need for such discretionary authority was a prime cause for dividing the South into departments. By the use of such a system,

[1]Davis to Humphrey Marshall, February 24, 1863, in Dunbar Rowland, *Jefferson Davis, Constitutionalist, His Letters, Papers and Speeches* (10 vols.; Jackson, Miss., 1923), V, 436.

the government hoped to deal with the vastness of the Confederacy. The matter of size was serious, and there seemed a danger in 1861 that the South would simply get out of control. The state of Georgia alone was larger in area than the combined states of Vermont, Rhode Island, New Jersey, New Hampshire, Massachusetts, Maryland, Connecticut, and Delaware. In early 1864 General Leonidas Polk, who commanded the Department of Alabama, Mississippi and East Louisiana, was responsible for an area larger than the combined countries of Austria, Hungary, Belgium, and the Netherlands.

Across such vast bodies of land southern generals had to control armies of far greater size than had been known previously in American history. For example, at the battle of Stone's River alone, General Braxton Bragg suffered more casualties than did the Continental army at the combined battles of Brooklyn Heights, White Plains, Trenton, Princeton, Brandywine Creek, Germantown, Saratoga, Monmouth, Oriskany, and Yorktown. Late in the summer of 1862, even such a modest command as General Edmund Kirby Smith's Department of East Tennessee possessed more troops than the combined American forces in the War of 1812 at the battles of the Thames, Chippewa, Lundy's Lane, the Plattsburg campaign, Bladensburg, and New Orleans.

In 1861 the Confederate rail system seemed hopelessly inadequate to bind together such vast territory. Texas and Florida possessed no rail connections with neighboring states, while there were few joining Louisiana and Arkansas with states east of the river. In 1861 the theater between the Mississippi River and the Appalachians had only two east–west rail lines. When General Albert Sidney Johnston's small army lay on a long defensive line stretching four hundred miles from the Mississippi to the Unaka Mountains, the nearest railroad which joined his flanks was the Memphis and Charleston— two hundred miles southward in northern Alabama. With the loss of that line in early 1862, the Western Department was thrown back to the only alternate route, a circuitous line which ran from the Great Smoky Mountains to the Gulf of Mexico and then northwest to the Mississippi Delta, via Atlanta, Montgomery, and Mobile.

There were other reasons to support the departmental system.

A system of well-organized, semi-independent departments seemed to provide a partial answer to basic logistical problems. Southern munitions works, foodstuff areas, and raw material processing areas were scattered widely in 1861, particularly in the most vital production regions of Tennessee, Alabama, and Georgia. What was to be surrendered? If east Tennessee were abandoned, 90 percent of the South's copper supply would be lost. A loss of the Cumberland River basin would surrender the government's only powder mill in operation during the summer of 1861. A loss of the lower Appalachian Valley of Virginia would produce a severe shortage of salt and lead resources, while a Federal seizure of the Tennessee River basin in west Tennessee would mean the loss of the South's largest center of iron production in 1861.

The departmental system, then, was intended to provide at least a semblance of control and protection for such widely scattered regions. For example, a principal objective of the department of Alabama, Mississippi, and East Louisiana, created in early 1864, was the protection of one of the South's few remaining areas of abundant foodstuffs, the Tombigbee River valley. A key objective of the Department of East Tennessee from its creation in early 1862 was to protect the Ducktown copper district in the Ocoee River gorge.

There was still another logistical motivation. In theory at least, the departmental system was to provide a more economical distribution of food and supplies. Although Federal advances in 1862 soon made this more theory than fact, it had been intended that each department be a self-sustaining logistical unit. Each maintained its own administrative bureaus for supply, thus relieving long-range shipment.

There were also political motivations. Such an organization seemed to provide balm for internal political tensions. The appearance of military organization within each state provided some defense mechanism for every inch of southern terrain. In theory, this would be a method of placating jealous local political officials who demanded that their region's interests receive priority. Such organization also seemed to be a means of controlling dissidents. Another key reason for the organization of the east Tennessee department in 1862 was the aim of squelching Unionist activity. It was hoped that a show of military organization in the Appalachian Valley would prevent a repetition of the disastrous 1861 autumn uprisings which had disrupted the vital East Tennessee Railroad between Bristol and Chattanooga. Likewise, a key mission of the Alabama-Mississippi department in 1864–1865 was to contend with the vast no-man's-land of deserters and Unionists who dominated north-central Alabama.

The system also meshed well with southern diplomatic aspirations in 1861. Essentially, the departmental organization was defensive and thus echoed the Rebel contention that the new government did not seek aggression. It also gave the appearance of a well-established nation which could maintain its independence through the broad network of military commands, though many were more apparent than real.

A decentralized territorial administration is essentially the only means by which military command can be exercised. Likewise, geography and communication facilities break military operations into distinct theaters which require unity of command and are in many essential respects isolated from adjacent theaters. The tests of the wisdom of Davis' management were how well the structure of these departments was adapted to logistical and strategic realities and also the measure and quality of the coordination which he supplied to these independent commands.

To achieve these various aims, Davis, in 1861, instituted a system of very small departments which stressed decentralization of defense. The President could not be severely criticized for the cordon defense evident in the summer of 1861. The war was still a small affair. The Rebel army possessed fewer armed men between the Mississippi and the Appalachians than General Robert E. Lee would lose in the Seven Days' campaign of 1862. Confederate intelligence and cavalry arms were still in their infancy as well. News of Federal strength, location, and objectives was frequently contradictory, and the lack of an overall commanding general or a general staff produced uncertainty as to Federal objectives. In a sense, the Confederates in these early months seemed to believe that all objective points were equal. Both the Virginia and western fronts responded with a broad, dispersed cordon defense. For example, in the autumn of 1861, General Albert Sidney Johnston's infant intelligence network completely lost touch with General Don Carlos Buell's army in Kentucky, and knew almost as little of the location of two companion armies led by Generals U. S. Grant and George Thomas. Johnston's response was an almost pitiful exhibition of cordon defense stretching four hundred miles from the Mississippi River to the Unaka Mountains.

In short, the war effort of early 1861 exhibited a strong sense of localism. The government's response to this picture was an impossible network of small departments. In June, 1861, General P. G. T. Beauregard's first Virginia command, the Department of Alexandria, embraced only a three-county area south of the Potomac River. To Beauregard's right, General T. H. Holmes led the Department of Fredericksburg, which guarded the Northern Neck and the lower Rappahannock River areas. Farther south, General John B. Magruder's Department of the Peninsula protected Richmond. Meanwhile, the Appalachian-Allegheny sector of Virginia was also protected by several miniature departments. General Joseph E. Johnston guarded the northern end of the Shenandoah Valley with the Army of the Shenandoah, which functioned as a department. General John B. Floyd protected the lower Virginia Allegheny front with the Army of the Kanawha, while General W. W. Loring led the Department of Northwestern Virginia.

In the West there was some of the same division of effort for local defense. The defense of the lower Mississippi River and of New Orleans was the duty of General David Twiggs's Department Number One. Alabama was divided among three departments: Twiggs's command extended along the western coastal area, merging with General Braxton Bragg's Department of Alabama and West Florida; Bragg's responsibility embraced the defense of Mobile and Pensacola; and General Leonidas Polk's Second Department was held responsible for northern Alabama.

The upper portion of the West, on the other hand, was provided with an enormous department, a real theater command. In September, 1861, General Albert Sidney Johnston assumed charge of the Second or Western Department. Held in trust by Polk until Johnston's belated arrival from California, the Second Department's limits were staggering. Under Johnston, the department was extended to include the region from the Unaka Mountains of Tennessee into Kansas and the Indian Territory.

Davis' vision in establishing such a broad command probably has been overrated. Johnston's theater command was not a result of Davis' insight into the need for a western concentration. Instead, it probably exhibited Davis' lack of realization in 1861 that a threat existed in Tennessee as genuinely as in Virginia. Evidently the government merely desired to provide some semblance of command on the western front while it was preoccupied with affairs in Virginia. Johnston's management of his extensive department actually nullified Richmond's efforts to provide a unified command on this frontier. His department was effectively divided into miniature departments with little central direction.

In July of 1861 Davis had placed General Leonidas Polk in command of the Western Department, chiefly because his old friend Bishop Polk had expressed concern over the defense of the Mississippi River front. Polk responded to the new position by totally neglecting the defense of the central South. The bishop was so completely preoccupied with Mississippi River fortifications that he even allowed the Memphis Committee of Public Safety to issue departmental orders in his name.

By September of 1861, when Polk relinquished his command to Albert Sidney Johnston, the Western Department possessed only 27,000 troops. Some 21,000 of these were in six Mississippi River garrisons from Memphis to Island Number Ten. By October, 1861, the only fort on the Cumberland River, Fort Donelson, had only 300 men—untrained and almost unarmed. The fort's earthworks on the land side were not constructed, and the bastion contained not a single artillerist. Matters were worse at nearby Fort Henry, the only Confederate fort on the Tennessee River. By October, Fort Henry, the only impediment to a Union advance up the river into north Alabama, was manned by only 870 men. These were armed chiefly with muskets used by the Tennessee militia in the 1813 Creek campaign. The fort had been so poorly constructed by Polk that during the ordinary winter rise of the Tennessee River, the lower river battery would be under nine feet of water; meanwhile, the highest point of the fort, the parade ground, would be under two feet of floodwater.

Thus Polk set a pattern which Richmond permitted to be followed under his successor, General Albert Sidney Johnston. The vulnerable route to the central South via middle and east Tennessee continued to take second place to the priority of Mississippi River defense. Johnston, like Polk, adopted a policy of dispersing his troops into a cordon defense. The forces west of the Mississippi were virtually independent. Although Johnston did place more troops in middle Tennessee, the emphasis on Mississippi River defense continued. By January of 1862, only a third of the earthworks at Fort Donelson had been completed, and not a single trained artillerist was at the fort. Despite warnings of its danger during high water periods, Fort Henry had not been relocated. Other warnings that its guns were improperly mounted (all faced downriver) also went unheeded. The total forces at these two forts in January numbered only forty-five hundred troops. Of these, two thousand were completely without arms, and many of the remainder still used Andrew Jackson's muskets of 1813 from the state armory. Half of Johnston's departmental force was positioned in Polk's Mississippi River garrisons. Columbus, Kentucky, alone boasted 150 pieces of artillery, over 6 times the number of guns at Fort Henry.

In early February of 1862, P. G. T. Beauregard came to the Western Department as second-in-command to General Albert Sidney Johnston. He brought with him ideas of concentration and the offensive. Since 1861 Beauregard had been an exponent of concentrating for offensive operations against a single line of the enemy's advance. His June, 1861, proposal to the government had emphasized such a policy for use in Virginia, by his own army at Manassas Junction and by General Joseph E. Johnston's forces in the northern Shenandoah Valley. Beauregard emphasized the need to "crush in rapid succession and in detail, the several columns of the enemy."[2] The following month, Beauregard again suggested this policy. He urged

[2] *Official Records*, I, 77.

that Johnston's army be shifted rapidly to the Manassas front. The combined forces would take the offensive first against General Irvin McDowell's troops; if successful, the Confederates would then concentrate against the Federals in the Maryland-Virginia valley region.

Rebel intelligence indicated that three separate Federal columns were in Kentucky. Documents procured from army headquarters at Louisville indicated that Buell possessed at least seventy-five thousand troops in west-central Kentucky, on the Nashville-Louisville Railroad. On the west, a second Federal column in the Paducah-Cairo vicinity was estimated at anywhere between twenty-five thousand and one hundred thousand troops. On Buell's left in eastern Kentucky, General George Thomas possessed a force of unknown strength.

Johnston's response had been to continue a cordon defense. By January he possessed only forty-eight thousand poorly armed men. He spread these in four static positions across a defensive line four hundred miles wide, on the Mississippi River, at Forts Henry and Donelson, at Bowling Green, and in east Tennessee. The emphasis, was still on the Mississippi River front where the garrisons contained about half of Johnston's effective strength. Even here, however, there was a dispersal into minute garrisons. Columbus, Kentucky, with seventeen thousand troops, was the largest concentration on any front.

The static defensive positions of Johnston's men negated any hope of rapid concentration. It would have been better had Johnston placed the bulk of his forces at some rear position which had access by rail to adjacent areas, such as at Jackson, Tennessee, Corinth, or Nashville. Instead, his entire force was frozen into a series of outposts, each operating almost as a separate entity. Communication between these groups was so inadequate as to be almost ludicrous. Not until after he retreated from Bowling Green to Nashville, after Fort Donelson's fall, did Johnston even know that his engineers had failed to construct a second line of defenses at Nashville. Until he read the news in a Louisville newspaper, Johnston did not know that his east Tennessee wing had been demolished on January 19 at the battle of Mill Springs.

The Mill Springs disaster, which almost coincided with Beauregard's arrival, did little to alter Johnston's thinking. Beauregard urged unsuccessfully that Johnston concentrate the garrisons of Fort Henry and Donelson and the forces at Bowling Green into a single column. A disturbed Beauregard confided to a Richmond friend that "we must give up some minor points and concentrate our forces to save the most important ones, or we will lose all of them in succession."[3]

Within a few days, Beauregard's pessimism proved correct. By February 17 the Tennessee River and Cumberland River defenses had been swept away and Johnston's cordon defense was shattered. His departmental army was now isolated in two segments: the Mississippi River garrisons and the Bowling Green column, now pulling back to Murfreesboro.

The Confederate defeats at Mill Springs in January and at Fort Henry in early February, 1862, produced a reaction in Richmond camparable to McDowell's advance prior to First Manassas. Department Number One, now commanded by Mansfield Lovell, and Bragg's Department of Alabama and West Florida were ordered to send reinforcements to A. S. Johnston. The loss of Fort Donelson and the appeals of Bragg and Johnston soon produced an even more emphatic response from the War Department. Acknowledging that "recent operations in Kentucky render necessary a change in our whole plan of campaign," the Secretary of War noted that he and the President already "had in contemplation the necessity of abandoning the seaboard in order to defend the Tennessee line. . . ." Bragg was ordered to abandon both Mobile and Pensacola and to "hasten" to aid Johnston.[4]

Davis' decisive concentration was welcomed by the generals in the field. Beauregard, who had assumed de facto command of the Western Department, advocated an immediate concentration and soon took steps to add most of the departmental troops in Arkansas and Tennessee to those sent from Alabama, Florida, and Louisiana, planning to concentrate them at Corinth, Mississippi.

Although it is not clear who selected Corinth, it was Beauregard

---

[3] Beauregard to R. A. Pryor, February 14, 1862, in P. G. T. Beauregard Papers, Duke University.

[4] *Official Records*, VI, 824–28, 894.

who effected there the concentration of the army which would fight at Shiloh. By late February Johnston was at Murfreesboro with the remnants of the middle Tennessee command. The loss of Fort Donelson, totally unexpected by a stunned Johnston, had been followed by the debacle of Nashville's abandonment. There, Johnston's poor judgment in placing his supply depot so close to the front lines had cost the Confederates staggering losses of food, munitions, and equipment. General William J. Hardee later estimated that half of the Second Department's stores were left behind when Nashville was abandoned.

A dazed Johnston seemed close to a mental collapse, and by the end of February, it was obvious that Beauregard was directing the affairs of the Western Department. Later, Johnston's son and biographer, William Preston Johnston, contended that his father masterminded the concentration at Corinth. This seems erroneous. At Murfreesboro, Johnston was not thinking of concentration, but instead he still planned a cordon defense. Although Beauregard's column in west Tennessee was isolated by Grant's presence on the Tennessee River, Johnston at first did not contemplate a union with the Creole. Instead, his first plan was a retreat along the Nashville and Chattanooga Railroad to Stevenson, Alabama, slightly west of Chattanooga. This move would have taken him away from the Beauregard-Polk column in west Tennessee.

Although his motives may have been selfish ones, Beauregard did save the situation by assuming control of the army's affairs. A passive Johnston allowed Beauregard to implement the desired concentration. Beauregard drew back the west Tennessee defenses along the Mobile and Ohio Railroad to Jackson. He convinced Johnston that he should not march to Stevenson, urged instead a concentration, and eventually drew Johnston to north Mississippi. Beauregard, too, was responsible for the mass of urgent appeals to Richmond and the governors of the Mississippi Valley.

The ensuing battle of Shiloh was also an application of Beauregard's strategy. In essence, what occurred was a concentration of Rebel strength from five lines of operation (middle and west Tennessee, New Orleans, the Gulf, and Arkansas) against the single Federal column under Grant on the Tennessee River. By late March, Grant's army lay on the river above Savannah, Tennessee, poised for an advance on the rail junction at Corinth. Buell's army at Nashville was marching southwest to join Grant. By March 18 Buell had advanced forty miles forward to Columbia on the Duck River. At Shiloh all Confederate forces had concentrated except the Arkansas contingent. Grant and Buell were still separated.

The geographical area involved in the Davis-Beauregard concentration was greater than post–World War I Germany, and the military frontier over which it took place was more than double the distance from Prague to Stettin or from Ulm to Cologne. Beauregard's engineering background and his imagination, combined with his study of Napoleon and Jomini and his participation in the campaign of First Manassas, enabled him to think readily in terms of applying the strategy employed by Napoleon within a theater to wider areas. After the war, at least, Beauregard listed the railroad and the telegraph, along with mountains and rivers, as defensive advantages for the South. Feeling that the "great principles of war" were "the same today as in the time of Caesar or Napoleon," Beauregard thought that their applications had been "but intensified by the scientific discoveries affecting transportation and communication of intelligence."[5]

Thus Beauregard and the War Department, using the telegraph and, where available, the railroad, brought about a concentration unprecedented in geographical extent. Troops which had been deployed *en cordon* in five different and virtually independent packets were concentrated for the offensive which would culminate at Shiloh. Bragg enthusiastically supported this concentration. He felt that Confederate "means and resources are too much scattered," and that important "strategic points only should be held." Consequently, he advised that "all means not necessary to secure these should be concentrated for a heavy blow upon the enemy where we can best assail him" so that, "whilst the enemy would be weakened by

[5] *Ibid.*, VII, 899–901; G. T. Beauregard, "The First Battle of Bull Run," in C. C. Buell and R. U. Johnson (eds.), *Battles and Leaders of the Civil War* (New York, 1887–88), I, 223.

dispersion," the concentrated forces of the Confederates "could then beat him in detail instead of the reverse." President Davis, kept informed of the progress of the concentration, perceived the strategic opportunity presented by the continued Union double line of operations which would soon be opposed to a single Confederate line of operations. He pointed out to Johnston the advantage, realized on the first day at Shiloh, of meeting "the division of the enemy moving from the Tennessee before it can make a junction with that advancing from Nashville."[6]

Realizing, after Shiloh, the magnitude of the Federal threat on the Tennessee front, Davis revised his departmental system to accommodate the need for reinforcement. By mid-July, both Department Number One and the Department of Alabama and West Florida had been abolished. They were incorporated in a new supercommand, still called the Second or Western Department. For the only time in the war, the Second Department and its military force, the Army of Tennessee, had adequate logistical support. The department now embraced middle and east Tennessee, all of Alabama and Mississippi, northwestern Georgia, and parts of Florida and Louisiana. It was not by coincidence that during this period the Army of Tennessee achieved its greatest period of strength.

Consolidation had already been effected in Virginia. Beginning in the autumn of 1861, many of the smaller departments were eliminated. In October, 1861, a new organization, the Department of Northern Virginia, was established. Initially, this department, commanded by General Joseph E. Johnston, assumed control of three older commands in north-central Virginia: the Department of Fredericksburg, the Department of Alexandria (renamed the Potomac District), and the Shenandoah Valley District. By the late spring of 1862 the Federal threat in Virginia had shifted from the northern frontier to the Peninsula, and further consolidation ensued. Magruder's Department of the Peninsula and General Benjamin Huger's Department of Norfolk were incorporated into Johnston's department in April, 1862.

---

[6] *Official Records,* VI, 826, 836, 894, X, Pt. 2, pp. 302, 327, 361, 365.

To the south, there was also concentration in the Carolinas. The old Department of North Carolina was discontinued. It was replaced by the Department of North Carolina and Southern Virginia, which embraced all defense in North Carolina and into Virginia as far north as Petersburg. In South Carolina, small commands were also consolidated in late 1861 and early 1862. General R. S. Ripley's old Department of South Carolina, intended for coastal defense, was abolished in November, 1861. A new department under General Robert E. Lee was inaugurated—the Department of South Carolina, Georgia, and Florida. Lee's new command steadily absorbed smaller departments in the region. In November it took control of General A. R. Lawton's Department of Georgia. In the spring of 1862, the department was further extended, taking control of the old Department of Middle and Eastern Florida. In October, 1862, the Department of South Carolina, Georgia, and Florida had jurisdiction over all of South Carolina and Georgia, and that part of Florida east of the Apalachicola River.

Concentration was also visible west of the Mississippi in early 1862. Plagued with ineffectual commanders and loss of terrain west of the river, Davis moved toward consolidation in May. A new super-department, the Trans-Mississippi Department, was created. Commanded by General T. H. Holmes, this new organization consisted of several older ones created in 1861. The Department of Texas (created in April, 1861), the District of Arkansas (created in June, 1861), and some scattered Louisiana districts were merged into Holmes's department.

Davis had initially organized what, without constant intervention from Richmond, would necessarily have been a cordon defense. After First Manassas he had reorganized Virginia and after Forts Henry and Donelson he had reorganized the West. Other reorganizations had centered Confederate military operations under five large commands: northern Virginia; North Carolina and southern Virginia; South Carolina, Georgia and Florida; the Trans-Mississippi; and the Second Department. Thus Davis sought to avoid a cordon defense and provide for concentration through restructuring his departmental system. For example, the departments which had supplied all of the troops that had actually been present at Shiloh were consolidated under one departmental command. The new organization in Virginia provided Lee with the scope of authority he needed to conduct the Seven Days' and First Manassas campaigns, though the former had required War Department intervention to secure reinforcements from departments south of Virginia. From a departmental structure appropriate to Europe or to the prerailroad and telegraph era, Davis had moved to one which enabled Lee and Beauregard to apply the strategy taught by Jomini and practiced by Napoleon. The principal Confederate disaster, defeat in Tennessee, had come, ironically, in the one theater where Davis had avoided miniature departments. His commander, Sidney Johnston, had established a cordon defense within his department and, unlike Davis, failed to compensate for this by prompt concentration, meeting with disaster when Grant had concentrated against one of his detachments at Donelson.

Whereas Lee succeeded at Seven Days', Sidney Johnston, guided by Beauregard, failed at Shiloh and was killed. The new commander, Beauregard, was discredited by the government. Part of President Davis' disgust may have been well justified. Beauregard's dispatches from the field at Shiloh and his subsequent notes from Corinth misled and embarrassed the government. For almost two months Richmond believed a victory had been won at Shiloh. In late May, Lee and Davis still spoke of a victory at Pittsburg Landing. Beauregard's communications were sparse and vague, so much so that Richmond was shocked to learn that on May 30 Beauregard had abandoned Corinth for a fifty-mile retreat southward to Tupelo.

Another key source of Davis' resentment was the loss of territory incurred by Beauregard. On June 21 the President angrily confided to his wife that "we must make a desperate effort to regain what Beauregard has abandoned in the West."[7] Davis also sent his aide, Colonel William Preston Johnston, to Beauregard on July 14 with a list of questions. Most of the questions, which Beauregard was

---

[7] Davis to wife, June 21, 1862, in Rowland, *Jefferson Davis*, V, 282–83.

supposed to answer, were concerned with why territory had been abandoned. Later, in September, when a petition of almost sixty congressmen asked for Beauregard's reappointment in the West, Davis' reply was revealing. Part of his explanation for removing Beauregard on June 20 was concerned with the legal technicalities concerning Beauregard's taking a leave of absence without properly informing Richmond. The bulk of Davis' reply, however, was a complaint on the amount of territory lost during Beauregard's service in the West.

After his removal, Beauregard would not be concerned directly with the West until October of 1864, when he was given command of the Division of the West. Yet, during this period of over two years, while serving mainly in the Carolina department, Beauregard became the leading voice—if not the inspiration—of the western concentration bloc. He was their strategic oracle and provided a rationale for their ruling ideas: the critical importance of the central South, and the need for a concentration and offensive in that area.

That Beauregard's influence was the guiding light behind this group cannot be proven conclusively. It is apparent, however, that by two methods Beauregard expounded such ideas and discussed them freely with others, and that other generals sought his advice. First, from mid-1862 until 1864, Beauregard submitted both to the government and to various departmental commanders several strategic plans embracing these ideas. He also constantly elucidated his views in his vast correspondence with generals and politicians.

Beauregard's first such effort to influence strategy came in the summer of 1862. His successor in command of the Army of Tennessee, Braxton Bragg, was pondering his eventual junction at Chattanooga with Kirby Smith. Bragg's subsequent concentration with Kirby Smith was preceded by his seeking advice from Beauregard. His later enmity for Beauregard has clouded his fairly close relationship with the general during this period. On July 17 Bragg had confided to a friend that "no two men living ever served together more harmoniously, or parted with more regret" than did he with "so pure a man and eminent a general as Beauregard." Furthermore, "our intercourse was daily, free, unrestrained, and as harmonious as if we had been brothers."[8]

Both Beauregard and Bragg perceived the opportunity presented by Halleck's very unorthodox conduct of operations. On the first day of Shiloh, Grant's army had had to face a Confederate attack while still separated from Buell's force, the other principal Union army in the theater. Halleck, as the new supreme commander in the West, had concentrated both Buell's and Grant's armies under his personal command and used this very large army to force Beauregard back and to capture Corinth. Halleck, perhaps made overconfident by the uninterrupted string of Union victories in the West, then divided his forces. One part was to remain on the defensive in north Mississippi while the other, under Buell, marched away to the east toward the Confederate forces in east Tennessee. Buell's advance was to be very slow as he moved toward Chattanooga, rebuilding the railroad as he went. The effect of this plan was not a Union concentration against the east Tennessee line of operations; it was more a preparation for a further advance in Mississippi, one which was more in accord with Archduke Charles's injunction that the width of the base of operations must be proportionate to the depth of the projected advance.

With Halleck's removal to Washington to assume the post of general in chief, the Confederates were faced with three uncoordinated Federal lines of operations; one facing south in west Tennessee and north Mississippi, one facing east along the Memphis and Charleston Railroad, and one facing southeast in east Tennessee. The Beauregard-Bragg plan to exploit this situation was to concentrate three armies against the east Tennessee line so as to outflank Buell. Half of Bragg's army would be used together with all of Kirby Smith's east Tennessee command and Humphrey Marshall's small force from southwestern Virginia. The plan, like that of Shiloh and Seven Days', involved the use of the railroad, and was one to concentrate several

---

[8] Bragg to John Forsyth, July 17, 1862, in Alfred Roman, *The Military Operations of General Beauregard in the War between the States, 1861 to 1865; Including a Brief Personal Sketch and a Narrative of His Services in the War with Mexico, 1846–48* (New York, 1884), I, 592.

forces from more than one department against a single line of operations. Its distinctive feature was that, by concentrating against and overwhelming a weak enemy force—a major Union army—Buell's would be outflanked.

Thus on July 22 Bragg submitted to Beauregard his proposal to join Kirby Smith for the Creole's "candid criticism." He asked his advice "in view of the cordial and sincere relations we have ever maintained."[9] Bragg's views essentially jibed with those of Beauregard. He explained that his only alternative to maintaining a stationary defensive position at Tupelo was to join Kirby Smith against a single line of the Federal advance.

Beauregard sent Bragg two replies. Both emphasized the principles of the developing western concentration bloc. Bragg should concentrate against a single line of the Federal advance. Also, while the Federals were thus divided, Bragg and Kirby Smith should take the offensive. Finally, Beauregard stressed a viewpoint which he often repeated: any Rebel advantage in the West would be gained only by a surprise concentration on one line of operations. Although he mentioned this briefly in his July letter, Beauregard on September 2 explained it to Bragg in greater detail. By outflanking and defeating Buell, Bragg and Kirby Smith were provided with an opportunity to force the withdrawal of the other Federal column in north Mississippi by a lateral move against its communications. Having defeated Buell or forced his retreat into Kentucky, Bragg and Kirby Smith could force the Federals from the Mississippi River front by jeopardizing their communications.

As in earlier Confederate successes, the Bragg-Beauregard Kentucky campaign utilized the railroad and the telegraph to concentrate dispersed Confederate troops against a single Union force. In the absence of interior lines of operation, surprise and the railroad were substituted. Although the principles are essentially the same, the spirit and vocabulary seem more Napoleonic than Jominian. Beauregard, for example, wished to make "a proper combination of our still latent forces and resources," endeavoring "to divide the enemy's

---

[9] Bragg to Beauregard, July 22, 1862, in Roman, *Beauregard*, I, 592.

forces, if possible, and then to unite ours rapidly for a sudden blow on only one of his fractional commands." Perceiving that Halleck had divided his forces, Bragg desired to move "before they can know of my movement," to exploit Halleck's pause and dispersal after the fall of Corinth. He rapidly shifted half of his army by rail to Chattanooga so as, "in conjunction with Major General [Kirby] Smith, to strike an effective blow through Middle Tennessee, gaining the enemy's rear, cutting off his supplies and dividing his forces so as to encounter them in detail." [10]

Fully adequate unity of command was lacking, however, for President Davis had, in the spring of 1862, complicated western defense by establishing a separate Department of East Tennessee under General Edmund Kirby Smith. Thus Chattanooga and east Tennessee were placed in Kirby Smith's jurisdiction, where only eighty-six hundred Confederates defended a line from Cumberland Gap to Chattanooga. Cooperation with Kirby Smith did not work well, and that which Kirby Smith secured from the third participating force, Humphrey Marshall in southwest Virginia, was never effective. Yet, with little more than the goodwill of Secretary of War Randolph and President Davis, Bragg embarked on a campaign which involved moving his forces by rail from Tupelo, Mississippi, to Mobile and then north to Atlanta and Chattanooga. The speed of this surprise move was to be accelerated by incorporating the garrison of Mobile in the movement. This garrison would start immediately and be replaced by the last forces to leave Tupelo. These troops from Mississippi and Alabama were to march north from Chattanooga to Kentucky, meeting there Kirby Smith's forces from Tennessee and Marshall's command from Virginia. Forces left in Mississippi were to occupy the Union troops facing them. Thus, in a campaign somewhat reminiscent of Marengo, Bragg attempted to unite Confederate armies on three separate lines of operations, first driving back the Federal force in east Tennessee and then, with the combined force, to penetrate Kentucky in Buell's rear. Bragg's execution was not equal to his conception, nor was cooperation between him and

[10] *Official Records*, XV, 752, 794, XVI, Pt. 2, p. 701, XVII, Pt. 2, p. 656, III, Pt. 2, p. 331.

Kirby Smith a substitute for a single commander for the participating forces.

President Davis contributed to the difficulties of this campaign because his attention in the early summer of 1862 was drawn to General George McClellan's threat on the Peninsula. Instead of ordering a union of the two isolated western forces, Davis in June relied again upon his concept of the autonomous workings of the departmental system. He merely expressed confidence that Bragg would aid Kirby Smith if he could do so. The War Department did not order the junction but merely asked Bragg to send reinforcements to Kirby Smith if he thought it desirable. It was on his own initiative, then, that Bragg on July 21 notified the government that he was moving his troops into the east Tennessee department.

Davis' chief interest in the invasion was the political hope of regaining Kentucky, and not the attempt to thwart Buell's seizure of the Chattanooga-Atlanta route. The President later admitted that his expectation that Kentucky would rise en masse "alone justified an advance into that state." [11]

Actually Davis was completely out of touch with the concentration effected by Bragg and Kirby Smith. The lines of authority were thus confused. Davis himself termed the command agreement merely as one of "cordial co-operation" between the two generals. [12] As late as September 17, thirty-one days after Kirby Smith's wing had advanced into Kentucky, Davis admitted that he was ignorant of the two generals' plans.

The results were disastrous. Kirby Smith, unwilling to cooperate with Bragg, took advantage of the split authority and shunned a concentration with the Army of Tennessee. Not until early October were the movements finally combined under the senior general, Bragg. By then, however, Buell had concentrated at Louisville with his support forces, and the initiative had passed to the Federals. Meanwhile, unknown to Bragg, the government in September and October continually readjusted Bragg's departmental boundaries, removing vital supporting areas in middle Tennessee and Mississippi.

[11] Davis to Holmes, October 21, 1862, in Rowland, *Jefferson Davis*, V, 356.
[12] *Official Records*, LII, Pt. 2, p. 335.

For example, on October 1, without Bragg's knowledge, Davis created another department. The Mississippi portion of Bragg's command was removed, and Davis styled it the Department of Mississippi and East Louisiana, under General John C. Pemberton. No small part in Bragg's decision to abandon Kentucky in mid-October was the failure to receive reinforcements from these supporting areas.

A complete reorganization of the West resulted from Bragg's campaign. The creation, in October, 1862, of Mississippi and eastern Louisiana as a separate department had come as a result of the incredibly confused situation he had left behind in Mississippi. Earl Van Dorn and Sterling Price were operating independently in the same theater of operations. This new organization, however, destroyed much of the unity which had been provided in the spring when the Western Department was enlarged. At the same time, it was clear that Kirby Smith's Department of East Tennessee was within the same theater of operations as was Bragg's army, now that the latter's line of operations lay along the Chattanooga-Nashville axis.

President Davis soon took the logical step and provided unity to the three departments by establishing a superdepartment embracing all three. The new organization, called the Department of the West, was organized in November, 1862, and command was given to an experienced senior officer, General Joseph E. Johnston.

The organization of the Department of the West also received an impetus from Bragg's activities after his retreat from Kentucky. By late October, his army recrossed the Cumberland Mountains into east Tennessee. Quickly Bragg ordered another offensive thrust, so quickly that the orders were issued before he had received the government's permission for the move. In late October, before entraining for Richmond to explain his plan, Bragg ordered his army to take the offensive into middle Tennessee. Ultimately, his tactics were to be defensive—to await an assault at Murfreesboro by the Federal army at Nashville. Strategically, however, Bragg's new proposal embraced what were evolving as the western bloc's principles. With Buell still in east-central Kentucky, the weakest line of Federal advance lay in middle Tennessee. Bragg realized also that this was the critical route into the central South. Already in

September and early October, Bragg had ordered Breckinridge's division and Forrest's cavalry to Murfreesboro, to prepare for an assault on Nashville. Then, in late October, he intended for his army to unite with Kirby Smith's and take the offensive in middle Tennessee. Although his movement eventually became a defensive position at Murfreesboro, the thrust was offensive in nature and initially gave hope of a forward move on Nashville.

For a number of reasons, including Bragg's poor management of cavalry strikes against the Federal communications, the campaign ended with the Murfreesboro defeat in early January. Yet two matters are significant. In late October, Bragg visited Richmond to explain his past campaign and his new offensive. There he pinpointed the basic western flaw—several departmental armies with no unified operations or concentration. Within a month, the government had created Joseph E. Johnston's new supercommand, the Department of the West. Bragg's Murfreesboro campaign also contained the same elements discussed during the previous summer with Beauregard. It involved a concentration of two armies (Bragg's and Kirby Smith's) against a single line of enemy advance, and evoked a concern for the Chattanooga route.

Again Davis had found major departmental reorganization necessary. He could now hope, however, that he had fully provided departments which coincided with strategic realities and were of adequate size for strategic maneuver. Thus, within the Department of the West, for example, Johnston understood that he was "intended to operate in Napoleon's manner" by uniting "the forces in Mississippi and Tennessee in whichever might be first attacked." In this way Davis sought to avoid a cordon defense and to provide for strategic concentration through his departmental organization. [13]

Meanwhile the western concentration bloc was beginning to take form. It solidified around the strategic ideas of Beauregard and a concern for the central corridor—Nashville to Chattanooga to Atlanta. In fact, the western bloc solidified in 1862–1863 chiefly

[13] Johnston to Beverly R. Johnston, May 7 1863, in Robert M. Hughes, "Some War Letters of General Joseph E. Johnston," *Journal of the Military Service Institution of the United States*, L (May–June, 1912), 319.

out of a concern for the disastrous effects of the government's early western policy. Until at least mid-1863 Richmond did not share the western bloc's concern for the central invasion route via Nashville and Chattanooga in spite of the fact that much of the South's logistical strength lay vulnerable along this route on the Tennessee frontier. By the end of 1862 much of this logistical base had been lost and the remainder was in serious jeopardy. The east Tennessee copper mines in the Ocoee River gorge furnished almost all of that precious metal required for percussion caps and bronze artillery. The South's most important powder mills in 1861 lay exposed along the Cumberland River northwest of Nashville. The Confederacy's largest production center for pig, bar, and sheet iron lay between the Cumberland and Tennessee rivers in the so-called western iron belt of Tennessee. The Confederacy's most productive nitre areas were the Cumberland Mountain front of Tennessee and its extension, the Sand Mountain region of north Alabama. Nashville and Memphis in 1861 vied as two of the most important production centers for munitions, equipment, and heavy ordnance. The fertile middle Tennessee basin produced more pork in 1861 than any other Rebel state east of the Mississippi River. Tennessee supplied more mules than any other Rebel state, and more horses than any other southern state east of the Mississippi, excluding Kentucky. With the exception of Kentucky, the most important corn-producing district east of the Mississippi was also in middle Tennessee.

To members of the western bloc the government's war policy appeared to underrate the value of the central South. Evidently the government did not fully grasp until 1863 that the Federals in the West possessed sufficient strength for a multifront advance. Nor did the government until 1863 seem to consider the seizure of the Chattanooga-Atlanta route as a prime Federal objective, but instead saw it as an appendage to the main front on the Mississippi River. Thus, as late as December of 1862, President Davis saw only two principal Federal objectives: "one to get control of the Missi. [*sic*] River, and the other to capture the capital of the Confederate States."[14]

---

[14] Davis to T. H. Holmes, December 21, 1862, in Rowland, *Jefferson Davis*, V, 386–87.

Johnston's appointment added a third member to the western bloc. Like Bragg, he thought well of Beauregard and part of his rapport with the Creole was their common belief that they had been given commands of secondary importance because they were disliked by President Davis. Johnston frequently expressed a warm friendship for Beauregard, which was reciprocated by the Louisiana general.

The two generals also expressed similiar ideas on strategy. The two key points on which Johnston disagreed with the government while commanding the Department of the West—the need for a western concentration and the importance of the Tennessee front—were salient ideas of the western bloc. Even before arriving in Tennessee, Johnston in August had voiced agreement with Beauregard. He wrote Beauregard that the "true principle" was "an attack against one of the enemy's fractions in superior force." [15]

Yet the war would reveal fundamental differences between the military thought of Johnston and of Beauregard. Johnston's ideas rarely had the breadth of Beauregard's. Whereas Beauregard was often too sweeping and too optimistic, Johnston was too narrow and almost always pessimistic. Beauregard was far more able than Johnston to see "the whole theater of war as one subject of which all points were but integral parts." [16] Whereas the defense-minded Johnston thought in terms of abandoning territory to get a defensively strong concentration, the offense-inclined Beauregard wished to combine dispersed forces for an unexpected attack against an enemy weak spot. Johnston emphasized that "by attempting to defend all valuable points at once," Confederate forces were "being beaten everywhere." [17] Beauregard's approach was different: "You ask," he wrote a friend, "what should be done to end this exhausting war. We must take the offensive, as you suggest, not by abandoning all other points, however, but by a proper selection of the point of attack—the Yankees themselves tell us where." [18]

Johnston seems to have failed to perceive that dispersal was a

[15] Johnston to Beauregard, August 6, 1862, in York-Beauregard Papers, Columbia University Library.

[16] Beauregard, "The First Battle of Bull Run," 223.

[17] Johnston to Beauregard, August 6, 1862, in York-Beauregard Papers, Columbia University Library.

[18] *Official Records*, XIV, 995.

necessary prelude to concentration and that any deliberate concentration would have merely elicited a corresponding move from the enemy and so not have changed the situation at all. Beauregard, on the other hand, clearly recognized the essential element of a surprise concentration against an enemy weak point: "the Yankees themselves" selected the point of attack by being more vulnerable at one point than the others. Beauregard's spirit is Napoleonic; Johnston's is more like that of Jomini in his *Précis.*

Johnston encountered a number of administrative and personal difficulties in his command of the Department of the West. His constituent commanders, Bragg, Pemberton, and Kirby Smith, were still to report directly to Richmond. Often Johnston learned of their activities through rumor or from a personal friend with an army. For example, he did not even know that Bragg had engaged General William S. Rosecrans' army at Murfreesboro in December until rumors circulated at his headquarters in Mississippi. Also, the limits of Johnston's authority were vague. The ever suspicious Johnston felt that his old enemy Davis had deliberately placed him in a position with much responsibility but little authority. Johnston's November 24 orders empowered the general to go to any part of his command "whenever his presence may, for the time, be necessary or desirable." Yet there were flaws in this arrangement. The main advantage of a western theater command was to superintend moves across a vast territory, so that meager resources could best be utilized against rising Federal strength. Unless his department commanders supplied Johnston with information, on their own initiative, he would be without adequate knowledge. For example, from January, 1863, until mid-May, Johnston was absorbed with problems in Bragg's army at Tullahoma. A communication gap between Johnston and Pemberton resulted. Pemberton remained uncommunicative, but Johnston's complaints to the government elicited little but sympathy. Thus, in May, while Grant bypassed Vicksburg, occupied Grand Gulf, and crossed to the east bank, Johnston knew little. By May 7, days after Grant crossed the river, Johnston still did not know if the main Federal army had crossed or that Pemberton had already engaged Grant's men.

There were other flaws. The government did not specify whether Johnston was to visit his several armies at his own initiative or by governmental order. Left unsaid also was whether or not he could issue field orders to an army when he was not present within a particular department.

By February the government finally had taken pains to assure Johnston that he possessed actual authority. Johnston relished self-pity, and was still convinced that his appointment was an administrative plot to shelve him. Also, he was embarrassed at the rising tide of anti-Bragg sentiment in the Army of Tennessee. He feared that any exercise of genuine authority in Tennessee would smack of personal intrigue for Bragg's command. Thus the general refused to be convinced, and continued to complain during the spring of a lack of authority. Johnston's position was complicated by his preexisting relations with many of the generals and his sharing of mutual friends and ideas with Bragg. Pemberton, on the other hand, was an outsider not linked to Johnston by any associations other than Pemberton's not particularly popular tour as commander in Charleston.

Even without these personal motives, the powers of Johnston's command would still have looked weak. Again Davis exhibited that peculiar contradictory dualism which characterized his concept of departmental command: a localistic arrangement coupled with sporadic intervention from Richmond. Although Davis assured Johnston of his powers, it was the President who in December had peremptorily ordered one fourth of Bragg's infantry to reinforce Pemberton. Twice, in January and March, Davis ordered Johnston to proceed to Bragg's department and take command—again a violation of the government's repeated assurances that Johnston had full power in the West. Then, in February, the War Department, without Johnston's knowledge, had planned a cavalry invasion of Kentucky by troops from the east Tennessee department. Again, on May 9, Davis ordered Johnston to proceed from Bragg's headquarters to Pemberton's department, thus violating an earlier assurance that the President "had felt the importance of keeping you free to pass from army to army in your Department." That same month the government twice intervened to order almost twelve thousand reinforcements from Bragg to Pemberton.

Again departmental chaos contributed to disaster. When Johnston went to Mississippi in May, he assumed from the government's attitude that he no longer commanded Bragg's department. Not until the second week of June did he learn that he was still a theater commander. An angry Davis on June 30 ridiculed Johnston's misconception, yet contradicted himself again by attempting directly to obtain more reinforcements from Bragg for Pemberton.

Johnston also disagreed with Davis about the organization of departments in the West. Johnston felt that Mississippi and the Trans-Mississippi should be joined and thought that Lieutenant General T. H. Holmes, the commander in Arkansas and western Louisiana, should join Pemberton for an offensive against Grant. Davis agreed, in part, urged and even ordered Holmes to send ten thousand men to assist in the defense of Vicksburg. Holmes successfully resisted this pressure, and Davis, fearful of the loss of territory with its attendant loss of supplies and the desertion of troops whose homes had been abandoned to the enemy, declined to compel Holmes to obey. Although it is doubtful that without railroad communication many of the scattered and disorganized forces of the infirm and ineffectual Holmes could have reached Vicksburg, both Davis' strategy and his respect for departmental autonomy are reflected. Perhaps because of the Shiloh campaign and the late arrival of Van Dorn's forces from Arkansas, the president saw the area from the Appalachians to the Mississippi region as a strategic unit. This, added to his reluctance to overrule a local commander except in a dire emergency, led to Davis' refusal to order Holmes to reinforce. In addition, at the time he discussed this with Johnston, Davis had already ordered a reinforcement from within the Department of the West and troops were on their way from Tennessee.

While Davis was with Johnston in Tennessee and Mississippi in December, 1862, they apparently discussed the problem of coordinating operations in those two states. Johnston stressed the difficulties; Davis, apparently recollecting the Shiloh and Kentucky campaigns, was impressed with the strategic unity of the Tennessee and Mississippi fronts. The route of reinforcement by rail was circuitous, the same one through Mobile which Bragg had employed during the previous summer. Implicit in these discussions must have been the nature of "Napoleon's manner" and how it could be implemented. Davis' concept, like the Napoleonic, was that troops not actively engaged with the enemy were available for detachment and concentration with another force. These troops are reserves, though not in the conventional sense of the subtracted reserve, troops held back and not potentially engaged anywhere. Johnston's emphasis on the distance between the Tennessee and the Mississippi armies led Davis to suggest to Johnston the employment of a subtracted reserve, the placing of a division of troops at Meridian, Mississippi, or Selma, Alabama.[19] Johnston did not adopt this plan but he did evolve a "pipeline" concept similar to that used by Bragg the previous summer. This concept involved sending the garrison of Mobile either to Mississippi or to Tennessee as the leading contingent of any reinforcement. Although Mobile would be evacuated, it would be safe as long as the reinforcements were passing through and it could be regarrisoned by the last reinforcements to leave Mississippi or Tennessee. If the movement was toward Tennessee, troops at Jackson, Mississippi, would participate in the same way. Thus a plan, pioneered by Bragg, was evolved which would increase the mobility of reserves by setting troops in motion simultaneously all along the reinforcement route, just as all water in a pipe moves simultaneously when water is introduced at one end.

Though Johnston did his best to facilitate concentration on either the Mississippi or the Tennessee fronts, he remained skeptical of the workability of his department. How much his disagreement stemmed from his desire to develop massive concentrations in key areas is not clear. Johnston's and Davis' differences seem to go beyond the feasibility of the plan. Davis' approach seemed to be a compromise between that of Johnston and of Beauregard. Like Beauregard he anticipated a rapid concentration when the occasion demanded; like

[19] Davis to Johnston, January 8, 1863, in Joseph E. Johnston Letters, Miami (Ohio) University Library.

Johnston he perceived it as a defensive concentration only. Another difference between Johnston and Davis was, of course, the latter's optimism and Johnston's pessimism about the likely outcome of a well-conducted enemy offensive. Perhaps equally important was Johnston's concern for Tennessee and his membership in the western concentration bloc.

During the spring of 1863 Johnston continued to insist that Bragg and Pemberton were too far apart to aid one another, and he pressed Richmond for a commitment as to which territory should be considered as more valuable, middle Tennessee or Mississippi. Johnston saw Tennessee as more vital because its possession would give the Confederates a rich food-producing region, and because its loss would open the Chattanooga front to Rosecrans.

Davis did not share Johnston's regard for Tennessee as a gate to the central South. He saw its importance only as a food producing region and did not regard it as a primary Federal objective. Therefore, in December when Bragg protested the transfer of ten thousand infantry to Pemberton, Davis' reply was merely for Bragg to fight if possible and if not, to retreat to Alabama. Too, Davis shrugged off Johnston's request for guidelines as to which area was to be considered more vital. The President considered this a moot question since he believed both Tennessee and Mississippi could be defended simultaneously. However, in January, in reply to Johnston's query, Davis' terse reply was "to hold the Mississippi is vital."[20] Subsequent events indicate Davis' western interest in 1863 lay chiefly in defending the Mississippi. In early May, the government ordered an additional eleven thousand troops from Bragg to Pemberton. This reinforcement, which brought Pemberton's accession from Bragg to almost twenty-two thousand, left the Tennessee army with barely thirty thousand infantry to face Rosecrans. The Mississippi army, as it turned out, was not strengthened sufficiently to insure success, while the Tennessee army was weakened badly.

Once his plan to employ men from Holmes's department had fizzled, Johnston had nothing to propose. In Johnston's lengthy

[20] *Ibid.*

correspondence with Richmond, there is a noticeable absence of a plan of grand strategy similiar to that offered by Beauregard. For several reasons Johnston in 1863 did not repeat his proposal of a western concentration made in November–December of 1862. He was doubtless confused by the government's refusal to state which region was considered more vital. Johnston's personality might also explain why he did not press the western bloc's ideas more vigorously during the spring of 1863. His poor relations with Davis seemed to prevent a free exchange of ideas. Johnston also possessed an almost neurotic self-pity. He was convinced the government had plotted against him by assigning him to a command of dubious authority. He spurned Richmond's January–February assurances that he had authority if he would only use it. After the initial rebuff of his proposals in November and December, Johnston seemed content to let the government see that their strategy would bring disaster. Convinced that his command status and the government's strategy were both wrong, he seemed almost determined to prove his point, and during the spring he spent much time sulking.

More important, Johnston was not fully in harmony with Beauregard's ideas. Although he shared Beauregard's view of the need for a concentration, Johnston disliked taking the offensive once that concentration was achieved. He favored instead the assumption of a defensive position, to await a forward advance by the enemy. In Beauregard's view, such a position was unsound because it lost the advantage of surprise, gave the enemy the initiative, and enabled the Federals to match the Rebel concentration by a like move. To Johnston, the defensive-offensive was more logistically sound. Later, Johnston's 1864 proposal for dealing with Sherman's army in Georgia evoked this same transitional strategy—to abandon territory, to concentrate at Dalton, and then to maintain a defensive position. Then, if the enemy were defeated, Johnston would take the offensive.

In spite of his negative attitude and the paucity and brevity of his communications, Johnston was an effective advocate for the western bloc. He impressed Davis and Secretary Seddon with the needs of the West and inspired them to conduct an active search for eastern troops which might be spared for permanently reinforcing the West. He was a potentially effective guardian of Tennessee as well, for in addition to his pipeline reinforcement, he placed an interdepartmental cavalry force at Columbia, Tennessee, commanded by General Earl Van Dorn. Van Dorn, with cavalry divisions from both Bragg and Pemberton, was authorized to operate either against Grant's or Rosecrans' communications. In April, Johnston's pipeline reinforcement arrangement was given a trial, and more than ten thousand men actually began a movement to reinforce Tennessee.

There were, at this time, three schools of strategy focused on the West: Beauregard's concept of concentrating against enemy weakness for a surprise offensive, Johnston's approach of concentrating to be prepared to resist an anticipated attack on a key point, and Davis' policy of defensive concentration once the point of enemy attack was revealed. Davis' ideas were best exemplified in the First Manassas and Shiloh campaigns, in the strategies of which he had been intimately involved. Johnston's pipeline reinforcement scheme was, ironically, an effective means of implementing Davis' strategy. Beauregard's ideas were best exemplified in Jackson's Valley and Lee's Second Manassas campaigns.

Johnston was an advocate of the ideas of the western concentration bloc because he viewed holding Tennessee as more important than conserving the Confederate position on the Mississippi. Bragg and the other officers of the Army of Tennessee naturally agreed, and the fact that Johnston spent so much of his time with that army helps explain his assignment of priorities.

Beauregard would give priority to Tennessee for a different reason. He would soon regard Rosecrans' army in Tennessee as the most vulnerable major Federal force and the fruits of any victory there the most attractive. He would, therefore, advocate a Tennessee offensive as an attack upon the enemy weak point.

Thus was the western concentration bloc formed, and in early 1863 Johnston would begin the long series of pleas by the westerners for reinforcements from Virginia. The thrust of Johnston's argument was that Tennessee was relatively the weakest and hence the most menaced position in the Confederacy. In accordance with his strategic views, he argued that some fundamental east-to-west redistribution of Confederate troops was needed to build up defensive strength in Tennessee. He buttressed his argument by pointing out that substantial Federal forces under General Burnside had been transferred from Virginia to Tennessee.

Davis was squarely in the middle between Johnston and the western concentration bloc on one side and his trusted adviser Lee on the other. To Lee's formidable authority and physical proximity to Davis, the westerners could oppose their many friends in Richmond who lobbied for their cause. By March, 1863, the western bloc was able to dominate the president's councils and place Lee on the defensive there. Lee, who had twice during the previous fall advocated that Virginia be reinforced from Bragg's army, was now resisting two requests from Richmond that he send troops to Bragg. Lee's arguments were much like Johnston's. He stressed that Virginia, rather than Tennessee, was to be the scene of the major Federal effort and, like Johnston with respect to his own department, emphasized that troops shifted from one distant line of operations to another would always arrive too late. He also stressed previous concentration at the point of impending attack which, in Lee's view, was clearly Virginia. He emphasized the impact of the climate to hinder Federal efforts in the Deep South and, his own intelligence about Hooker's strength and intentions. With these arguments he was successful in persuading the President in March and again in April, 1863, that no reinforcements should be sent from Virginia.

Thus neither of Davis' two principal commanders, Lee and Johnston, was ostensibly in agreement with his concept of shifting reserves in an emergency. Ironically, Beauregard, who was out of favor with Davis, was advocating ideas more congenial to the President. Lee's concern for Virginia, his conviction that it was to be the principal point of attack, and his lack of knowledge of the West led him to advocate ideas on grand strategy which were basically foreign to his own perceptions of strategy. Simultaneously Johnston was saying he could not operate within his own command as Lee had within his, while providing an effective means of doing so through his pipeline method of giving mobility to reserves. It was in the context of these conflicting theories on strategy, differing evaluations of enemy intentions, and varying estimates of the importance of Virginia and of two major western areas that Davis was to respond to pressures and guide Confederate operations during the spring of 1863.

Other individuals joined the western bloc in 1863. One was the Texas senator, Louis T. Wigfall, who had served with Beauregard at Charleston and with Johnston in Virginia. Yet Wigfall's motives for championing a western concentration were probably more political than strategic. By the late autumn of 1862 the fiery Wigfall had become a strong critic of Davis in the Congress. He had supported the removal of Bragg in September, and through the spring of 1863 again supported Bragg's removal and his replacement by Johnston.

Wigfall's interest in the West and in Johnston was thus somewhat selfish. In September it was Beauregard he had supported as Bragg's successor, and he shifted to Johnston only after Davis made it clear he would not reappoint Beauregard. Later, in 1863, Wigfall gave indication that his western interest sprang from political motivations. In early 1863 Johnston was sent by Davis to Bragg's headquarters at Tullahoma to investigate widespread reports of disaffection among the Tennessee army's generals. In essence, Johnston's laudatory reports to the government saved Bragg. An irritated Wigfall on several occasions berated Johnston for supporting Bragg. He insisted that Johnston's friends had moved heaven and earth to have Bragg replaced. Instead, Johnston had betrayed his friends by supporting Davis' friend. The incisive Johnston retorted that "the friends who have been irritated by my expressions of opinion are less my friends, I take it, than the President's enemies."[21]

Wigfall was a powerful adhesion to the western concentration bloc for he had influence with the new Secretary of War, James A. Seddon. He had so much influence, in fact, that on one occasion Seddon told him "when you write to me, mark you letter on the outside 'private' and then it will come under my own eye . . . I shall always receive with gratitude the suggestions of your fuller knowledge and riper experience.[22]

[21] Johnston to Wigfall, December 27, 1863, in Wigfall Papers, Library of Congress.
[22] Seddon to Wigfall, undated letter in Mrs. D. Giraud Wright, *A Southern Girl in '61—the War-Time Memories of a Confederate Senator's Daughter* (New York, 1905).

Johnston was aware of Wigfall's influence. Beginning in November both men, actually warm friends, were also using one another. Wigfall used Johnston as a standard bearer for the anti-Davis bloc in Congress. Johnston used Wigfall to advance the ideas of the western bloc in Richmond. When Johnston spoke to Wigfall of "what you are doing for us,"[23] he did so with cause. It was Wigfall whom Johnston asked to pressure Seddon to accept his idea of the Pemberton-Holmes offensive against Grant. Thus Wigfall pressed Seddon to accept this strategy, and urged "let us save Vicksburg and then crush Rosecranz [*sic*]." Wigfall then echoed a Beauregard sentiment, when he remarked that "I trust the last battle has been fought by us with inferior numbers. Whenever the enemy divides, concentrate and crush."[24]

During the spring of 1863 Wigfall responded as a member of two Confederate factions, the western bloc and the antiadministration faction in Congress. While he pressed Johnston's case with Seddon, Wigfall also pressed for Bragg's removal. On February 27 Wigfall wrote Johnston that Seddon was definitely interested in Bragg's replacement, and that if Johnston wanted the position, it would be his. That night Wigfall and Seddon met in a private conference that lasted until midnight. The following day, Wigfall again asserted that Bragg's position was Johnston's for the asking. Wigfall's prediction proved correct. On March 3 Seddon offered Johnston the position of commander of the Army of Tennessee.

By May it was no secret that the government was deliberating a major strategic decision—for Vicksburg was seriously menaced, and Lee had just won a signal victory at Chancellorsville. On May 15 Beauregard at Charleston sent to Johnston a new strategic proposal for the West. The following day he sent a copy to Wigfall, thanking him "for the defense I am told you made for me lately in the Senate."[25] Beauregard requested that Wigfall make "a desperate effort" to have his views adopted by the War Department. A shabby commentary on the status of personal relationships within the Rebel high command was Beauregard's request that his plan's authorship be kept secret.

[23] Johnston to Wigfall, January 26, 1863, *ibid.,* 104, 123.
[24] Wigfall to Seddon, December 8, 1862, in Wigfall Papers, Library of Congress.
[25] Beauregard to Wigfall, May 16, 1863, *ibid.*

Beauregard's plan truly involved viewing "the whole theatre of war as one subject of which all points were but integral parts." Forces from northern Virginia, southeastern Georgia and South Carolina, and from western Mississippi were to be concentrated with those in middle and east Tennessee for a sudden attack on Rosecrans' army, perceived by Beauregard as the most vulnerable Union force. The defeat of Rosecrans would have permitted a movement westward against Grant's communications. It was Napoleon's second defeat of Würmser, translated, by means of the railroad and the telegraph, to a geographical scale ten times as large and involving several rather than s single theater. It could also have come readily from Jomini's *Traité*, following, as it does so exactly, Jomini's and Napoleon's recommendations for Frederick's campaign of 1759. From his vantage point in Charleston, Beauregard was able to see how the principles exemplified by Napoleon, taught by Jomini, and used by Lee in Virginia could have a Confederacy-wide application. Initiative and control from the President together with Johnston's authority within the West would ensure that unity which had been lacking in Bragg's Kentucky campaign, and troops from Lee's army would assure that numerical superiority which had been missing at Shiloh. In this sense it was the 1862 western offensives repeated, but with the addition of a major reinforcement from Virginia which was made possible by the direct route of the Virginia and Tennessee Railroad and by Lee's victory at Chancellorsville.

Beauregard's plan was the ultimate development of his own ideas and of those of the western bloc. It involved the broadest possible application of those Napoleonic-Jominian ideas which he had advocated and practiced since the beginning of the war and which had been the foundation both of Confederate victories in Virginia and of that measure of success which had been gained in the West. It included an emphasis on what the western bloc regarded as a key area, the central corridor, and it included an eastern reinforcement for the West. Around this plan would rally the western bloc during the summer of 1863. In January, 1863, General James Longstreet had suggested to Lee that he maintain the defensive in Virginia while his own corps reinforced Bragg for an attack on

Rosecrans. At the same time Wigfall was pushing Longstreet as a possible replacement for Bragg. Longstreet apparently corresponded with Wigfall on the matter, and noted that he desired to go to the West because there seemed "opportunities for all kinds of moves to great advantages."[26]

In May, Longstreet revived his plan almost simultaneously with the arrival of Beauregard's plan in Richmond. On May 6 Longstreet conferred with Seddon in Richmond, and proposed the same plan as did Beauregard—a concentration at Chattanooga of Johnston's army and his corps from Virginia, to be followed by an attack on Rosecrans. This plan was strikingly identical both to Beauregard's plan and to that offered by Polk to Davis two months later. The combined forces were to defeat Rosecrans, and then to make a diagonal march against Grant's communications on the Mississippi River, to force his retreat.

While Seddon was deliberating Longstreet's proposal, Beauregard's plan arrived in Richmond. It is not impossible to conjecture that by means of intermediaries such as Wigfall, strategic views during the spring had been interchanged between Beauregard and Longstreet. Certainly such was the case with Johnston, Beauregard, and Bragg. On May 15 Beauregard had sent his plan to Johnston "for your consideration."[27]

Meanwhile President Davis had been taking advantage of his first respite as commander in chief. The organizational problems of 1861 had given way to a year of feverish activity in 1862 as Federal offensives in East and West penetrated and were ultimately halted. Then, after Confederate counterattacks, the situation was stabilized with the battles of Fredericksburg in Virginia and Murfreesboro in Tennessee and with Grant's withdrawal on the Mississippi. These campaigns had involved Presidential intervention in numerous ways. Although departmental restructuring was his principal method of strategic control, Davis had, in a sometimes tardy and haphazard manner, coordinated departments and shifted troops from one to

[26] Longstreet to Wigfall, February 4, 1863, *ibid.*
[27] Beauregard to Johnston, May 15, 1863, in P. G. T. Beauregard Papers, National Archives.

another, playing a personal role in almost every Confederate defensive or offensive operation of the year 1862: reinforcing Pemberton, Lee, and Kirby Smith, encouraging Bragg, and initiating the Shiloh concentration.

From these activities Davis was developing a concept of reserves, forces which could be shifted from department to department to meet the varying needs of each theater. To him the need had seemed primarily defensive, but movement of reserves could encompass the offensive plans of a department commander as had been the case of Lee's Seven Days' battle offensive of June, 1862. That Davis' concept of reserves included subtracted reserve is illustrated by his suggestions to J. E. Johnston that he place a force in the center of his department. Nevertheless, his concept of reserves placed primary emphasis on the Napoleonic approach of considering all forces not actively engaged with the enemy as "defensive reserves."[28] By the spring of 1863 Davis began to improve his reserve system by making explicit advance preparations. Generalizing his improvisations of the preceding year into a system, he consciously viewed forces available to be concentrated as reserves, and he sought to develop means for increasing their mobility.

During the winter of 1862–1863 the Confederacy was organized into four major regional commands: (1) Kirby Smith's Trans-Mississippi Department; (2) Johnston's Department of the West, embracing the commands of Bragg in middle Tennessee and Alabama, Pemberton in Mississippi and eastern Louisiana, and the Department of East Tennessee; (3) Beauregard's Department of South Carolina, Georgia and Florida; and (4) Lee's command in Virginia and North Carolina. Clearly Davis' main reliance was on this departmental organization. It had come a long way from the complex series of miniature departments which had been the organization the year before. Each embraced a major strategic theater; yet each had sufficient diversity for Davis to expect that not every part of each of these major commands could be attacked simultaneously. If Tennessee were menaced, for example, Mississippi might well be

[28] *Official Records*, XXV, Pt 2, pp. 708–809.

quiescent. When the Army of the Potomac advanced, Lee might secure reinforcements from the Virginia and North Carolina coasts. Simultaneous attacks along Beauregard's extensive coastline were not likely, so he could use the coastwise railroad to concentrate wherever he was threatened. Still there were joints between these major regional commands and there was the distinct possibility that one department might be attacked while others were left alone.

In a small but definite way Davis approached this problem. His inspiration could well have been the pipeline concept developed in the West. To secure mobility of reserves between East and West, the War Department relied on the Virginia and Tennessee Railroad. To provide added celerity in reinforcement, General Samuel Jones, commanding in southwestern Virginia, halfway between the Virginia and Tennessee armies, was alerted to be ready to move a portion of his forces to either department as ordered. It was intended to replace these troops in his department with the last detachment of reinforcements to pass through.[29] A reserve pipeline between East and West was thus to be kept half filled, though Jones's forces were, as were those at Mobile, minute compared with the numbers in the major departments on either side. The coastline provided a more fruitful place for the application of this idea, since it was dotted with small detachments which were adjacent to a railroad. When it was decided to transfer forces from South Carolina to the West, arrangements were made to shift troops from the North Carolina coast to Charleston and to replace the North Carolina forces with troops from Virginia, arrangements which, incidentally, were implemented and which proved highly successful at the time of the attack on Charleston in July, 1863.[30]

Thus, by the end of the winter, Davis had not only made two explicit arrangements for strategic reinforcements in advance of their possible need, but, also, in planning to shift reserves from South Carolina to Tennessee at a time when both fronts were inactive, had anticipated what the exigencies of a Federal advance would

[29] *Ibid.,* LII, Pt. 2, p. 691.
[30] *Ibid.,* XVIII, 1059, 1076, XVIII, 1058–59, XXVIII, Pt. 2, pp. 187, 194, 196.

require.[31] Clearly Davis had already made significant strides in securing unity of control over the Confederate war effort, while at the same time retaining a large measure of autonomy for department commanders.

In the late spring the President saw the possibility of further refinements. Having already provided for the eventuality of shifting reserves along the Atlantic coast, he was faced with the fact that reinforcements from Charleston had actually gone to Vicksburg rather than Tennessee. It was at this time that he contemplated an expansion and reorganization of his system of regional commands, inspired, it seems, by an effort to increase the efficacy of the pipeline approach to reinforcement and by the fact that troops committed to coast defense were necessarily passive and must await attack. He may also have been responding to General Lee's expressed conviction that the summer climate would prevent a Federal attack on the south Atlantic coast. In considering giving Lee command of the "Atlantic slope" and Beauregard command of the Gulf Coast, Davis may well have been groping for the best way to exploit the excellent rail connections which both Charleston and Savannah enjoyed with Atlanta and Montgomery, Alabama, as well as with Wilmington, North Carolina, and Richmond. This approach also would, in part, begin to supersede the Department of the West organization, one which Johnston had always insisted was unworkable. Even though this reorganization was not implemented for a year and a half, Beauregard was directed to prepare to assist Mobile or Vicksburg, thus tentatively linking the coast from Alabama to Virginia in a reserve chain or network.[32]

In May, 1863, Davis' contemplated strategic redistribution of forces from South Carolina to Tennessee was interrupted by Grant's effective move on Vicksburg. This crisis provided a test of Davis' developing interdepartmental reserve system. The already alerted South Carolina troops were redirected and promptly dispatched to Vicksburg. Troops were sent from Tennessee, also, but none from Virginia, in spite of the fact that reinforcement from Virginia had been under discus-

[31] *Ibid.,* XVIII, 923.
[32] *Ibid.,* XXV, Pt. 2, p. 842, XIV, 956, 959.

sion for several months. Grant's move precipitated a major confrontation between Lee and the western concentration bloc because reinforcements from Virginia were being sought both for an offensive in Tennessee and to assist in the defense of Vicksburg.

To the President's and the Secretary of War's request for reinforcements for the West, Lee was almost adamant in his refusal. On a number of occasions, General Lee had emphasized his belief that "the climate in June will force the enemy to retire": from Mississippi and from the coasts of South Carolina and Georgia, and that any troops "ordered from Virginia to the Mississippi at this season would be greatly endangered by the climate."[33] In addition, he had disparaged this effort to try to counter the enemy's move by shifting troops because it was "not so easy for us to change troops from one department to another as it is for the enemy, and if we rely upon that method we may always be too late."

In General Lee's view one solution to the problem of enemy concentrations was for the other armies to take the offensive since "greater relief would in this way be afforded to the armies" threatened by a Federal advance "than by any other method." The Confederate commander in Virginia again emphasized his precarious situation where his army was reduced by the casualties sustained in the battle of Chancellorsville at the beginning of May. The strength of the enemy, he said, was such that sending any force to the West would pose "a question between Virginia and the Mississippi."[34]

Having developed the reasons why a portion of his army should not be sent west, Lee began to make his plans and to strengthen his own army for the coming campaign. The situation was critical, for it was evident to General Lee "from the tone of the Northern papers that it is the intention of the administration at Washington to re-enforce the army of General Hooker" so as to make Virginia "the theater of action." If, however, adequate reinforcements could be supplied him, he might himself take the offensive. The logical

[33] *Ibid.*, XXV, Pt. 2, pp. 713, 725–26, 752–53, 782–83, 790. For Beauregard's and Seddon's comparable views on the South Carolina and Georgia climate, see *ibid.*, XIV, 932, 935, 940.

[34] *Ibid.*, XXV, Pt. 2, pp. 713, 725, 790.

place to secure reinforcements for the Virginia army was the southern coastline. Lee pointed out that troops would not be needed there because the climate would make South Carolina secure and, alternatively "a vigorous movement" in Virginia would make certain that the enemy withdrew his forces from the southern coasts. Faced with an enemy inaccessible because it was seaborne, the South Carolina troops must inevitably be idle unless moved to Virginia. General Lee's belief that the climate would compel the employment elsewhere of the Union troops on the southern coasts was confirmed by his intelligence that indicated that "every available man" was being sent to reinforce the Union army in Virginia. Lee was sure that the Army of the Potomac was "preparing for an early move" and that there was "no point in the country where we stand in greater need of troops than here." Lee's plan was thus to concentrate with his army as many men from the coast defenses as possible in order to withstand the Federal advance when it came. Actually Lee's preferred strategy was to "forestall" Hooker's advance.[35] A spoiling attack would have another major advantage for Lee; it would move his army into a new area for forage and subsistence, thus relieving his desperate supply problems.

The actual decision to make the movement northward, if made earlier, was not communicated to President Davis until early June and even then Lee proposed to move "cautiously, watching the result, and not to get beyond recall" until it was clear there would be no enemy attack in Tidewater Virginia.

So tentatively was begun the famous Gettysburg campaign. Its aim was defensive rather than offensive and the primary objectives were to upset Federal plans and to move the Army of Northern Virginia to new sources of supplies. Beyond these, the objectives were quite vague. There seems to have been some notion that the situation at Vicksburg might be favorably affected. Other objectives were even more elusive. At various times Lee alluded to the following: to "operate advantageously," to gain some "material advantage," to accomplish something "of importance," to "make some impression

[35] *Ibid.*, XVIII, 1063, 1066, 1070, XXV, Pt. 2, pp. 791–93, 815–16, 820.

on the enemy," to achieve "good results," to "give occupation" to the enemy, and to obtain "valuable and substantial results."[36]

Confirmation of the limited objectives of the campaign comes from the evaluation made of it upon Lee's return. Noting that it had been a "general success," Lee summed up the campaign, writing to Davis that "had the late unexpected rise [in the Potomac] not occurred . . . everything would have been accomplished that could reasonably be expected. The Army of the Potomac has been thrown north of that river, the forces invading the coast of North Carolina and Virginia had been diminished, their plan of the present campaign broken up, and before new arrangements could have been made for its resumption, the summer would have ended." In the favorable assessment of the campaign Davis later concurred, noting that the "wisdom of the strategy was justified by the result."[37]

Of course many Confederate leaders outside of Virginia thought that Lee's advance into Pennsylvania was an offensive move and believed it was a luxury the South could ill afford in view of the peril of Pemberton's army at Vicksburg and Rosecrans' advance in Tennessee. The members of the western concentration bloc increased their efforts and one of them, General Leonidas Polk, commander of Bragg's first corps, approached Davis directly. Polk was a good example of cross patterns of factions within the Confederate army. He shared Beauregard's views on the need for a western concentration, yet these men felt a mutual dislike. Polk also shared Bragg's strategic views, yet he was a leader of the powerful anti-Bragg faction within the Army of Tennessee.

Despite his spotty field performance and reputation for troublemaking in the army, Polk was a far deeper strategic thinker than historians have credited him with being. After the Kentucky campaign, Polk had also gone to Richmond to urge a unified western command. In March of 1863, when Davis sent an aide to inspect the Army

[36] *Ibid.*, XXV, Pt. 2, pp. 752–53, 842, XXVII Pt. 3, pp. 869, 931–33; Rowland (ed.), *Jefferson Davis*, V, 507, 539; Jefferson Davis, *The Rise and Fall of the Confederate Government* (2 vols.; New York, 1881), II, 438; Archer Jones, "The Gettysburg Decision Reassessed," *Virginia Magazine of History and Biography* (January, 1968), 65.

[37] Rowland, *Davis*, V, 543; Davis, *Rise and Fall of the Confederate Government*, II, 447; Jones, "Gettysburg Decision Reassessed," 65–66.

of Tennessee, Polk exhibited strategic insight. He repeated an old Johnston argument—that the western command was aligned improperly—and urged a concentration of the Second Department and east Tennessee armies under Johnston. After the twin disasters of Vicksburg's surrender and middle Tennessee's loss in July, Polk's views seemed very close to Beauregard's. On July 30, deeply troubled with the effects which dispersal had wrought, Polk proposed to his friend General William Hardee a plan of concentration. He suggested a massive concentration at Chattanooga of the three departmental armies in the West—Bragg's, the east Tennessee force, and the remnants of the Mississippi department now commanded by Johnston. Polk's plans for this force, which he estimated at eighty thousand men, seemed a carbon of Beauregard's. Once concentrated under Johnston, the Confederates would take the offensive against Rosecrans. If Rosecrans were defeated, a diagonal move against Grant's communications on the Mississippi would be effected. This move would reestablish communications with the Trans-Mississippi Department. Then Polk envisioned a second concentration in the region between Memphis and Island Number Ten, by the troops of Johnston and the Trans-Mississippi. This combined force would then launch a second offensive against Grant.

Polk also sent his proposal to President Davis, a warm friend of prewar days. Polk insisted that better use could be made of Johnston's army than merely retaining it on the defensive in Mississippi. On August 9 Polk repeated his plan to Davis and urged its acceptance. He argued that it was "more full of promise"[38] than any other available plan.

On June 21 Beauregard again sent Johnston a copy of his proposal of the previous month. Beauregard had also not only sent a copy to Wigfall, but to his former brother-in-law and strong congressional ally, Charles Villeré of Louisiana. In Beauregard's second letter to Johnston, he commented on what seemed to have been the government's policy decision of May—to maintain two defensive positions in the West (Bragg and Pemberton) and apparently to undertake

[38] Polk to Davis, August 9, 1863, in Leonidas Polk Papers, Duke University Library.

an offensive in the East. Beauregard insisted the proper course should have been the concentration against Rosecrans, followed by the diagonal move against Grant's communications. Then "the principles and maxims of war would then be observed."[39] Again, just before the battle of Gettysburg, Beauregard wrote Johnston to comment on the bad effects of the government's strategy. Thinking that Lee's advance into Pennsylvania was an offensive movement, he asked "of what earthly use is this 'raid' of Lee's army into Maryland, in violation of all the principles of war? Is it going to end the struggle, take Washington, or save the Mississippi Valley?" After the war Beauregard criticized Lee's offensives after Second Manassas and Chancellorsville, denouncing them as the result of a "timid policy . . . which . . . with characteristic mis-elation [sic], would push a victorious force directly forward into unsupported and disastrous operations, instead of using its victory to spare from it strength sufficient to secure an equally important success in another quarter."[40] To Johnston, Beauregard reiterated that the true course should have been the Chattanooga concentration against Rosecrans. Perhaps not by accident did Beauregard emphasize that the troops sent from Virginia would be Longstreet's corps.

In July the interchange of ideas continued. Beauregard sent to Bragg a copy of his proposal for the Chattanooga concentration. Bragg replied warmly, stating that their views were "identical" and that he had desired such a concentration in the spring, but was unable to convince "others who control."[41] Bragg also discussed strategy with Johnston. On June 22 he confessed to Johnston that he had been tardy in seeing that western concentration was the key, and commented upon "how we can now see the folly of last spring's operations in diverting you from your aims."[42]

Then, on July 17, Bragg proposed to Johnston a new plan of concentration. He wrote that "our success can only result from

[39] *Official Records,* XXIII, Pt. 2, p. 837.
[40] *Ibid.,* XXVIII, Pt. 2, pp. 173–74; Beauregard, "The First Battle of Bull Run," 223.
[41] Bragg to Beauregard, July 21, 1863, in Don Seitz, *Braxton Bragg, General of the Confederacy* (Columbia, S.C., 1924), 321.
[42] Bragg to Johnston, June 22, 1863, *ibid.,* 308.

concentration." Bragg's proposal was also almost a carbon of Beauregard's, save that he reversed the point of concentration. Bragg suggested a union of forces under Johnston in Mississippi, with an attack on Grant. Bragg argued that Rosecrans would not be ready to move until the first of September. Thus he unselfishly offered his entire army to Johnston, save for his cavalry and a few infantry brigades to garrison Chattanooga. Bragg's exhortation sounded much like those of Beauregard—"concentrate all else by the most rapid means . . . and strike at once. Success is our deliverance; failure would be no more than defeat in detail."[43]

Although Johnston was too engrossed in a puerile post-Vicksburg quarrel with Davis even to reply, support came from other quarters. In mid-August, Longstreet for the third time advanced a scheme of concentration. He urged Seddon to detach at least part of his corps to aid Bragg while Lee held a defensive position on the Rapidan River. By late August, Longstreet even approached Lee with the idea. Again on September 2, while Lee conferred with Davis in Richmond regarding future operations, Longstreet repeated his proposal. He urged that a corps be sent to the Chattanooga front.

Thus during the summer of 1863, the air must have been charged with the idea of a concentration in Tennessee as the western concentration bloc and many of the various informal organizations of Confederate soldiers and politicians pushed the idea through their myriad contacts in Virginia. Even Lee's influence was diluted by the adherence of Longstreet to the western bloc.

At the same time President Davis was plunged into "depths of gloom in which the disasters of the Mississippi River have shrouded our cause."[44] As well as seeking the cause of disaster, he must have been reassessing the Confederate situation. The thought of a counterattack to recover some lost territory must have come naturally to him, and recovery of middle Tennessee must have appeared the most logical and feasible operation. He certainly also had official as well as unofficial cognizance of Beauregard's ideas since they had been presented to Davis by Bragg on the latter's visit to Richmond

[43] *Official Records*, LII, Pt. 2, p. 508.
[44] Davis to R. W. Johnson, July 14, 1863, in Rowland, *Jefferson Davis*, V, 548.

in October, 1862, or on the President's visit to Tennessee in December. A westward shift of Virginia reserves had been under consideration in the spring, and Longstreet had presented a proposal comparable to Beauregard's to the Secretary of War in early May.[45]

The basic idea of applying Napoleonic theater strategy to unify the operations of all Confederate armies, of viewing "the whole theater of war as one subject of which all points were but integral parts" was not foreign to Davis, the strategist of First Manassas, since his system of reserves already embodied this concept. It would be easy for him to incorporate part of Beauregard's thinking into his own, and to continue his concept of reserves, merely extending it to an offensive initiated from Richmond rather than limiting it, as he had largely done in the past, to the defensive. Large-scale troop movements by rail were as familiar to Davis as they were to Lee, Beauregard, Bragg, and Johnston.

At the end of July, 1863, President Davis received from his friend Leonidas Polk, Polk's western concentration plan which he represented as the views of "the most intelligent circles" at Bragg's headquarters. Probably already familiar to Davis, this proposal coincided with the receipt of intelligence from Mississippi that there was no enemy near Johnston and that no enemy attack was probable. Immediately the commander in Mississippi was interrogated as to forces available for reinforcing Bragg and was directed to "prepare such force, if disposable, for early movement."[46] After many telegrams and a projected conference between Johnston and Bragg, the latter, who had just proposed a concentration in Mississippi, vetoed the President's proposal, saying that the forces of Johnston and Buckner were insufficient "to justify a movement across the [eastern] Tennessee mountains" to reach Rosecrans. Bragg felt, however, that "whenever he shall present himself on this side of the mountains the problem will be changed." Davis' disappointment is evident in his endorsement on Bragg's letter: "However desirable a movement may be, it is never safe to do more than suggest it to a commanding general,

---

[45] *Official Records,* XL, Pt. 4, p. 745; James Longstreet, "Lee in Pennsylvania," in *Annals of the War* (Philadelphia, 1879), 413–16.

[46] *Official Records,* XXIII, Pt. 2, pp. 932–33, 936–38, LII, Pt. 2, p. 514.

and it would be unwise to order its execution by one who foretold failure."[47]

By August 21 Bragg's situation at Chattanooga had become so desperate that assistance seemed imperative. On August 21 and 22 Bragg warned Richmond that a combined Union advance had begun. Rosecrans was crossing the Tennessee River below Chattanooga in order to outflank Bragg, while Burnside advanced against Buckner's small army at Knoxville.

The ensuing concentration of Confederate forces below Chattanooga developed slowly. Already in early August, Buckner's Department of East Tennessee had been placed under Bragg's authority. By August 21 Bragg had ordered Buckner to evacuate Knoxville. Soon Buckner's five thousand infantry began a slow retreat southward toward an eventual union with Bragg. From Mississippi, General Joseph E. Johnston also responded to the urgings of the War Department and an appeal sent to him by Bragg on August 21. The following day Johnston began forwarding two divisions, totaling nine thousand infantry, to Chattanooga.

By the last week of August, President Davis seemed to believe that Bragg needed further aid. Bragg's continual gloomy prognostications, urgent appeals from the governor and senators from Tennessee, and the threatened loss of the direct railway link between Tennessee and Virginia turned the President to consider other measures to assist the Army of Tennessee.[48] During Lee's long absence from Virginia with his army during June and July, Davis strongly felt the need of his "advice" and "counsel." Thus, during the last week of August, Lee was summoned by Davis to Richmond for a conference. For almost two weeks, Davis and Lee discussed overall strategic policy, as events steadily convinced the President that assistance for Bragg was required from the Virginia army. Knoxville fell to Burnside on September 3. The East Tennessee Railroad was now severed, and by September 6 two thirds of east Tennessee was in Federal hands. Worse, a junction of Rosecrans' and Burnside's

---

[47] *Ibid.*, XXIII, Pt. 2, pp. 848, 936, 948, 950, 952–53, LII, Pt. 2, pp. 508, 514.
[48] *Ibid.*, XXI, Pt. 2, p. 662, XXX, Pt. 4, pp. 526, 529–31, 541, 584, 561, 566, LI, Pt. 2, pp. 761, LII, Pt. 2, p. 519.

troops, approximately one hundred thousand men, now seemed inevitable.

Apparently General Lee at the Richmond conference did not support the idea of detaching part of the Army of Northern Virginia to assist Bragg. Already on August 31 Lee had ordered Longstreet to prepare the army for offensive operations against Meade. At Richmond, Lee argued that since Meade had been weakened by detachments to Charleston, an eastern offensive seemed desirable.[49]

Despite Lee's lack of enthusiasm for the proposal, Davis by September 7 had decided to detach part of Longstreet's corps to Bragg's assistance. Longstreet was ordered to move at once with two divisions to Chattanooga.

In some respects, the ensuing Confederate concentration below Chattanooga was probably less impressive than some historians have indicated it to be. Johnston could have sent more help from Mississippi. Earlier in the summer he had promised Richmond that if Bragg were threatened, he would send nine of his eleven infantry brigades to Chattanooga. Instead, after receiving Bragg's urgent appeal on August 21, Johnston sent only six brigades. Although affairs were generally idle in his department, Johnston retained nine thousand infantry and over six thousand cavalry. Too, the government actually never ordered Johnston to reinforce Bragg. After receiving Bragg's telegram and requesting advice from Richmond, Johnston was merely told to aid Bragg if he were able to do so.

Longstreet's reinforcement has also probably been overrated in some respects. Only two divisions, without supply wagons or teams, were sent. The long Richmond conference between Davis and Lee also consumed precious time. The first of Longstreet's troops did not leave Virginia until September 9—almost three weeks after Bragg's pleas for assistance. Due to impossible supply problems and poor rail communication, only five bragades, none possessing artillery, reached Georgia by September 20 in time to participate in the last day's action at the battle of Chickamauga.

Still, the concentration below Chattanooga was a signal event in

[49] *Ibid.*, XXIX, Pt. 2, pp. 660, 554–664, XXX, Pt. 4, pp. 607, 619, 623, LI, Pt. 2, pp. 742, 750, 761.

Confederate policy making. Two factors seem notable. The clash of opinion between Lee and the western concentration bloc had produced a significant event—a reinforcement for the West from Lee's army. More important, the concentration—however late and modest—indicated Davis' acceptance of a plan long advocated by the western bloc. It involved a junction of forces in the central South from several departments. Major reinforcements from the Department of Northern Virginia, and the Department of Alabama and Mississippi were sent to join Bragg's army in the Second Department. Another sizable reinforcement joined Bragg from Buckner's Department of East Tennessee. In addition, Richmond authorized General Sam Jones, commander of the Department of Southwestern Virginia, to advance into upper east Tennessee if practicable. In addition, President Davis sought to augment the concentration by calling out the militia of Georgia and Alabama for service in Tennessee.

This concentration marked the high point for Davis as generalissimo. It was a repetition, on a larger scale, of the basic pattern of Confederate strategy usually applied within a particular zone of operations such as in Virginia. Too, the genesis of this multidepartment concentration on a grand scale was certainly not a new idea. It was reminiscent of that first grand design for a western concentration sent to Bragg in the summer of 1862 by General P. G. T. Beauregard.

V
The Ghost
of Beauregard

Even though defensive in character, the Confederate concentration for Chickamauga represented an acceptance by President Davis of the ideas of Beauregard and of the western concentration bloc. It was the only instance of using the strategy applied by Lee in the East and by Beauregard and Bragg in the West in order to unify all Confederate operations, and to produce, on the widest possible scale, what was the basic pattern in Confederate strategy. Chickamauga also influenced the President's thinking, but not as much as one might expect. The most important influence was that Davis was impressed by the possibility and the potentialities of offensives instigated by or devised in Richmond.

Neither Davis nor Lee, for example, seemed to view the Chickamauga concentration in quite the same way that Beauregard and the western bloc did. Both were more concerned with the fate of east Tennessee than with Rosecrans' seizure of the Chattanooga-Atlanta corridor. Evidently the President simply misread the Federal objective. His correspondence with Bragg and Lee until after the battle at Chickamauga on September 19–20, indicates that Davis still had not accepted the seizure of the Atlanta route as a key Federal objective. He believed instead that the Federal objective in the campaign was a seizure of the east Tennessee valley where Rosecrans would join the independent corps of General Ambrose Burnside. On September 11, two days after Bragg had abandoned Chattanooga, Davis still believed that Rosecrans would halt and unite with Burnside. By that day, Rosecrans' center and right corps were already reaching far south of Chattanooga toward the Atlanta railroad. Then, on September 16, Davis asserted that he regretted that Chattanooga had fallen, mainly because it lost an opportunity to trap Burnside's corps in east Tennessee. By then, Rosecrans' right wing had penetrated almost seventy-five miles into north Georgia.

The battle of Chickamauga and the ensuing "siege" of Chattanooga again raised the question of what should be done in the West. Immediately after the battle, Bragg began formulating plans for an offensive. His strategy was vague for many reasons: his own declining health, the heavy Chickamauga losses, the absence of a pontoon train, and the lack of transportation for Longstreet's corps. Still, during the week after the September 20 victory, Bragg had decided to concentrate upon one of the two weak enemy fronts in Tennessee. By September 29 his determination was either to shift quickly to east Tennessee and crush Burnside, or to flank Rosecrans on the west and overwhelm the weak defenses in middle Tennessee.

While Bragg discussed these ideas with Richmond, other members of the western bloc were also busy. By the end of September, all four of Bragg's corps leaders—Longstreet, Leonidas Polk, Simon Buckner, and Harvey Hill—were conspiring to have Bragg replaced. They decided to undertake a letter writing campaign, and Polk and Longstreet were selected to plead their case in Richmond.

The famous September letters to Davis, Lee, and Seddon expressed more than dissatisfaction with Bragg. They also expressed a concern over the western situation. Longstreet not only urged that Seddon replace Bragg, but also called attention to the need to take the offensive immediately in Tennessee against a single line of Federal advance. Longstreet suggested a rapid strike against Burnside, to be followed by a diagonal move into middle Tennessee against Rosecrans' communications. That same day Longstreet proposed a similiar plan to Lee.

Polk, on September 26, wrote the President and Lee. He criticized Bragg's defensive policy, asked for Beauregard to replace him, and reiterated the proposals which he and the Creole had made during the summer. Polk urged that Lee should come to Tennessee for a thrust against Rosecrans. Once Rosecrans was beaten, a diagonal move would be made against Grant's communications. After reaching the Mississippi River the Army of Tennessee would then join the Trans-Mississippi army for a southward thrust against Grant.

Within a few days, a major crisis in Bragg's high command again stimulated proposals by the western bloc. By October 1 Bragg had suspended both Polk and one of his division commanders, General Thomas C. Hindman, which prompted President Davis to hurry to Bragg's headquarters. Davis had two reasons for the visit—to discuss future strategy and to attempt to stifle command disputes. Command friction was settled by a general dispersal of Bragg's enemies.

The question of strategy produced a resurgence of the western concentration bloc. There was good reason for concern. By September 28 intelligence sources indicated that two corps were en route from the Army of the Potomac to relieve Chattanooga. By October 1 two corps from Grant's Mississippi army were reported moving eastward through north Alabama.

Thus, after he completed talks on October 10 relative to the army's internal matters, Davis called a war council to discuss future policy. Here the influence of Beauregard was felt. On October 7 Beauregard, from his Charleston vantage point, had completed a new plan of grand strategy. He quickly dispatched it by his brother Armand to Bragg's headquarters. Beauregard stated that he had "just been informed, from Richmond, that the army of Virginia is about to take the offensive again to prevent Meade from re-enforcing Rosecrans, thus repeating to a certain extent, the campaign of last July into Pennsylvania, which did not save Middle Tennessee and the Mississippi Valley." Beauregard prefaced his new plan with a review of how the government's policy of cordon defense had resulted in piecemeal defeats. Then, stating that the war should be a contest of "masses against fractions," he proposed almost the same plan that he had sent Bragg in July. Now twenty-five thousand men from Lee's army and ten thousand from Joseph E. Johnston's in Mississippi were to be sent to Chattanooga. Bragg would then strike Rosecrans before he was reinforced from Meade and Grant. After Rosecrans was defeated, Bragg would then fall upon other isolated Federal columns in Tennessee, such as Burnside's corps. Again Beauregard sensed that his signature on any proposal might doom it in Richmond, so he urged Bragg to present the plan as his own.[1]

---

[1] *Official Records*, XXVIII, Pt. 2, pp. 399–400.

Although inspired by his belief that if Lee was strong enough to advance, then he was strong enough to spare reinforcements, the plan is not typical of Beauregard. The letter is more in accord with Johnston's than his own ideas, for, rather than proposing a concentration against weakness, it advocates a counter-buildup against the Federal strength which was rapidly accumulating in Tennessee. The tone of Beauregard's letter is one of despair. He was clearly at his wit's end, and he stuck to his orginal idea long after the conditions which would have made it successful had ceased to exist. Since the plan advocated further reinforcement of Bragg's army, it would be unlikely to receive a very critical appraisal from Bragg to whom Armand Beauregard was to deliver it.

Armand Beauregard reached Bragg's headquarters on the evening of October 9. Ironically, Davis arrived that same evening, and Armand sensed an opportunity for quick action not anticipated by his brother. Immediately he held a conference with Bragg, and presented the new proposal. Bragg expressed "strong friendship and admiration" for Beauregard, alluded "with pleasure to past association," and mentioned the "great intimacy" between the two generals "in the exchange of views upon national topics." Bragg also indicated high approval of the plan and promised to submit it to Davis.

Other matters indicated Bragg's admiration for Beauregard's ideas. On October 14 he replied directly to Beauregard, stating that "your views . . . are so nearly in accordance with my own that a presentation of them to the Department would be almost a renewal of my recommendation." Bragg admitted that from the time he had received Beauregard's July strategic proposal, "my efforts have all been directed to the policy you indicate on this line, and I am daily strengthened in the views first formed of its importance."

That same day, Beauregard's brother sent a report of a second conversation with Bragg, held after that officer's meeting with Davis. Bragg referred to the July, 1862, plan sent by Beauregard, prior to Bragg's Kentucky invasion. He told Beauregard's brother that he had "strongly advocated" this, so much so that Bragg admitted that the Kentucky campaign was based on Beauregard's principles. Moreover, Bragg had always kept it in view "to act on whenever the opportunity would present itself," since "it was and is the only plan which can save the Confederacy."[2]

Beauregard's new proposal was also advocated by Bragg. At the council of war, probably held on October 11, Bragg presented Beauregard's plan as his own, but did mention that it was sustained by Johnston and Beauregard. Little resulted from the council. Davis rejected Beauregard's new plan, claiming that Lee could spare no more men. Instead, he insisted that Bragg must take the offensive only with those troops now available at Chattanooga. Even here little was settled. No plan was produced by the council, save for a vague agreement that Bragg would remain on the defensive until strong enough for a forward move, probably across the Tennessee River west of Chattanooga.

The disaster at Missionary Ridge in November and Bragg's subsequent resignation in December did not stifle planning by the western concentration bloc. By January, General Joseph E. Johnston, the new commander of the Army of Tennessee, was busy at Dalton, Georgia, with the arduous task of rebuilding his army for the spring campaign. These preparations, which lasted until May, were accompanied by the most widespread discussion yet on Confederate western policy. Some writers have oversimplified this policy debate by depicting it merely as a disagreement over strategy between Johnston and Richmond. Actually, what was involved was the climax of the influence of the western concentration bloc. From December, 1863, until March, 1864, four basic plans of western strategy were offered by Beauregard, Polk, Johnston, and the faction of Kentucky generals. All of them— even a fifth plan proposed by the government—contained elements of the western concentration bloc's thinking.

Characteristically, Beauregard was the first to write his views. Since October, he had returned to his basic concept of the surprise concentration against the enemy weak point. After repining for opportunities lost "irretrievably" since Chancellorsville and deploring the losses at Gettysburg and Vicksburg, he advanced the idea that it would be best for Longstreet's forces to join "Lee's, to crush Meade

---

[2] *Ibid.*, XXX, Pt. 4, p. 745.

before the return of the latter's three corps sent to defeat Bragg
. . . ." Longstreet, he pointed out, could "move on interior lines,
while Meade's three corps have to go around the circumference
of the circle."[3] Yet in December the general returned to what was
now his *idée fixe,* a concentration on the Nashville-Atlanta line of
operations, and forwarded a new proposal to a Richmond friend
and lobbyist, Pierre Soulé. A copy was also sent to Johnston at Dalton.
Beauregard's rambling proposal quoted freely from Napoleon's
maxims and emphasized all of the Louisiana general's previous ideas.
He stressed "a sudden and rapid concentration upon some selected,
decisive, strategic point . . . to crush the forces of the enemy. . . .
This must necessarily be done at the expense or hazard, for the
time, of other points less important." Beauregard argued that we
"will never win a signal, conclusive victory until we can manage
to throw a heavy and overwhelming mass of our forces upon the
fractions of the enemy, and at the same time successfully strike at
his communications without exposing our own."

The plan itself revealed that Beauregard's ideas had undergone
a change. Rather than concentrating to take advantage of weakness,
he was concerned about Atlanta, the loss of which would be "the
most injurious blow" the South could receive. He thought, therefore,
that the Confederates must regard Atlanta as "the actual objective
point" of the Federals at Chattanooga. To prevent this terrible
occurrence, Beauregard again suggested a massive western concentration involving twenty thousand troops from Lee's army, ten
thousand from the Carolinas, and ten thousand from Polk's Alabama-
Mississippi command. "Let this army take the offensive at once"
to defeat the "scattered" Federals in Tennessee, before they completed
concentrating at Chattanooga. Again he stressed that "the whole
science of war" was "placing in the right position at the right time
a mass of troops greater than your enemy can there oppose to you."

A critical feature of Beauregard's plan was his stress on striking
Sherman's communications, "without exposing our own." While he
suggested that the western concentration be effected at Dalton, he

[3] *Ibid.,* XXVIII, Pt. 2, pp. 523–24, 564, 580–81.

stated that the proper place to begin the campaign would be from east Tennessee. From here Beauregard envisioned a lateral thrust into middle Tennessee, severing Sherman's communications. Thus would be achieved Napoleon's maxim, Beauregard argued, that "that part of the base of operations is the most advantageous to break out from into the theater of war which conducts the most directly on the enemy's flanks or rear."[4]

Johnston replied with a formidable critique of Beauregard's plan. After emphasizing the logistical difficulties of Beauregard's proposed campaign, he pointed out that "our troops to be concentrated are now spread over the whole Confederacy, while" those of the enemy "could be united in two or three days, and that after our army is formed it must march with great trains over a barren and mountainous country inhabited by people many of whom are disloyal, so that no movement could be concealed." He then suggested that it "would be easier to penetrate into middle Tennessee from northern Mississippi than from Georgia." Although such a maneuver "would involve the abandonment of this route into the interior of Georgia," any enemy army would not get too far because "the progress made from Mississippi would compel its return."[5] It was an unusual turn about for Johnston to point out to Beauregard that a concentration should aim at an enemy's weakness and avoid his strength, especially when the latter was advocating a Johnston style buildup for Johnston's own army.

Other proposals for the West also entailed some concentration on the middle-east Tennessee line. In mid-January, a group of prominent Kentucky generals, including John C. Breckinridge, presented Davis with their plan for a concentration in east Tennessee of some eight thousand mounted Kentucky troops. They would invade Kentucky via the Cumberland Gap and strike Federal communications there while Johnston advanced from Dalton. Breckinridge, who only two months previous had corresponded with Beauregard concerning strategy, joined General Simon Buckner and others in stressing such

---

[4] Beauregard to Pierre Soulé, December 8, 1863, in Beauregard Papers, National Archives.

[5] *Official Records*, LII, Pt. 2, p. 597.

familiar ideas as a concentration on a weak line of Federal advance (east Kentucky), a diagonal thrust at enemy communications, and the importance of the mid-South region.

Yet another strategic proposal was emitted by the western bloc. By January of 1864 General James Longstreet's corps lay in winter quarters in upper east Tennessee where he temporarily commanded the department. Longstreet's campaign against Burnside had ended only in the miserable, bloody assault against Knoxville. Evidently he relished independent command. His correspondence during this period indicates no great desire to concentrate at Dalton with Johnston, nor did he appear to want to return to Lee's army. On January 11 Longstreet proposed to Lee a plan not unlike that being advocated by the Kentuckians, a mounted invasion of that state. The only difference was the makeup of the invading force. Longstreet did not plan to use Kentuckians, but would mount his own infantry corps on horses and mules.

The government did not laugh at this unconventional idea. Lee also evidently took it seriously. Although he questioned whether enough animals could be secured, Lee did not discourage the project. On January 16, he suggested to Longstreet, "Let us both quietly and ardently set to work; some good may result and I will institute inquiries."[6] By early February, Lee had made inquiries in Richmond as to how much equipment and livestock could be sent to east Tennessee. Lee also approached Davis with Longstreet's plan, and asserted that such an offensive would force the Federals at Chattanooga to detach troops to pursue Longstreet. This move, Lee suggested, might enable Johnston to take the offensive.

In February, Longstreet kept pressing for a Kentucky invasion. On the second, he revised his original proposal and came up with an almost fantastic plan. Johnston's army would be shifted to Virginia, while Lee's army would join Longstreet in east Tennessee. Meanwhile, Longstreet's own mounted corps would invade Kentucky, where it would be joined by all of the cavalry in the Tennessee and the Alabama-Mississippi departments. Before this proposal, Lee had been

[6] Lee to Longstreet, January 16, 1864, in Confederate Miscellany Collection, Emory University Library.

working seriously to obtain equipment and had already been promised five hundred horses and fifteen hundred saddles and bridles. But by mid-February, Lee was backing away from the proposal. Now he suggested that Longstreet might do well to consider a joint invasion of Tennessee with Johnston's army.

Still, Longstreet kept up the pressure for a Kentucky offensive well into March. In late February he pleaded with Lee, Davis, and Seddon for permission to make the move. Again on March 4 he repeated his plan to Lee. Then, four days later, Longstreet went to Richmond to confer with Seddon, Bragg, Davis, and Lee on western strategy. He carried to Richmond a new Kentucky plan. This, the third strategy devised by Longstreet within two months, called for a three-pronged invasion. Beauregard would bring twenty thousand men from the Carolina department to southwestern Virginia. He could cross into Kentucky via the lower Virginia gaps. Meanwhile, Longstreet's corps would invade Kentucky via the Cumberland Gap. When the enemy fell back from Chattanooga to protect its communications, Johnston would follow. Basically, this was the old Bragg–Kirby Smith–Humphrey Marshall strategy of the 1862 invasion with increased numbers. Like Bragg in 1862, Longstreet now suggested that the three colunms should unite near the Ohio River.

Longstreet's proposal had scarcely been presented, when, within a week he came up with a fourth plan. Longstreet had proposed to Beauregard on March 7 the plan he presented at the Richmond council. But immediately after leaving the Richmond meeting, Longstreet altered his plan for using Beauregard's troops. Instead of the three-column invasion, Longstreet's and Beauregard's forces should unite at Abingdon, Virginia. From there, they would march across the Cumberland Mountains to Louisville, while Johnston from Dalton advanced northward into Kentucky.

Neither Richmond nor Beauregard accepted Longstreet's ideas. Beauregard thought the logistical problems of a move through east Kentucky would be too severe. By mid-March, Lee, Davis, Bragg, and Seddon had ruled out Longstreet's plan.

From Mississippi, General Leonidas Polk submitted his own strategic proposal. Polk's idea, sent to President Davis in February, also contained some familiar items, and was extremely imaginative. It was based on the idea that the Federals in Tennessee had not yet concentrated at Chattanooga, but were dispersed from north Mississippi to the Unaka Mountains. Polk suggested that the Federal concentration at Chattanooga could possibly be broken up by a two-pronged forward move. While Johnston's main army remained stationary at Dalton, reinforcements were to be sent to Polk from Johnston. Polk would then cross the Tennessee River and operate against Grant's right flank and communications in middle Tennessee. Meanwhile, from east Tennessee, Longstreet, with Morgan's cavalry, would cross the Kentucky-Tennessee Cumberlands on Grant's left flank, and would also harass his communications. Polk believed that Grant would be forced to abandon his designs of a massive concentration at Chattanooga. Polk surmised that perhaps then "we might take the offensive and invade his territory."[7]

Polk's plan was probably the most realistic of all the spring proposals, because it did not require much strain on Rebel logistics and did not envision an attempt to overwhelm Sherman with a counterconcentration. Rather, it reverted not only to the Kentucky campaign but to December, 1862, when Grant had been forced to withdraw from Mississippi after Van Dorn and Forrest cut his communications. Polk's forces were adequate to the proposed campaign, for he already possessed twenty-six thousand cavalry and infantry in the Alabama department. He proposed that four thousand infantry from Johnston's army be added.

Meanwhile Davis had been in consultation with Seddon, Bragg, Lee, and Longstreet, and a plan had been formulated calling for the union of Johnston and Longstreet in east Tennessee for an offensive against middle Tennessee. Already on March 5, before the Richmond conference, Davis had sent an aide to Longstreet with the plan. Then, in a conference at Richmond, the new plan was adopted. Johnston was to march from Dalton to some point south of Knoxville, join Longstreet, and then cross the Cumberland Mountains into middle Tennessee. On March 18 Colonel John Sale

---

[7] *Official Records*, XXX, Pt. 2, p. 814.

arrived at Johnston's headquarters at Dalton with the new western plan.

The plan elicited enthusiasm from the President and his advisers. Lee said of the potential Johnston-Longstreet success in middle Tennessee, "a victory gained there will open the country to you to the Ohio," while Davis intended for Longstreet and Johnston to march into the eastern portion of middle Tennessee in the vicinity of Sparta. There "you will be between the enemy's divided forces at Chattanooga, Knoxville and Nashville, and be in condition to strike either one of them, or move forward into Kentucky." To Longstreet, Davis added, "It is needless to point out to you the value of a successful movement into Tennessee and Kentucky." Bragg also was enthusiastic. On March 12 he wrote to Johnston, giving the government's plan for the West. The letter, which was borne to Johnston by Colonel Sale, stated that a chief aim of the invasion into middle Tennessee was "reclaiming the provision country of Tennessee and Kentucky."[8]

For the President to send a plan at all was a major innovation in the conduct of Confederate operations for, in the past, intervention by the President and the War Department had been limited to ordering reinforcements. Events of the spring and summer of 1863 had called forth a larger measure of central strategic direction, and this plan indicated there was to be no reversion to the older laissez faire methods. That the plan was for an offensive was also a departure from the largely defensive point of view which had dominated Davis' thinking before the previous summer. The President had evidently absorbed this common element in the thinking of Lee and Beauregard. This is not surprising, nor is it remarkable that the plan had much in common with the others proposed. The western bloc no longer needed to rely on lobbying by outsiders to promote their ideas with the President and the War Department, for General Bragg was now in charge of military operations. His concern with strategy and his constant advocacy of the ideas that had borne fruit at Chickamauga

---

[8] *Ibid.*, XXXII, Pt. 3, p. 594, LII, Pt. 2, 634; Bragg to Johnston, March 12, 1864, in Johnston Papers, William and Mary.

may have suggested to Davis that this post was appropriate for Bragg when he had resigned after the Chattanooga disaster. The plan itself had been the result of weeks of consultation between Davis, Seddon, Longstreet, Lee, and Bragg.

The impractical nature of the Richmond plan has clouded some other important matters. The plan did not seem workable. It called for Johnston to march his army east of Chattanooga, and up the east Tennessee valley for a junction with Longstreet near Kingston, Tennessee. There the two armies would combine between Burnside at Knoxville and the Federals accumulating at Chattanooga. Two alternatives were available. If the Chattanooga Federals moved from their entrenchments to protect communications with Burnside, Johnston and Longstreet would attack them. If not, the Confederates would make a lateral move across the Cumberlands into middle Tennessee. There they could perhaps capture Nashville, isolate Federals in that region, and force a retreat from Chattanooga.

Logistics, as Johnston had pointed out earlier to Beauregard, made such a plan almost impossible. Colonel Arthur Cole, Inspector General of Field Transportation, visited Johnston in late March. He reported back to Richmond that among Johnston's other shortages, he lacked three thousand mules for his wagons, and he needed an additional 900 wagons and teams for such an expedition. Longstreet had brought no transportation from Virginia and would have to rely heavily upon Johnston. In essence, Johnston would be forced to march over 250 miles up the already well-foraged east Tennessee valley to join Longstreet, and then move through more than 75 miles of barren mountain country to middle Tennessee. He would also be forced to locate an additional 150 wagons for his pontoon train. Additional artillery animals would also be needed. Already many of his field pieces, usually drawn by six animals, were being drawn by four.

Regardless of the plan's feasibility, it was important because it did represent the western's bloc's influence in Richmond. It was essentially Bragg's, one he described as having "long been my favorite one."[9] It was evidently composed by him and was delivered to Johnston by his trusted aide, Colonel John Sale.

[9] Bragg to Johnston, March 12, 1864, in Johston Papers, William and Mary.

Even if the government's plan was primarily the work of Bragg, it showed Beauregard's influence. Actually Bragg's plan differed from several previous proposals by Beauregard. Essentially the government's plan was the same as Beauregard's proposals of July 28 and September 2, 1862, proposals which, as mentioned, Bragg admitted he continually tried to follow. Beauregard's 1862 proposals had called for a junction in east Tennessee, similar to the government's 1864 idea. Both plans also called for a union of the troops from the Army of Tennessee and the east Tennessee department. Beauregard's plans had then urged an offensive against a single line of the enemy's advance. Bragg's plan called for Longstreet and Johnston to attack the Federals at Chattanooga, isolated from Burnside, if it proved feasible. Also, both Beauregard's 1862 proposals and the government's 1864 plan called for a lateral thrust from east Tennessee against Federal communications between Nashville and Chattanooga.

There was also similarity between Beauregard's proposals of May and October of 1863 and the government's plan. Beauregard's May plan was warmly praised by Bragg, who in October said he had continually attempted to implement it. Beauregard's October plan, advocated by Bragg in the October 11 council with President Davis, called for a multidepartmental concentration in lower east Tennessee, a thrust into middle Tennessee, and an attempt to defeat the Tennessee Federals in detail.

There were also similarities in Beauregard's December proposal and the government's plan. In December, Beauregard also favored a concentration in the Knoxville vicinity. Both stressed the lateral drive into middle Tennessee, a defeat of the Federals in detail, and a severing of the Nashville-Chattanooga supply line. Both Bragg and Beauregard were particularly enthusiastic about the origin of the invasion being in the Knoxville vicinity, as a device to gain the shortest route upon the enemy's communications.

In fact, almost all of Beauregard's plans, those of Longstreet, and the government's March, 1864, proposal contained this common element: a movement against the enemy's communications. Bragg no doubt was partial to it because it had worked so well for him in the summer of 1862, when he joined Kirby Smith in east Tennessee. His subsequent letters to Beauregard and the October conversations with Beauregard's brother give solid proof of this belief. In fact, a shift into east Tennessee was at the heart of most proposals of the western bloc. There is considerable irony here. A pattern seems to be evident. In Richmond was General Braxton Bragg, nominal general in chief of Rebel forces and President Davis' chief adviser on western policy. Bragg by his own admission had been strongly influenced by Beauregard's ideas, especially the key principle of a shift to east Tennessee and a lateral thrust behind the enemy's main position into middle Tennessee. The plan had worked for Bragg in 1862, and doubtless in 1864, sick and depressed, he remembered the halcyon days of his command. Thus, in early 1864, when Davis asked him to help to prepare a western policy, Bragg produced what was essentially the old 1862 policy—a combination of the Second and east Tennessee departmental troops in east Tennessee.

There was also a good military reason that Bragg and Beauregard should now emphasize a movement on the enemy's communications. With both Union and Confederate forces well concentrated on only two lines of operation in north Georgia and east Tennessee, the opportunities for the employment of their traditional strategy were quite limited. Shielded by the long Cumberland Mountain front, a movement in from this region seemed to achieve Beauregard's desire to break out into the war zone on the enemy's communications, into the area "which conducts the most directly on the enemy's flanks or rear."[10] Visions of Napoleon's Marengo campaign could well have been Beauregard's inspiration. Nor was this approach uncongenial to Lee, another collaborator in the development of the plan. It involved concentration against the weaker of two Union lines of operation and, like his recent invasion of Pennsylvania, included passing around the flank of the enemy's principal army.

Johnston was more of a realist in logistical matters. Bragg, naturally, refused to admit that his army had been so badly beaten on the Chattanooga front that its transportation had been wrecked. Beauregard never seemed to give weight to problems of supply when he

---

[10] *Official Records*, XXXVIII, Pt. 5, p. 149; Beauregard to Soulé, December 8, 1863, in Beauregard Papers, National Archives.

suggested such proposals. But Johnston, the former quartermaster general of the United States Army, knew that such a junction with Longstreet below Knoxville was impossible. Johnston also feared the effects of stepping aside and opening to Sherman the corridor via Atlanta into the Georgia-Alabama production areas.

Thus, when Colonel Sale brought the government's plan in March, Johnston sent back to Richmond his own proposal. Again a touch of irony is evident. The government's plan more closely resembled Beauregard's ideas than Johnston's plan did. Johnston had never sought a surprise offensive concentration against a weak Union front and did not do so now. Nor is there any element of the offensive or reliance on mobility in his plan. Instead Johnston suggested what he had always preached, to match concentration with concentration. His plan also harked back to his idea of the previous year and the effective 1862 raids on Grant's communications. He recommended the use of cavalry to break up Sherman's communications and thus force his retreat. He would assemble the Confederates at Dalton, opposite the main Federal front massing under Sherman at Chattanooga. Johnston planned to bide his time in a defensive posture at Dalton and await an advance by Sherman before giving battle. This plan was a far cry from Beauregard's ideas of throwing masses upon fractions of the enemy after a surprise concentration. His ideas could not have been very well received in view of the strategic plans current in Richmond, where Bragg and Lee collaborated with Davis in devising plans.

Yet in other respects, Johnston's plan, as the others offered in late 1863 and early 1864, represented ideas of the western bloc. It called for a combination of Johnston's and Longstreet's departmental armies. It was based upon a concern for the Chattanooga-Atlanta corridor. It was keyed upon striking the enemy communications between Nashville and Chattanooga with cavalry. By this means he hoped to force Sherman to fight on open ground to protect his communications.

Still, Richmond's plan of March, 1864, as well as the other proposals, represented the apex of the western bloc's influence. In this last great dialogue on strategy by Confederate leadership, the western bloc's old ideas loomed again. That they might no longer have been feasible, due to dwindling manpower and transportation, is beside the point. What is significant is that at this late hour of Confederate fortunes, key men still discussed the value of the central South, a concentration in that vicinity against the weak line of Union advance, a subsequent offensive to defeat the enemy in detail, and a lateral or diagonal thrust against Federal supply lines. These were old dreams of a better day, when the Confederates had talked surely of a defensive line on the Ohio River.

Obviously, Davis had absorbed many of these ideas. He was planning offensives from Richmond which involved a surprise concentration of forces from two departments. This plan had been followed in 1862, but only to halt major Federal advances. In 1864 the proposed concentrations involved Confederate initiatives against a quiescent enemy. Although the means were lacking, Davis had, by 1864, incorporated into his thinking all of the key concepts advocated by Beauregard and the western bloc two years before.

During this winter of feverish planning, Lee clearly played a new role. Instead of feeling he must oppose the weakening of his army in Virginia, he sought to make the most of sending Longstreet to Tennessee. He involved himself in planning for the West and not only collaborated with the President but with his old subordinate, Longstreet, lobbying to help him get the horses and mules he needed for his proposed invasion of Kentucky. He became a proponent of western reinforcement, if only of animals rather than people. His influence must have been formidable, as it worked to reinforce the western concentration bloc, and it was, perhaps, decisive in fully converting Davis to the concept of offensive rather than defensive concentration. Lee's advice could, in these circumstances, only have been in accord with his practice in Virginia and thus in harmony with the ideas long espoused by Beauregard and Bragg.

The President's concern with strategy and his increased involvement with strategic planning may have caused him, during the last year of the war, to overlook or to deemphasize the role of his departmental system. Perhaps, too, the strain of responsibility, overwork, and the burden of defeats weakened Davis' perceptions. In any case, the quality of his handling of strategy through adapting the departmental structure declined markedly during the last days of the war. Gone was the high level of responsiveness and effectiveness of 1862. Response to change was tardy and the departmental organization was often quite unrealistic even after a change which should have been an adjustment to a new situation. Davis' organization became an impediment to the war effort.

From steadily increasing centralization up to the spring of 1863, Davis turned more and more to greater decentralization. It may be that he had been disillusioned with the concept of theater command when Vicksburg and middle Tennessee were lost. At any rate, thereafter, the more terrain lost by the South, the more the President further divided the Confederacy into a departmental structure which made victory more difficult.

With John C. Pemberton's surrender, Bragg's was the only major army between the Appalachians and the Mississippi River. Bragg's department had long provided a wholly inadequate logistical base for his army. With Pemberton's surrender, much territory should have been released to Bragg for subsistence. Instead, by August, the Second Department had been restricted ridiculously. On August 25, 1863, Bragg's department was reorganized and renamed the Department of Tennessee. The legal bounds of the new organization did not keep step with the military situation. Where would Bragg obtain his manpower? All of Georgia remained in Beauregard's coastal department save the upper northwestern sector. Yet it was Bragg on whom Davis counted to defend the Georgia industrial complex of Augusta, Macon, Columbus, and Atlanta. Likewise, all of Alabama remained in neighboring departments save for that thin strip of barren country north of the Tennessee River. Thus, for supplies and reinforcements, Bragg's recruiting agents under General Gideon Pillow and his commissary officials were restricted to extreme north Alabama, northwestern Georgia, and what could be obtained from Tennessee, a state which the Confederates had almost completely evacuated.

The government made only one shift in departmental boundaries to accommodate Bragg. Since mid-1862 the Second Department and the Department of East Tennessee had experienced command confusion, duplication of effort, and discord. Finally, on July 22, 1863, the government notified Bragg that he now controlled the east Tennessee department, then commanded by General Simon Buckner. The government did not, however, say whether the east Tennessee department was officially abolished. Buckner was allowed to remain during the summer as an independent commander who corresponded directly with Richmond.

By August it was essential that Bragg's territory be enlarged. He faced General William S. Rosecrans' army poised for a thrust on Chattanooga. Also, a corps of twenty-five thousand troops, commanded by General Ambrose E. Burnside, was preparing to invade east Tennessee from Kentucky. But Davis responded with a half-measure. Bragg, on August 6, was allowed to assume control of Buckner's department formally, and the east Tennessee troops were designated as the third corps of the Army of Tennessee. Yet Buckner was commanded to remain in east Tennessee and be in charge of administrative matters. Confused, Buckner appealed to Richmond on August 11 for clarification. Ten days later the government began reversing itself, and suggested that the east Tennessee department be retained. Bragg agreed, and the department was revived under a curious arrangement. "For administrative purposes" it was to exist as a separate department; yet it was designated as part of Bragg's command.

A fierce misunderstanding ensued during September and October between Bragg and Buckner. It raged even as Rosecrans crossed the Tennessee River. After the battle of Chickamauga, when Bragg attempted to reorganize Buckner's corps, the Kentuckian argued that this was not within Bragg's authority, but was an administrative matter. Finally, on October 20, after a fiery confrontation at Chattanooga, Davis wisely abolished the east Tennessee department. Yet, Davis reinstated the department in December. It survived to be led by six more generals, making a total of fifteen east Tennessee commanders during the war.

Although decentralization appeared to predominate in both the eastern and western theaters, there were significant differences in the East. The main eastern department, the Department of Northern Virginia, was allowed far more control over neighboring commands than was the Second Department under Bragg and General Joseph E. Johnston. Since the summer of 1862 Lee had exercised a semblance of command over North Carolina. Although in September, 1862, the Department of North Carolina and Southern Virginia was established, and in April of 1863 was divided into the three departments, those of Richmond, of southern Virginia, and of North Carolina, Lee still controlled affairs as far south as the Cape Fear River.

Such was in accordance with the President's wishes. Davis had consistently believed that Lee should control operations on the Atlantic slope. Although Lee demurred, he never hesitated to offer advice on sending reinforcements from the Carolina departments to Virginia and continued to have a special interest in Beauregard's Department of South Carolina, Georgia, and Florida. As early as June, 1862, Lee had suggested that this region be stripped of troops to be sent to the Virginia army. In December, 1862, Lee had suggested that Beauregard send troops from his department to reinforce Wilmington, North Carolina. In January, 1863, Lee again urged that the South Carolina department reinforce Wilmington against an expected assault by General Ambrose Burnside. Again, in February, Lee suggested that Beauregard shift troops from Savannah to reinforce the northern sector of the Creole's department and Wilmington as well. Later, in April, Lee suggested to Davis that Beauregard's departmental troops be shifted to the Virginia front. In June, Lee again suggested either this move or that Beauregard take a heavy reinforcement to Johnston in Mississippi. The following day, June 8, Lee appealed for Beauregard's troops to be brought to Virginia. After the Gettysburg defeat, Lee appealed for another shift by Beauregard from Charleston to Virginia to divert attention from the retreat from Pennsylvania.

The culmination of Lee's many suggestions came in May, 1864. Hard pressed by Meade in Virginia, Lee convinced Davis of the need for a major reinforcement by Beauregard. On May 15, all organized cavalry and infantry in the Department of South Carolina,

Georgia, and Florida were ordered to Virginia with Beauregard in personal command.

Davis ultimately got his way and Lee steadily assumed direction of all Atlantic coastal forces. By the progression from advice to outright reinforcement by Beauregard, the two departments, North Carolina and Southern Virginia, and eventually the Department of South Carolina, Georgia and Florida existed for the purpose of feeding reinforcements to Virginia. Thus Lee became responsible for a quasi-theater command on the Atlantic slope and used this position to concentrate forces to oppose the major Federal advance in Virgina.

Still, unification in the East was not complete. The satellite departments were not disbanded. Beauregard came to Virginia as the new commander of the Department of North Carolina and Southern Virginia. His troops were at first not merged into Lee's army, but were responsible for the geographic district which embraced that part of Virginia south of the James River and all of North Carolina east of the Blue Ridge. Nor was the South Carolina department abolished; in Beauregard's absence, General Samuel Jones held command until replaced by General William J. Hardee in November, 1864.

Although the effects of this unification under Lee were extremely beneficial in providing mobility to reserves and in permitting concentration in Virginia, the departmental structure along the coast became increasingly anachronistic and seriously handicapped operations in the West. The South Carolina department retained vast amounts of land for logistical support but had virtually no army. In contrast, when General Joseph E. Johnston's Department of Tennessee faced Sherman in northern Georgia in 1864, the geographic restrictions were most burdensome. The limits of the almost vacant Carolina department extended northward beyond Atlanta. Technically, even the Atlanta defenses were not at first in Johnston's department. Nor were either the bridge guards on the vital railroads to Alabama under Johnston's authority, or the defenses of the Macon-Columbus munitions area. Also, through the early summer, Johnston was prevented from drawing subsistence and recruits from south-central Georgia, an area not under his jurisdiction.

Davis' half-way policy of coastal theater command did seem a substantial innovation. Directly controlling troops in Virginia and North Carolina, Lee by mid-1864 also controlled the troops from the South Carolina department. Yet no such rule applied in the West. Davis retained a fragmented command system. The surrender of Pemberton's army almost ended Confederate military strength in the Mississippi department. By the late summer of 1863, the acting commander, General Joseph E. Johnston, had no more than twenty-three thousand men, most of them cavalry.

Since the main incentive for the creation of the Mississippi department—protection of the Mississippi River—was now gone, it seemed logical to abolish or reorganize the department. Too, since Bragg's Second Department had lost all of Tennessee by October, a union of Johnston's command with Bragg's would produce not only reinforcement but also additional territory in Alabama and eastern Mississippi for Bragg's support.

In January, 1864, Davis revamped the old Pemberton command. Now it was titled the Department of Alabama, Mississippi, and East Louisiana. The new commander, General Leonidas Polk, was given charge of all of Alabama save that thin strip north of the Tennessee River mainly in Federal hands, which was allotted to Johnston. Davis also beefed up Polk's command. Although Johnston desperately needed reinforcements at Dalton, the President seemed determined to revive a sagging department. Paroled prisoners from Vicksburg were channeled into Polk's command, which also included recruits from Alabama and Mississippi, a heavy column of cavalry, and Johnston's old command from Jackson, Mississippi. By the late spring of 1864, Polk's department contained some thirty thousand effective troops, in spite of having sent substantial reinforcements to the Army of Tennessee.

On Johnston's right flank, a similiar situation prevailed. The Department of East Tennessee was revived in December, 1863, when General James Longstreet invaded the Knoxville region. During the early spring of 1864, Longstreet balked at returning to the Army of Tennessee, which by now had retreated to Dalton, Georgia. Much of the misunderstanding between General Joseph E. Johnston and

Richmond in regard to a strategy for the West was produced by the continued presence of an east Tennessee department. Longstreet still exhibited that lust for an independent command which had colored his activities while under Bragg after the battle of Chickamauga. Since December he had balked at returning to the Army of Tennessee. Instead, during the early spring, Longstreet, shielded by his departmental authority, represented a curious, independent second front in the West.

This reversion to three departments in the West immensely complicated Confederate strategy. Coordination and planning had to be done in Richmond, and the result was a plan which ignored the logistical realities of the situation and proposed not a unified effort but a joint invasion of Tennessee by the armies of Johnston and Longstreet. Even after Longstreet's recall to Lee's army in Virginia, a split command continued in the West. By the early summer of 1864, the east Tennessee department, now led by General John Morgan, comprised four thousand effective cavalry. Despite many appeals from military and political figures for cavalry to assist Johnston against Sherman's communications, none were ever sent.

At the time these plans were being formulated Polk's Alabama and Mississippi department was thought to be threatened, and reinforcements were sought from Johnston's army at Dalton, although none were sent because the supposed crisis passed. The lack of a unified command in the West had obviously imposed upon Richmond the need for coordinating these two separate lines of operation. It was characteristic of the proprietary feelings of departmental commanders that Polk's request for reinforcements was couched in terms of the return of four brigades loaned the year before to the Army of Tennessee. This approach to the reinforcement problem elicited from the President a firm statement of his concept of reserves and of reinforcement: "Troops are to be sent where most needed and only returned to former positions when they are more useful there." Yet Davis at the same time exhibited the weakness of his too fragmented and too decentralized organization in the West. Instead of decision by a theater commander or emphatic orders from Richmond, reliance was still placed on requests from Richmond and collaboration by the department commanders. Between the latter, Davis wrote Johnston that he still relied on "entire co-intelligence . . . to secure such co-operation between you as will render the forces most available for the general defense."[11]

A significant reinforcement from Polk's department was sent to Johnston in May, after Sherman had already moved against Dalton. Davis had consented to a partial reinforcement, and Polk was ordered to send one division and any other available troops to Johnston's assistance. In what was probably Polk's finest hour, he moved personally with three divisions, fourteen thousand troops, to Johnston's aid. Despite a prolonged grumbling in Richmond, it was obvious that Polk saved Johnston from near disaster at Resaca in late May.

Yet it was after this reinforcement that the greatest misuse of the Alabama departmental troops ensued. With Polk's death in June, the permanent command of his department devolved upon General Stephen D. Lee. Lee's conduct exhibited the fatal weakness in the departmental system. Despite his sporadic interference, as with Bragg and Johnston in late 1862 to 1863, Davis in theory left to the departmental commander the discretion of how best to use his troops. The possession of such autonomy by a departmental general placed a premium on the abilities of the officer. Lee, a former artillery officer in Virginia, seemed incapable of broad ideas on strategy, either within his vast Mississippi-Alabama department or in terms of cooperative effort with Johnston. Like many such generals, once in power Lee became both possessive and overcautious. Already in 1863 he had failed badly as commander of Polk's departmental cavalry. During the late summer and fall of that year, Lee let slip a splendid opportunity to strike the soft underbelly of Rosecrans' communications in northern Alabama.

Again in 1864 Stephen Lee waived an excellent chance to strike Sherman's line of supply during the Chattanooga-Atlanta campaign. In May, when Polk moved to Johnston's assistance, both Johnston's and Polk's headquarters had ample intelligence reports of the vulnerability of Sherman's supply line along the single track from Nashville

---

[11] *Official Records*, XXXII, Pt. 2, p. 554.

to Chattanooga. Reliable reports indicated that only four Union cavalry regiments protected the entire Nashville-Chattanooga supply line. By June, Confederate intelligence had reported a further weakening of Union troops along the railroad, particularly at critical bridging points. For example, only eight hundred Federal troops, of which only two hundred were cavalry, protected the entire rail link between Nashville and Athens, Alabama.[12]

Despite numerous pleas to Richmond from western generals and politicians, Davis did not choose to directly order Lee to strike Sherman's supply line with almost fourteen thousand effective cavalry in the Alabama department. The matter was left to Lee's discretion. In early May he actually began planning such a strike, but quickly canceled it when he became fearful of a Federal cavalry advance from Memphis. By May 18 Lee had informed the government that he could not assist Johnston, despite Lee's admission to Forrest that departmental intelligence indicated the Nashville-Chattanooga Railroad was weakly guarded. Some historians have indicated that Lee could not help Johnston because of Sherman's repeated ordering of cavalry raids from Memphis in order to neutralize the Alabama cavalry. Actually such raids had already occurred, mainly in the late winter and early spring. By May, Lee's headquarters had intelligence that only forty-five hundred Federal cavalry were reported at Memphis. Still, left to his own discretion by the strictures of departmental command, Lee hesitated and did nothing.[13]

Thus Davis sought opportunities to repeat the old pattern in Confederate operations by attempting first to combine the forces of Johnston in Georgia and Longstreet in Tennessee, and second to seek then to concentrate those of Johnston and Polk, first on Polk's line of operations and then, in spite of a concern over exposing Mississippi, he actually accomplished part of a desirable concentration against Sherman. Still the old vice remained; the President never

[12] For examples of detailed Confederate intelligence reports, see Lee's headquarters to Polk, April 20, 1864; A. B. Coffey to Ferguson, April 21, 23, 1864, in Polk letters and telegrams, 1861–64, National Archives; also see Wheeler's scouts to Wheeler, June 22, July 4, 1864, in Joseph Wheeler Papers, Alabama State Library and Archives.
[13] *Official Records*, XXXVIII, Pt. 4, pp. 685, 719, 723, 729, XXIX, Pt. 2, p. 606.

ordered, only asked. This emphasis on preserving local autonomy and delegating important decisions to local commanders gave decisions to officers who, though they knew their own situation well, were neither knowledgeable nor, presumably, competent enough to make decisions of this importance. There is in this behavior, besides a laudable concern with decentralization, an element of indecision if not a disinclination to assume responsibility. When considered in relation to Davis' reluctance to remove a commander, it seems that he shied away from difficult decisions. He had tried to delegate Bragg's removal to Johnston and in fact never removed Bragg. His appointment of Johnston to command the Army of Tennessee was the path of least resistance, and his removal of Johnston was preceded by long and agonizing deliberation. Davis has been accused of obstinacy and excessive concern with local defense. Indecisiveness was also a part of his makeup. One of his few orders, rather than requests, for concentation had been to Mansfield Lovell prior to Shiloh. The loss of New Orleans had soon followed. Perhaps his excessive decentralization of decision-making was a way of avoiding decisions fraught with the risk of disaster.

Many factors contributed to Johnston's removal in the summer of 1864. His corps commanders were not happy with him, and they used their contacts in Richmond to undermine what little confidence in him Davis may still have felt. Johnston's own indecisiveness, lack of plans, and secrecy contributed importantly to the government's concern about his performance. Yet Davis was urging Johnston to attack and repulse Sherman. The President had taken this position with respect to the appropriate course for Johnston's army ever since the general had been given the command in the previous December. To press an offensive on a general was quite uncharacteristic of Davis. It was contrary to all of his laissez faire practices with departmental commanders. Although Johnton had failed to attack in order to save the Vicksburg garrison, why should Davis suddenly insist that an outnumbered general attack, and then replace him with a commander who was committed to taking the offensive?

Davis' behavior in 1864 may well reflect the concentration which had taken place in Georgia. Most of the forces of the east Tennessee department were with the Army of Tennessee and that army had been twice reinforced from Mississippi, first in August and September, 1863, and again when Polk joined it. Davis doubtless felt not only that Mississippi had contributed enough to the Army of Tennessee but that this force represented a very large concentration, the kind of concentration which had always in the past been the prelude to an offensive. This may help to explain Davis' reluctance to press for more assistance from Mississippi and his constant pressure upon Johnston to take the offensive, something he had never before urged upon a commander. Considering his belief that Sherman had been weakened by strengthening Meade in Virginia, Davis' conduct is more explicable; the West had already been denuded to strengthen the Army of Tennessee; instead of standing pat or retreating, Johnston should have led this concentration against the weakened Sherman, as Lee had constantly suggested. Just as Johnston's pessimism made him anticipate defeat, so Davis' optimism enabled him to hope for victory if only Johnston would use the large force at his disposal. As in the Vicksburg campaign, their difference in outlook contributed to misunderstanding.

To some degree a western offensive had become as much an *idée fixe* with Davis as it had with Beauregard. Like the Creole, Davis ignored the fact that Sherman's army no longer represented an enemy weak point. Even after the fall of Atlanta and the heavy casualties suffered by John B. Hood's army, the President still entertained the idea of an offensive. It seemed then that the Confederacy faced complete defeat. From his position astride Rebel communications at Atlanta, it appeared that Sherman could move at will, either against Hood or the Georgia munitions complex. Rebel intelligence indicated that Sherman intended to thrust even deeper, in search of a new base, perhaps to Charleston or to Savannah. Yet the offensive which had been sought when Bragg was at the gates of Chattanooga was begun after Atlanta had fallen. Nor was it a conventional offensive; it involved no concentration and aimed at Sherman's communications rather than at his army. Perhaps a somewhat inconventional offensive at an apparently unpropitious time was the wisest course. Perhaps only in a long shot was there hope to save the Confederacy.[14]

On the other hand, Davis continued to neglect his departmental organization. Although the perilous situation indicated a need for consolidation, he took the opposite course. The Department of Alabama and Mississippi continued independent and Davis revived the dormant Department of South Carolina, Georgia, and Florida. In late September, General William Hardee was sent there to assume command. Troops were pared from the Army of Tennessee, until by December, Hardee had managed to acquire a force of almost twenty thousand men. Thus the Confederates continued to face Sherman with three different forces. In spite of the projected offensive, Davis' organization had clearly deteriorated into a cordon defense. To coordinate these separate forces was a task which could be neither appropriately nor effectively performed from Richmond even had the President been willing to order rather than request the needed concentrations.

This fragmentation involved more than manpower. With the loss of northern Georgia, the departmental limits of Hood's Army of Tennessee were only slightly altered. In August the southern portion of Georgia was removed from the South Carolina department and given to Hood. The remainder of Hood's department, now renamed the Department of Tennessee and Georgia, was that thin strip in Alabama north of the Tennessee River.

There were two obvious flaws. The two regions of Hood's command were separated by Sherman's command in north-central Georgia. Also, it was a repetition of the situation existing in late 1863 while Bragg commanded the Army of Tennessee. The chief western Confederate army found itself restricted within a narrow territory. Meanwhile, needed recruits and supplies in Alabama were within the province of Stephen D. Lee's command.

Realizing that opposition to Sherman required coordination, the

---

[14] For a favorable evaluation of Davis and of his relation to this and Hood's later offensive into Tennessee, see William J. Cooper, Jr., "A Reassessment of Jefferson Davis as War Leader: The Case from Atlanta to Nashville," *Journal of Southern History,* XXXVI (May, 1970), 189–204.

President finally moved to remedy the situation. In October, 1864, General Beauregard was sent to take command of the Military Division of the West, embracing the departments of Hood and Stephen D. Lee. Yet Beauregard's authority was both vague and weak, and Hardee's South Carolina command was omitted from his jurisdiction. Hardly more than an adviser, he could take immediate command of troops only when present with a particular army. Davis specified that even this was to be done only when "expedient." There were other problems. Beauregard never understood his powers, and the government did not clarify them. Probably Davis had not given extensive thought to the limits of the Creole's authority. Beauregard may have been appointed in part to stifle criticism of the failures of Davis' handpicked successor to Joe Johnston, General John B. Hood.

An example of the clouded nature of Beauregard's authority is his failure to understand whether he was expected to take the field command of an army when present with it. When asked to clarify, Davis responded with confused terminology. Beauregard, when present with an army, was to exercise "immediate command" but "not relieve the general of the particular army." Moreover, Davis demolished any hope of coordination by allowing both departmental commands to communicate directly with the government.

The results were almost humorous. For three months after appointment on October 3, Beauregard seemed constantly attempting to learn what was occurring in his theater. A few days prior to appointing Beauregard, Davis had visited with Hood at Palmetto to confer about a new western strategy. Although he had already decided upon Beauregard's appointment, Davis did not wait to seek his views. Instead, Hood and Davis agreed upon an offensive into northern Georgia. Hood would seize the Western and Atlantic Railroad in order to draw Sherman north from Atlanta into a fight. By October 2, when Davis conferred with Beauregard at Augusta, the new strategy was already being effected. On September 29 Hood had begun to cross the Chattahoochee.

The situation now became ludicrous. Without informing the government, Hood abandoned the initial scheme to force a fight on the railroad, and began a long series of revisions. Meanwhile, for almost a week, the commander of the Military Division of the West, ignorant of the new strategy, pursued his major army across northwestern Georgia. Finally, on October 8, Beauregard caught up with Hood at Cedartown, Georgia.

The same failures of the theater command under Johnston now occurred under Beauregard. Throughout his stay in this new command, Beauregard obviously felt embarrassed at his position, and behaved more as an adviser than a theater commander. Hood's direct communication with Richmond often left Beauregard ignorant of what his major army was planning. For example, even after he joined the army at Cedartown, Beauregard did not know that Hood had altered his plan to include a possible crossing of the Tennessee River and an invasion of middle Tennessee. Nor was Beauregard consulted when about October 15-16, Hood made a firm decision to invade Tennessee. Only by hearsay did Beauregard learn that Hood had begun the march without him, and again the commander of the Division of the West was forced to ride in pursuit of his main army. Not until October 21 did Hood inform Beauregard of his plans.

Throughout the remainder of the march across north Alabama, it was obvious that the third attempt at a western theater command was a sham. Hood, in notes to the government, all but stated that he considered Beauregard's counsel a mere formality. Many dispatches were exchanged between Hood and Richmond which Beauregard did not see. Thus, after informing Beauregard that he would move across the river at Guntersville, Alabama, Hood revised his plans for a crossing further westward. Only after October 27 did the pursuing theater commander reach his army to learn of the change of crossing points. By October 31, due to this lack of coordination, the Army of Tennessee had made a useless lateral march completely across northern Alabama nearly to the Mississippi border—hardly a strategy for an army committed to a swift move into middle Tennessee.

The final blow to the new western design came at Hood's new base at Tuscumbia. Amidst a continual feud over authority, Hood almost completely cut Beauregard off from information regarding his proposed Tennessee offensive. Richmond did nothing to remedy the situation. By November 13 relations had broken down completely. Determined to be rid of Beauregard's influence, Hood quietly folded his tent and moved his headquarters to the north bank of the Tennessee River at Florence, Alabama. The commander of the western theater, desiring to converse with Hood, was forced to send a staff officer to search out the general. By now Beauregard was so demoralized that he did not order Hood to come to his headquarters for a needed conference. Instead, he asked Hood to drop by when it was convenient. At last the envoy found Hood on the north bank of the river, but the general did not think it was convenient to visit Beauregard. Two days later, the generals remained on opposite banks, with a stubborn Hood refusing to come to Beauregard's headquarters. Within a few days the invasion of Tennessee began amidst total confusion.

By 1865, though the Confederate cause was hopeless, the object lesson of how the departmental structure had often affected the war effort was again obvious. Even in these desperate hours, Davis refused to consolidate departmental organizations effectively. Instead, he continued with an extensive system of departments east of the river.

The final campaign in North Carolina was an example of how badly out of joint the departmental system was and how ineffective Beauregard's appointment had been. After Hood's disaster of November–December, 1865, in Tennessee, the remnants of his Army of Tennessee assembled at Tupelo, Mississippi. Quickly they were ordered eastward under Beauregard to join Hardee's departmental forces. By January, 1865, Savannah had fallen, and both Carolinas appeared vulnerable to Sherman's invasion.

There was no shortage of men in the western Confederacy. But they were so fragmented among several departments that a concentration in front of Sherman became impossible. Almost twenty thousand of Hood's old command were sent eastward under the general charge of Beauregard. His command status was circumscribed by the departmental structure. His authority as commander of the

Division of the West did not extend east or southeast beyond Augusta, Georgia, where Hardee's authority began. Not until February 16 was Beauregard's authority extended into South Carolina. Because of this duplication of authority and Richmond's insistence that Hardee continue to occupy Charleston, no concentration was effected until February. As Sherman moved northward through South Carolina, Hardee, with some sixteen thousand departmental troops, fell back through central South Carolina desperately seeking a junction with Beauregard. In the meantime, from Augusta, Beauregard was leading some fourteen thousand men northeast for the same purpose.

There were other divisions of forces. General Richard Taylor, Stephen D. Lee's successor, retained in Alabama between twenty thousand and thirty thousand men scattered at outposts from eastern Louisiana to the Georgia border. Although Hood's army had been ordered to North Carolina, Richmond saw fit to continue Hood's old Department of Tennessee and Georgia. Concentration in the Carolinas was further hampered by the Department of North Carolina, revived in 1864. In February, 1865, General Braxton Bragg, commander of the department, had at least fifty-five hundred infantry, with which he was conducting independent operations in eastern North Carolina.

In this final campaign, the departmental structure had again adversely affected the military effort. Division of forces among four departments, without counting the Department of East Tennessee, seriously inhibited any concentration against Sherman. Even without any men from Taylor's command in Alabama, a concentration of the forces from Bragg's, Hood's, and Hardee's commands would have produced no less than fifty thousand troops to impede Sherman's approach toward Lee's rear.

Thus President Davis' departmental organization ended as it began, with a major segment functioning as a cordon system. After steady improvement, the President's management deteriorated. In part this decline stemmed from Davis' failure to quickly enough adapt to changed circumstances. He clearly overestimated the threat presented by the Federal forces based at Memphis. This error led him, in 1864, to allocate too many resources to S. D. Lee's department which, with the brilliant field leadership of Nathan Bedford Forrest, was doing an excellent job of defending Mississippi. His delay in including South Carolina in Beauregard's Military Division of the West must have been, in part, a response to the fact that traditionally the coast was in R. E. Lee's sphere of influence and the source of reserves for the Army of Northern Virginia. A major part of Davis' troubles stemmed, of course, from a change in Union strategy. Atlanta became the major Union objective in the West, and, for the first time, the army operating on that line was the stongest Federal army in the West. The President was tardy in perceiving this change and understanding the magnitude of the Federal concentration against Georgia.

Perhaps equally important in explaining Davis' failure was the role the offensive had assumed in his thinking. From Chickamauga onward a western offensive had become a staple in Confederate strategic planning. This was a change, for the response to western disasters from Fort Donelson through Bragg's retreat from Tennessee in September of 1863 had been one of concentration and counterattack, culminating, at Chickamauga, in the western bloc's long-advocated counteroffensive. But after Chickamauga, and until Hood's retreat from Tennessee, the offensive, rather than the counteroffensive, dominated the President's thinking. Reinforcements had been at last lavished on the Army of Tennessee. The east Tennessee department had been virtually abolished; most of the infantry in Mississippi had been sent east in August and September of 1863; and soon after Longstreet had returned to Virginia, Polk had joined Johnston. Yet Bragg had failed, and as long as Johnston remained in command no offensive materialized even though the President took the unprecedented step of sending him a plan for an offensive from Richmond. Although failure to realize how much stronger and better supplied Sherman was than Rosecrans had been was undoubtedly a factor, Davis clung to the concept that the reinforced Army of Tennessee must implement the long-planned offensive.

At last, in John Bell Hood the President found the man who would take the offensive and, just prior to the appointment of Beauregard to command the new western division, Davis and Hood had agreed on a plan of offense. By now the offensive must have seemed more a last gamble than an exploitation of Union weakness, but was the culmination of a year of planning in which an offensive had taken precedence in Davis' thinking.[15]

A poorly managed departmental system partly resulted from a change in Davis' emphasis: from defensive to offensive, from a concept of counteroffensive to offensive, and from defensive to offensive concentration. In a sense Hood's Tennessee campaign was the final triumph of the western concentration bloc, for Davis initiated an offensive from a newly unified western command and had placed Beauregard in overall command, though by now the Creole lacked enthusiasm for the offensive. It is not, perhaps, too much of an exaggeration to say that a western offensive had become even more of an *idée fixe* for Davis than it had been for Beauregard and that Davis, the convert, was more devout than Beauregard, the prophet.

[15] *Ibid.*, 197–204.

VI
The Politics
of Command

Two factors clearly had fundamental influence on the formulation of Confederate strategy—the informal organization of westerners opposing Lee and the conflicting strategic ideas.

To a marked degree the factional struggle was that of an informal organization of western generals and politicians seeking to counteract the influence of Lee with his formal position as adviser. Of course, though Lee had the formal access to the President that the westerners lacked, most of the substance of his influence was derived from his personality and the prestige which his victories gave him.

This is not a unique situation. Policy determination and decision making usually include some element of conflict resolution, and the interests which compete and the pressures which are exerted are often not represented in the formal organization at all. In the case of the Confederate dilemma, even when only military factors were considered, a variety of interests and ideas sought attention. Equally, when one views only four of the myriad interrelated southern informal organizations, there is revealed a significant degree of informal access to power and influence over decisions.

Although this was not the only struggle within the Confederate organization and nonmilitary factors played an important role, the impact of the factional struggle and of the competing strategies can be reasonably well isolated. Yet the decisions were made in the context of the departmental system and of the President himself. Davis brought certain concepts and methods to his management of the war and developed others during his service as commander in chief. In an account of conflict resolution, of decisions which were the product of many pressures, it is well to note that there were many things about which there was agreement.

There was substantial harmony among all Confederate generals and politicians on the importance of territory. Davis, Lee, and the members of the western bloc agreed on the need to defend or regain the land area of the Confederacy. Whether political, diplomatic, logistical, or manpower considerations were the foremost at a particular time or for a given individual or group, or whether, as in the case of Kentucky, the territory represented a sentimental allegiance, all agreed that its conservation was the overriding consideration. On the other hand, except for logistical considerations, the security of individual Confederate armies was not a source of concern. Except in the case of Pemberton's army at Vicksburg, the safety of no Confederate army was ever a primary consideration. Neither Lee's nor Bragg's army was ever in that type of danger; they could always find safety by retreat.

Yet, except for Pemberton's own solicitude for Vicksburg, the enemy's armies were always the focus of attention for Davis and Confederate generals. There was no thought that territory could be protected or regained except by operations directed at the Union armies which menaced or protected the territory. Disagreement was limited to which territory was the most important or which was the most endangered.

Another shared assumption was the propriety of the departmental system and the desirability of interdepartmental troop movements. Although Lee at one time argued that these troop movements would "always be too late," he was fundamentally in agreement with the concept which he practiced within his department and the implementation of which he often urged upon the President. All Confederate generals, as might be expected, had attachments to the area where they were asssigned, and they developed proprietary feelings about the troops who served under them. President Davis probably never realized the degree to which his commanders developed these local attachments and perspectives.

There was a major conflict about the relative merits of three principal theaters of operations. Each area had as partisans its local commanders. The distant Trans-Mississippi was not one of these controversial theaters, nor was the Atlantic seaboard, which was never a major competitor for resources since only its ports, important as they were, were endangered. The coastline of Georgia and the Carolinas was, therefore, usually viewed as a place from which to draw troops rather than as one needing reinforcement.

There was general agreement that Virginia was of primary importance; disagreements centered around the degree to which it was menaced by enemy action or whether it was to be the object of a major Union offensive effort. Lee, naturally, was the advocate of Virginia, and the strength and persistence of the Federal effort there amply supported his contention that it was constantly and seriously endangered.

After Shiloh, the Mississippi had comparatively few influential adherents. Most western generals focused their attention on the middle Tennessee line. Yet the traditional importance and immense prestige of the river, together with Davis' long residence in Mississippi and the initial Union emphasis on the Mississippi line of operations, caused the President to assign it a primary defense priority. The members of western bloc thus had to compete both with Virginia and the Mississippi in their struggle to convince Davis of the primacy of their area. Even after the fall of Vicksburg, the old Mississippi front probably received from Davis a higher priority than its intrinsic merits warranted.

The strategy debate was never as explicit as the one over territory. Beauregard and Bragg were the advocates of a surprise offensive concentration on an enemy weak point and made their principles fairly explicit. President Davis was also an exponent of mobility, but for a long time limited his thinking to the defensive or the counteroffensive. Only in the summer of 1863 did he begin to think in terms of the offensive and of taking the initiative. Joseph E. Johnston was increasingly the implicit partisan of a defensive buildup at the expected point of enemy advance, and he influenced Davis' thinking in the early spring of 1863. Lee's concern for Virginia led him often to advocate a strategy much like Johnston's while at the same time he thought in terms of the offensive and sought to take the initiative.

The story of Confederate strategy can be perceived as a belated triumph for the western concentration bloc and for Beauregard's ideas. Throughout 1861 and 1862 Davis functioned through a laissez faire management of his departmental system, tempered by suggestions and occasional orders for interdepartmental reinforcements. Intrinsic to his departmental system was the continual restructuring and the substantial improvement in organization which took place. Although the informal organizations of Confederate generals and politicians revolved around personalities, state, family, and personal loyalties, several of these were able to unite as a western concentration bloc and display a common concern about a geographical area and the implementation of a strategic idea. It is doubtful whether all the generals understood the strategic principle, though Beauregard coached them continually. It is ironic that the influence of this group should be directly opposed to that of Lee, the ablest executor of the ideas so eloquently advocated by Beauregard.

The President naturally became the focal point as these generals sought, in various ways, to influence strategy. They talked to Davis in Richmond and when he visited them in the field, they used their political and personal contacts, and they worked through Secretary Seddon. Always their task involved counteracting Lee and soon focused on seeking reinforcements from Virginia. Gradually they convinced the President of the importance of middle Tennessee and, by effectively countering Lee's influence, also persuaded Davis that Virginia could spare some troops to reinforce Tennessee. In September, 1863, Davis made a doubly unusual decision. He overruled a local commander in sending Longstreet's corps to Tennessee and also disregarded Lee in the one area where his advice had hitherto always been heeded, removal of troops from Virginia.

Once Longstreet was committed to a substantial stay in the West, Lee became an exponent of the ideas advocated by Beauregard, urging on the western generals the kind of strategy he had practiced in Virginia. Davis and his new adviser, Bragg, became, with Lee's participation, active proponents of surprise offensive concentrations. Thus the President had first been persuaded of the importance of the central south and had begun to think in terms of an offensive concentration while the western bloc was still contending with Lee's influence. Then Davis' approach to the war was completely altered when Lee's influence at last reinforced the westerners, at least in the realm of the kind of strategy they had long advocated. An offensive, first urged on Johnston and then realized by Hood, became the cornerstone of Davis' western policy and seems to have partially superseded in his thinking both departmental restructuring and defensive mobility of reserves as the primary reliance for a successful defense.

Whereas the strategic ideas of Lee and Davis are made fairly clear by their writings and their actions, they never enunciated their principles clearly nor showed to whom, if anyone, they were indebted. If it could be demonstrated that southern leaders had absorbed the teachings of Jomini's *Traité,* Confederate strategy would clearly show that Lee's operations during the summer of 1862 and Thomas Jackson's valley campaign as well were fully in consonance with Jomini's principles. Interior lines were employed in bringing Jackson from the valley for the Seven Days' battle and in concentrating against Pope for Second Manassas. These operations by Lee have, in addition, a distinctly Napoleonic flavor. Jackson's operations in the valley were used to distract the enemy, occasioning the development of a strong cordon of forces for covering Washington and driving Jackson from the valley, thus permitting Lee's dispersed forces to concentrate for a blow against McClellan. Like Jackson's valley campaign itself, Lee's operations bear a strong resemblance to Napoleon's Italian campaign, particularly the operations around Mantua.

Later, Lee was not presented with many opportunities to apply his Napoleonic combinations. His effort to create such an opportunity was unsuccessful when Early's valley campaign failed to distract the enemy adequately. Lee's own dispatch of Longstreet to Suffolk worked out to be a detachment *en cordon.* On balance, Lee's operations in Virginia seemed to transcend the influence of Jomini, and, whether or not they were directly inspired by a study of Napoleon's campaigns, they clearly exhibit the same fundamental characteristics.

Likewise, if it could be shown that Union leaders were influenced by Jomini's *Précis,* their operations within theaters would, after the campaigns of 1861 and 1862, show this influence. It was, for example, the Union generals' Jominian avoidance of detachments, cordons, and multiple lines of operation that deprived Lee of the opportunities he had enjoyed in the summer of 1862. In the sense that Jomini's system of concentration provided security against serious defeats, Jomini's influence would also have resulted in the prolonged and indecisive character of the operations. More important, Jomini's disciples, having no concept of dispersion nor any means of luring the enemy into dispersal, would have been without any offensive technique.

Were the leaders on both sides in the Civil War effectively indoctrinated with Jomini's principles, what would be the result? Each group of generals would be likely to avoid dispersion, to eschew cordons and multiple lines of operation, and to remain concentrated. In other words, one could expect a retrogression to the seventeenth century, and again unitary armies would maneuver against one another. With both generals applying Jomini's prescriptions for safe and sound strategy, the power of the defense would be paramount. Neither general would have in his Jominian background any means of inducing the other to divide his forces. With the exception of viewing the enemy's (and one's own) flank as the weak point and believing that it was desirable to break the enemy's communications, Jomini would have little to say.

The influence of Jomini has usually been considered a chief cause for these Civil War military conditions. The reason given is not that a following of his security-conscious rules would have enhanced defensive power without any comparable augmentation of the power of the offense. Rather it is that Jomini had a positive preference for this type of warfare and had preached a limited eighteenth-century type of warfare. In view, however, of Jomini's emphasis upon the offensive and his disparagement of Daun's type of warfare, it seems that the limitations of his strategy would have contributed to indecisiveness. It was only his strategy, the branch of the Art of War that he preferred and emphasized, which would have been influential, since his limited tactical suggestions were largely obsolete by the time of the Civil War.

Jominian battle tactics, which were more eighteenth-century than

Napoleonic, clearly had little effect. In the sphere of grand strategy or the strategy of coordinating the operations of various theaters or lines of operation, Napoleon and Jomini were at variance very little if at all. Since separate lines of operation were inherent in the grand strategic situation, Jomini's failure to indicate a means of securing an enemy dispersal was not, in this sphere of operations, a critical weakness. Even a reading of Jomini as prescribing a concentration of all forces could not eliminate the need of some dispersal, since it was difficult to envision the abandonment of whole theaters of operation.

Yet the European influence in the Confederacy is clear only with Beauregard and, perhaps, Bragg. Only they showed by their words as well as their deeds that they were explicitly applying what the European inheritance could teach. The degree to which others were influenced cannot be ascertained. Although Lee's actions speak louder than words, generals long before Jomini and Napoleon implicitly applied the principles which Jomini sought to abstract and articulate.

Nevertheless two things are clear: Confederate strategy's strong conformity to the teachings of Jomini and Napoleon, and the prominent role of Beauregard in securing this conformity. Beauregard, by his wartime writings and correspondence, indicated he was consciously viewing military operations in terms of the military science he had studied, and showed he was influenced by Napoleon as well as by the Jomini of the *Traité*.

Jomini's writings have much to do with how to exploit mistakes made by Austrian generals in the Seven Years' and early Napoleonic wars. Napoleon made his reputation fighting against the Austrians who employed the very strategy which Jomini deplored. Confederate successes for which Beauregard was the strategic mentor were won against a strategy dominated by Henry W. Halleck whose military writings were dominated by the Jomini of the *Précis* and by that literary exponent of the strategy of Field Marshal von Daun, the Archduke Charles. Halleck's background caused him to emphasize places and to shift his attention from the enemy army.[1]

---

[1] David Donald, *Lincoln Reconsidered* (New York, 1956), 88–102; T. Harry Williams, "The Military Leadership of North and South," in David Donald (ed.), *Why the North*

Both Beauregard and Halleck exercised great influence over strategy, and on three occasions they were, indirectly at least, opponents. On each of these occasions Beauregard devised a campaign directed at Halleck. In each case neither was in command, though Beauregard was on the field at Shiloh and in command the second day. In fact, in the three instances after First Manassas in which Beauregard was able to influence major strategy decisions, the operations were directed at forces influenced by Halleck. At Shiloh, Beauregard was to attack Grant, Halleck's subordinate, before Buell could join him; in Bragg's Kentucky campaign he was to exploit the dispersion ordered by Halleck by attempting to outflank Buell while Grant, as ordered, remained on the defensive; and at Chickamauga the presence of Johnston's troops was made possible by Halleck.

The basic pattern of Confederate strategy from 1861 through 1863 was one using the railroad and the telegraph to bring about surprise concentrations on a single line of operations. This pattern, which has not been entirely evident to historians, was quite clear to contemporaries, and it is not surprising that Halleck, from his vantage point as general in chief in Washington, was one of those who perceived it most clearly. Immediately after the fall of Vicksburg, Halleck had written Grant: "If Johnston should unite with Bragg, we may be obliged to send Rosecrans more troops than the Ninth Corps," though "Johnston may be so re-enforced as to require all our means to oppose him. . . . In other words, wherever the enemy concentrates we must concentrate to oppose him."[2]

Halleck generalized his previous experience to anticipate what was in fact being discussed by Confederate leaders. Yet he immediately proceeded to create the conditions which the Confederates needed in order to do exactly what he had anticipated. He repeated the blunder of the previous year. Because of his concern for territory, he passed the initiative to the Confederates with his reply to Grant's

---

Won the Civil War (Baton Rouge, 1960), 37–54; Baron de Jomini, *Summary of the Art of War, or a New Analytical Compend of the Principal Combinations of Strategy, of Grand Tactics and of Military Policy,* trans. Major O. F. Winship and Lieutenant E. E. McLean (New York, 1854), 104, 150–51; Stephen E. Ambrose, *Halleck: Lincoln's Chief of Staff* (Baton Rouge, 1962), 55–56, 145.

[2] *Official Records,* XXIV, Pt. 3, pp. 497–98.

suggestion that the initiative be retained by an attack on Mobile. Halleck suggested that the Federals should first "clean out" Mississippi, Arkansas, and Louisiana, and then "when these things are accomplished there will be a large available force to operate either on Mobile or Texas."[3]

While Halleck was busy directing "clean up" operations and Grant was utilizing the consequent period of inactivity to give extensive leaves in his army, the Confederates were provided with an opportunity to carry out their concentration according to the plan advocated by Beauregard for more than three months. In spite of the fact that Halleck clearly had foreseen Confederate plans, that Rosecrans was advancing, and that Halleck knew forces had been withdrawn from Johnston to reinforce Bragg, the Union general in chief relied on intelligence from deserters that Lee's army was to be the point of Confederate offensive concentration. When he learned that Longstreet's corps had gone west, Halleck wrote Grant ordering counter-concentration:

> It was early apparent that while you and General Banks were operating west of the Mississippi, the enemy would concentrate his available forces on General Meade or General Rosecrans. It was believed from all information we could obtain that Lee's army was to be greatly reinforced. It now appears that all of Johnston's forces and at least three large divisions of Lee's army have joined Bragg. Probably the advance of Burnside and Rosecrans into East Tennessee and the danger of the rebel arsenals at Atlanta have changed their plans. At any rate Rosecrans is now the main object of their attack and he must be strengthened by all the means in our power.[4]

It seems evident that General Halleck saw rather clearly the recurring pattern in Confederate strategy. This is not too surprising since the first instance of its application in the West, the Shiloh campaign, had been directed against forces under his command. In the case of Bragg's Kentucky campaign as well as that of Chickamauga, it was Halleck's "Austrian" strategy and his passion for tidiness that had given the Confederates the opportunity to concentrate and

[3] *Ibid.*, 542, See also 513, 530, 557, XXIX, Pt. 2, p. 187, XXX, Pt. 2, pp. 35, 38, Pt. 3, pp. 693–94.

[4] *Ibid.*, XXX, Pt. 3, p. 693.

to strike a formidable blow. Halleck had, as Beauregard expressed it, shown the Confederates where to strike. Although his motive in driving back Confederate forces in Arkansas was to eventually permit the release of additional forces to join the main Union armies, the three main Federal armies east of the Mississippi were, in essence, disposed *en cordon,* and not working together as a whole, at the very time when all Confederate forces were coordinated and the Confederate strategists were viewing "the whole theater of war as one subject of which all points were but integral parts."

Once the point of concentration was revealed, Halleck set to work vigorously, and on an unprecedented scale, to apply his principle that "wherever the enemy concentrates we must concentrate to oppose him." The resulting concentration under Grant and the defeat of Bragg at the battle of Chattanooga moved Beauregard to comment that "Halleck is just finding out what can be done with sudden and rapid concentration of troops."[5]

The dominant theme in Union strategy for 1864 was to deny to the Confederates any more opportunities for the application of their basic strategy. After the Chickamauga experience, Halleck was no longer content to concede the initiative to the southern armies. Not only must the Federal command "act with caution and keep our troops well in hand, so as to prevent the enemy from catching us in detachments," but he agreed with Grant as to "the great importance of being able in the next campaign to select our theatre of operations and fields of battle instead of having them forced on us by the rebels."[6]

Grant had been the object of the Shiloh concentration, had been on the defensive during the Kentucky campaign, had been inert during the Chickamauga campign, and, finally, had, at Chattanooga, salvaged the debacle resulting from Rosecrans' defeat. On assuming overall command, it is not surprising that Grant perceived the degree to which the Confederates had been able to hold the initiative and sustain themselves through successive surprise concentrations. He

[5] *Ibid.,* XXVIII, Pt. 2, p. 580.
[6] *Ibid.,* XXXII, Pt. 2, p. 127.

identified the cause as a failure in Union strategy when he noted that the Union forces had "seventeen distinct commanders. Before this time these various armies had acted separately and independently of each other, giving the enemy an opportunity often of depleting one command, not pressed, to reinforce another more actively engaged. I determined to stop this." Grant immediately provided for a coordinated simultaneous advance of all forces. The main armies were strengthened as much as possible by reducing subsidiary forces which had been cordoned for defensive purposes, but these latter were also to contribute by advancing, enabling them to guard "their special trusts when advancing from them as well as remaining at them."[7]

In his concern to immobilize the enemy's reserves and prevent more Shilohs and Chickamaugas, Grant's emphasis was naturally on the main Confederate armies of Lee and Joseph E. Johnston. To prevent Lee from ever being able to detach any troops, he instructed George G. Meade: "Lee's army will be your objective point. Wherever Lee goes you will go also."[8] Sherman was pleased with Grant's plan, feeling that to act in a "common plan converging in a common center" was "enlightened war."[9] He understood the mission of his army, telling Grant that he "would ever bear in mind that Johnston is at all times to be kept busy that he cannot, in any event, send any part of his command against you or Banks." Even such complete understanding by his trusted subordinate could not banish Grant's fear of Confederate strategic maneuver. The counterconcentration used after Chickamauga did not appeal to him since, presumably, he did not want to abandon the initiative and, with a subordinate like Sherman, did not feel the need to do so. Writing from Virginia, he warned against loss of the initiative and explained to Sherman his contingency plan in case Sherman failed to hold Johnston's forces in Georgia.

> What I now want more particularly to say is, that if the two main attacks, yours and the one from here, should promise great success,

[7] U. S. Grant, *Personal Memoirs* (2 vols.; New York, 1886), II, 127–29.
[8] *Official Records*, XXXIII, p. 328.
[9] *Ibid.*, XXXII, Pt. 3, p. 312, See also 409.

the enemy may, in a fit of desperation, abandon one part of their line of defense, and throw their whole strength upon the other, believing a single defeat without any victory to sustain them better than a defeat all along their line, and hoping too, at the same time, that the army meeting with no resistance, will rest perfectly satisfied with their laurels, having penetrated to a given point south, thereby enabling them to throw their force first upon one and then on the other.

With the majority of military commanders they might do this. But you have had too much experience in traveling light, and subsisting upon the country, to be caught by any such *ruse*. I hope my experience has not been thrown away. My directions, then, would be, if the enemy in your front show signs of joining Lee, follow him up to the full extent of your ability. I will prevent the concentration of Lee upon your front, if it is the power of this army to do it.[10]

Throughout the spring and summer campaign of 1864, Grant and Sherman were haunted by the specter of Chickamauga. On July 16 Grant warned: "The attempted invasion of Maryland having failed," and all enemy troops in Virginia "beyond a sufficiency to hold their strong fortifications will be an element of weakness to eat up their supplies." Sherman should expect Johnston to be reinforced by twenty-five thousand men from Virginia. Telling him to "select a point that you can hold until help can be had," Grant committed himself to try to "hold the enemy without the necessity of so many men. If successful, I can detach from here for other enterprises, looking as much to your assistance as anything else." Sherman did not assume the defensive, however; he continued instead his advance, though fearful of a momentary arrival of troops from Virginia.[11]

Their fears were groundless. The beleaguered Confederates were dominated by the condition, foreseen by P. G. T. Beauregard, that there were "no more troops to concentrate. . . ." With two major theaters, both under heavy pressure, the Confederate armies were insufficiently dispersed to permit any significant concentration.[12]

This interpretation of Confederate strategy is that of the contemporaries, not just Beauregard and Bragg, but of their opponents

---

[10] *Ibid.*, 409.
[11] *Ibid.*, XXXVIII, Pt. 5, p. 149.
[12] *Ibid.*, Pt. 2, p. 580.

as well. There is a curious relationship between these two military scholars, Beauregard and Halleck, one which enabled Beauregard to implement his ideas. These key campaigns were thus inspired by antagonists whose military thought was derived from comparable opponents of a previous century. Halleck was too poor a disciple of Napoleon and Jomini to prevent Beauregard and the Confederates from defeating him with the methods of these two mentors of the "Napoleon in gray," but he was a good enough soldier to perceive what was happening to him. Similarly, Grant, innocent of any theory, perceived, as Beauregard did, the defects in Halleck's strategy and keyed his operations in the last year of the war to avoid these same errors. Grant's insight into the nature of northern and southern strategy and his acknowledgment of the effectiveness of that of the Confederates constitutes an endorsement of Beauregard's ideas.

Beauregard's ideas on strategy were influential because of a fortuitous grouping of Confederate factions. Although the informal organization of southern generals and politicians revolved around personalities, state, family, and personal loyalties, they were able to unite as a western concentration bloc and display a common concern about the implementation of strategy. The struggle of the western concentration bloc to overcome the influence of Lee aggravated hostilities among the Confederate high command. Although Bragg was the object of the most widespread antipathy and Davis was the object of detestation by Johnston and his partisans as well as by the antiadministration political faction, there seems also to have been some hostility toward Lee. This grew, in part, out of their perception that the Gettysburg campaign had been an offensive move. They blamed the Gettysburg campaign for the losses in the West, feeling that Pennsylvania was the wrong place for an offensive and that the troops used there could have been better employed in the West.

Beauregard was emphatic in his criticism. Although during the war he was not explicit as to whether he blamed Davis or Lee, he was clearly hostile toward the strategy which overlooked his "brilliant campaign" and substituted, "instead . . . the march across the border into Pennsylvania, the check at Gettysburg, the loss there of some 20,000 of the flower of the Army. . . ." His criticism has a personal flavor when he says that "the right course was so plainly laid down by the rules of the art of war that the veriest tyro ought to have seen it."[13] Mrs. Chesnut's account of the remarks of Dick Manning, one Johnston's aides, suggests that many who criticized the strategy of both Davis and Lee may have blamed Lee: "He talked Joe Johnstonism run mad. He coupled Lee and Davis and abused them with equal virulence. Lee was a solemn hypocrite; he used the garb of religion to mask his sins, but his iniquities were known!"[14]

If, with Beauregard as their mentor, informal organizations of Confederate generals and politicians were able significantly to influence strategic decisions, then some evaluations of these decisions are needed. What judgments may be made of the results of the interaction of these factions and ideas with other military and personal factors?

Since the departmental organization was so important to the conduct of the war, it is well to ask how responsive to strategic needs was the structure; how effective was the management of it? As administered by Davis, the departmental system did display a tendency to overemphasize the minor theaters of action, though there were important roles for subsidiary departments. In areas such as western North Carolina, southwestern Virginia, and east Tennessee, it gave a semblance of authority to areas which would otherwise have been dominated by Unionists. In areas of extreme isolation, such as the Trans-Mississippi, the centralization of strategic and supply matters on a regional basis was effective. The presence of even a skeleton military force within every foot of Confederate territory was not only politically advantageous, but also gave the government a sounding board for local needs and discontents. The foremost evil of the system, then, was that gradually it became not just the instrument to implement strategy but, to a degree, a strategy itself. The means often seemed to take precedence over the end. There were numerous instances when Richmond's war policy seemed to be more tailored to fit within the departmental framework than the opposite. For

[13] *Ibid.*, XXXVIII, Pt. 2, p. 524.
[14] Mary Boykin Chesnut, *A Diary from Dixie*, ed. Ben Ames Williams (Boston, 1961), 421.

example, Davis' strategy for Mississippi and Tennessee in 1862–1863 was shaped to allow General T. H. Holmes to maintain discretion in reinforcement from his Trans-Mississippi command. To accommodate Holmes, Davis may have been motivated to attempt to manipulate troops between Bragg and Pemberton. Likewise, the strategy for the 1862 Kentucky offensive was modified to fit departmental boundaries, and became a joint, cooperative effort. Richmond's proposed strategy for General Joseph E. Johnston in early 1864 was based upon maintaining the autonomy of General Leonidas Polk's Alabama department. Later, both in the summer and autumn of 1864, the lack of operations against Sherman's line of communications was colored by the government's determination to allow discretion to remain with the commander of the Alabama department.

Another serious flaw was the injection of personality into the departmental system. In theory, such organization gave wide discretion to the local commander, in matters such as departmental defense, reinforcement, and other matters. Usually, the response depended heavily upon the individual commander's personality. General Leonidas Polk was given almost free rein of the old Western Department in the summer of 1861, with such disastrous results as his unauthorized invasion of Kentucky in September, 1861, and his failure to fortify the Tennessee and Cumberland rivers. Later, the young, ambitious General Edmund Kirby Smith aided in wrecking the 1862 Kentucky invasion by his desire for independent power. A seeker of personal glory, Kirby Smith consistently shunned concentration and cooperation with General Braxton Bragg. In another way the slow, cautious General T. H. Holmes remained lethargic amidst the Vicksburg crisis of late 1862. Later, in 1864, General Stephen D. Lee exhibited overcaution in his timid attempts to destroy Sherman's communications.

There were other matters of personality. The departmental system displayed an innate conservatism—an expensive luxury amidst a revolt. Frequently a general preached a concentration and mutual support until he gained his own department, then became overpossessive and too cautious, even selfish. This proprietary feeling about one's forces was displayed by General Beauregard, whose several strategic proposals offered throughout the war stressed a massive concentration, particularly in the central Confederacy. Yet in 1863, when the War Department sought a major shift of troops from his South Carolina department to Mississippi, Beauregard wrangled incessantly. General Joseph E. Johnston also exemplified the difference between theory and practice. In late 1862 and early 1863, when he supervised Bragg's Second Department, Johnston had urged assistance for the Tennessee front. By the late summer of 1863, when Johnston commanded the remains of Pemberton's Alabama-Mississippi department, his tone had changed drastically. A reinforcement of Bragg at Chattanooga was effected only after repeated prodding by the government. Later, in the spring of 1864, Johnston showed great unwillingness to reinforce Polk's Alabama-Mississippi department against a threatened invasion by Sherman.

There were, of course, many instances in which forces were not utilized to great advantage because of Davis' usual allowance of discretion to departmental commanders. For this reason Holmes's troops were wasted in late 1862. The extensive cavalry organization in the Alabama-Mississippi department could have been better utilized in 1863–1864. Lee's logistical problems might have been better aided by sending Longstreet west after Chancellorsville. In late 1863 Johnston's Alabama-Mississippi troops could well have been used in wholesale reinforcement of Bragg in north Georgia. Taylor's departmental army might well have united with Hood in the 1864 Tennessee campaign, or with Beauregard and later Joseph E. Johnston in the Carolinas.

There was also waste involved in duplication of effort. Many seasoned field commanders needed elsewhere were siphoned off into routine administrative affairs. For example, in the early autumn of 1863, the Alabama-Mississippi department after Vicksburg's surrender possessed little *raison d'etre*. Yet it was commanded by General Joseph E. Johnston, whose second-in-command was a recent transfer from the Army of Tennessee, the able and experienced Hardee. The services of the capable division commander General Patton Anderson were lost to the Army of Tennessee by his transfer to command the District of Florida in 1864. Another competent officer,

General Daniel Ruggles, was lost to administrative duties in the Department of Mississippi and East Louisiana. Beauregard's long tenure as commander of the Department of South Carolina, Georgia, and Florida, from August, 1862 to mid-1864 seemed a waste of an experienced field commander.

In addition to the waste of seasoned field commanders, considerable manpower was absorbed by the system itself. Numbers of officers and men were lost in various subcommands. Every department, however unimportant, usually possessed an extensive staff connected with departmental headquarters, a second body of officers serving in district or subdistrict commands, and a third series of outpost commands. For example, in the early winter of 1864, General Richard Taylor's Alabama-Mississippi department possessed not only several district commands, but also maintained numerous outposts.

Sometimes, there was also a duplication of administrative and military effort between departments. During 1862–1863, the Second and east Tennessee departments were jointly charged with Tennessee's defense. Both possessed field armies, an extensive staff organization, and numerous district and outpost officers. The defense of the lower valley of Virginia, particularly the Abingdon-Saltville region, was the joint responsibility of the east Tennessee department and the Department of Southwestern Virginia (later renamed the Trans-Allegheny Department). Separate organizations were maintained completely until May, 1864. Then, although a single general commanded both organizations until the end of the war, separate administrations were continued. Such waste was probably far more serious than has been appreciated by historians. During the war, the South experimented with at least thirty-eight different departmental organizations, embracing over eighty-five district and subdistrict commands.

Another serious flaw was the inconsistency of departmental responsibility. Although Davis generally followed a policy of delegating authority to the departmental commander, the government frequently intervened in an inconsistent manner which only muddled the command problem. A classic example was the Kentucky invasion of 1862. Here Davis at first granted too much local authority, refusing to provide either Bragg or Kirby Smith with a clear-cut objective of the invasion, and abstaining from settling the issue of who would be in command.

Yet, after the invasion began, the government frequently interfered. Without Bragg's knowledge, the Mississippi portion of his department was detached and reorganized into a separate command under Pemberton, with the goal of recapturing New Orleans. In effect, this diverted some of Bragg's force from the invasion effort. Again without informing Bragg, the government removed middle Tennessee from his jurisdiction and gave it to the east Tennessee department. Both troops and supplies assembled there for support were thus lost to the campaign.

As mentioned previously, during General Joseph E. Johnston's tenure as commander of the Western Department, the government frequently intervened amidst avowals that Johnston possessed total authority. Against Johnston's wishes, troops were shifted from Bragg to Pemberton. Without Johnston's knowledge the War Department attempted to implement a cavalry invasion of Kentucky from the east Tennessee department. To further confuse the general, Johnston was several times directly ordered by the government to a particular field command within his jurisdiction.

There are abundant examples which indicate that the government's inconsistent policy confused its generals, created tension between departments, and hampered cooperative efforts. A lack of guidelines for departmental authority hampered cooperation between the departments of Bragg and Kirby Smith in the autumn of 1862, and after the Kentucky campaign produced outright hostility between the generals. A lack of clear-cut authority produced both tension and confusion between Pemberton and Joseph E. Johnston during Grant's spring operations against Vicksburg in 1863. R. E. Lee and Samuel Jones constantly bickered over the ownership of troops and supplies. This same failing created hostility and a lack of coordinated effort between Bragg and General James Longstreet during the Chattanooga-Knoxville operations of late 1863. In early 1864 a lack of guidelines or clear authority muddled attempts to combine operations between the departments of Johnston, Longstreet, and Polk.

The inconsistent governmental policy also seemed to create insecurity among the high command. Some officers seemed fearful of assuming the initiative, unsure of the extent of their powers. Even General Robert E. Lee was not immune from this feeling. On November 5, 1861, Lee was assigned to command the Department of South Carolina, Georgia, and Florida. He was fresh from a three-month bitter experience in command of the Allegheny sector of Virginia. There, with seemingly clouded authority, he had unsuccessfully sought to coordinate operations between several miniature commands. Prior to departure for his new department, Lee took pains to inquire of Davis the exact limits of his new authority, to avoid a repetition of the West Virginia disaster.

Joseph E. Johnston's spotty performance as theater commander in 1862 and 1863 was partially due to a lack of understanding of his authority. Beauregard's lack of firmness as theater commander in 1864 also was symptomatic of this problem. Because he did not understand the limits of his authority, Beauregard manifested an almost total lack of initiative and exerted little of his vague authority in dealing with Hood's Tennessee campaign.

Davis' concern with strategy, though it was geared to the protection of territory and the Confederate logistic base, seems to have involved a neglect of logistics. Although a failure to understand logistical realities was a part of his failure to perceive the lack of realism in the early 1864 proposals to advance through east Tennessee, this neglect of supply problems is most clear in the departmental organization. His military experience and background should have insured an appreciation of supply problems, and his close association with Lee's always critical supply situation would surely, if nothing else, have sensitized him to this issue. Yet his organization in the West constantly overlooked the need for departmental lines which would include supply areas adequate to the size of departmental armies. Ignorance of western problems, an assumption of abundance, and a concern with the strategic rather than the logistic function of departments seem the most logical explanation for what was surely a serious failing in Confederate departmental structuring throughout the war.

The natural tendencies and the inertia inherent in such a regional system are responsible for many of its defects. The regional system, with the dispersal involved, was essential and highly desirable, as long as it did not become a cordon defense. Such dispersal must necessarily be a prelude to the concentration of a substantial portion of the field forces for an offensive or defensive blow. Yet there is a built-in tendency toward a cordon approach. Departmental commanders necessarily viewed their own problems as the most pressing facing the country. This, together with the inevitable inertia of any organization, would have made response slow. This situation was immensely aggravated by Davis' policy of decentralizing decisions and placing too much responsibility on departmental commanders. They were often asked to compare the urgent and familiar needs of their own commands with those of some distant force of whose problems they were ignorant. If even R. E. Lee failed in this Herculean task, it is not surprising that S. D. Lee and others did also. Yet the President was possibly influenced by more than indecisiveness and concern for Confederate territory and logistical base. Staffs and staff principles were not well developed in the Confederate Army. The Confederate War Department not only lacked an adequately organized staff, animated by modern principles, but there was a deficiency of skilled and trained manpower to assemble necessary data, evaluate them, and formulate alternatives. Adjutant General Cooper even lacked reliable data on the numbers of men in the various Confederate forces. The reports of field commanders were often inadequate in frequency and in extent. Undoubtedly an important cause of the badly structured departmental organizations and of President Davis' apparent passing the buck to departmental commanders was a real lack of knowledge of both the Union and Confederate situations and the President's consequent unwillingness to take a leap in the dark. Davis should certainly have seen to it that he was better served. Yet if he had done so, he would have been many years ahead of the United States Army in which he was trained and ahead of all Europe except Moltke's Prussia.

The many instances of excessive decentralization of decision making almost invariably accentuated the vice of localism which any decentralized system must have. And there were instances of unwise intervention. The departments within Johnston's Department of the West, for example, probably received as many orders from Richmond as they would have had there been no Western Department. There were also many examples of anomalies in the departmental structure and instances when the departmental structure was unresponsive or inadequately or tardily responsive to the realities of the logistical or strategic situation.

On the other hand, hardly a month passed that some significant and at least potentially valuable interdepartmental movement of reserves was not accomplished. Likewise, the departmental structure was constantly reshaped to meet new situations and, increasingly, unified direction was supplied. Finally a decentralized system is the only satisfactory one yet devised. If the management of the Confederate departmental system was, on balance, too laissez faire, the greater evil was avoided: departmental commanders were not put in a straitjacket, nor was their initiative stifled through insistence on prior approval of their plans or by prescribing their campaigns from afar. The principles were sound even if the management was often uneven and quite imperfect.

The principal pressure exerted on Davis by Lee and the western concentration bloc had not primarily to do with the structure of the departments but with the allocation of troops among the departments as they existed at any given time. In addition there was disagreement over strategy and also an implicit argument concerning enemy capabilities and intentions and the opportunities and dangers presented by these.

As with the management of the departmental system, the President's understanding of the enemy's own strategy was a major factor conditioning the contests over Confederate strategic decisions. As also with his management of the departmental organization, President Davis' performance was also a mixture of good principles and imperfect execution. He had more difficulty than Halleck and Grant in perceiving the nature of the enemy strategy. From 1861 through much of 1863 Davis was slow to realize that Union forces in the West were advancing along two major lines of operations. Perceiving clearly the advance along the Mississippi, he only slowly understood the significance of middle Tennessee and the central corridor into the Mid-South. By the fall of 1863 the President had grasped the danger to Atlanta and was adding to rather than subtracting from the Army of Tennessee. Yet he failed to see that the front in Mississippi had ceased to be of major significance. Although he agreed with R. E. Lee's contention that Virginia was to be the scene of the main Union effort and for much of early 1864 thought that Union forces in the West were being seriously depleted to strengthen those in Virginia, he failed to assign to any theater an entirely subsidiary role.

Grant's 1864 strategy of simultaneous advances on all fronts was particularly effective in distracting Davis' attention from the main Union concentrations and principal offensives in Virginia and Georgia. Widespread Union activity diverted the President's attention to many subsidiary theaters of operation. Nowhere was Grant more successful than in Mississippi. The Federal commander at Memphis launched a series of advances into Mississippi which were really nothing more than raids. Yet Davis vastly overestimated their significance. In view of the importance which operations in Mississippi had held while the navigation of the river was in dispute, and in view of the size of Union forces that had been deployed there, it is not surprising that he failed to perceive that the Union was no longer making a major effort in Mississippi. Just as Lincoln became overly concerned about Confederate operations in the Shenandoah Valley, so Davis was as easily distracted by events in Mississippi. Whereas, in the period 1861–1863, Davis had seen only one major Federal effort in the West when there were really two, he made, in the critical year 1864, the opposite error and perceived two major efforts, Georgia and Mississippi, when in fact there was only one— Sherman's advance into Georgia.

President Davis was the victim of Grant's successful application of distraction through dispersion, the always necessary prelude or concomitant to concentration. Davis' reaction to Grant's strategy would also affect Davis' organization of his departmental structure during 1864 and 1865. Grant's strategy was perhaps one of the major factors in what was a degeneration of the Confederate defensive effort into a cordon system.

The President's misconception may also explain his long insistence on an offensive by the Army of Tennessee, even when it faced a major Union concentration in the form of Sherman's army. Since the Army of Tennessee possessed most of the east Tennessee troops and, in the form of Polk's corps and previous reinforcements, a major part of the Mississippi forces, Davis naturally thought it strong enough to attack what had traditionally been the weakest of the two major Union armies in the West. Lee, in urging this offensive, stressed that the major Union effort for 1864 was in Virginia and so reinforced the President's misconception of Grant's grand strategy for 1864.

Davis' own application of the ideas of Napoleon and Jomini did not come spontaneously; his understanding and application of them came as much because of the activities of his generals as because of the knowledge and receptivity which his West Point education provided. In Davis' own formal organization, neither the departmental structure nor the War Department staff was able to supply the ideas or the impetus for their application. Again the primitive state of the military staff was the source of problems. Departmental commanders were necessarily parochial-minded, and the War Department, between the tenures there of Lee and Bragg, lacked any leaders who could reasonably be expected to supply a Napoleonic or Jominian synthesis to Confederate operations. Assistant Secretary John A. Campbell was a lawyer, as were Secretary Seddon and Bureau of War Chief Kean. Elderly Adjutant General Samuel Cooper, a pre-Mahan graduate of West Point, largely confined his activities to administrative detail. Although Secretary George W. Randolph, trained as a sailor and educated for the bar, knew something of European military organization and campaigns, his term was apparently too short for him to do more than press for greater departmental coordination. Thus the President's formal organization could not provide the means by which Davis could have received the ideas which came ultimately to animate his strategy.

Although judgments about the proper strategy have been avoided because they depend so much on ifs, certain assumptions are implicit. One of these is that, although Beauregard's plans were often extravagant and impractical, his concept of operations was the proper one. It was the foundation of so many Confederate successes that, even though it was the basic pattern of Confederate strategy, it should have been applied even more frequently than it was. If Confederate strategy is viewed in the context of the need, as T. Harry Williams has expressed it, for a "national application of the one principle which might have brought success," Beauregard is the principal advocate of that application, urging that the "whole theatre of war be viewed as one subject of which all points are but integral parts." Lee was long the principal obstacle to a complete national application of the principles he applied so brilliantly in Virginia. Yet many successful applications were made and contemporaries on the Union side recognized this consistent pattern in Confederate operations. That they perceived it and sought to guard against it is some confirmation of its worth. Implicit also is the assumption that since the South survived the loss of the Mississippi but not defeat on the Nashville-Atlanta line of operations, the partisans of that area were correct in their concern.

R. E. Lee, as Davis' adviser, was a major obstacle to the realization of more frequent national applications of Jominian-Napoleonic concepts and to the strengthening of the Nashville-Atlanta line. Not only does the quality of his advice invite criticism, but more important, he might have provided advice of a high quality that he did not in fact supply. And as already emphasized, he had unequaled oportunities to influence Davis. The high order of his strategic insight is amply demonstrated by his operations in Virginia. Yet he never made any general statements of the principles implicit in those operations. It may be that his understanding was intuitive rather than learned and that he did not have the kind of mind which would have enabled him to abstract those principles which underlay his action. Or perhaps he never gave to another theater of operations or to the Confederacy's problems as a whole the kind of sustained attention which would have led to the generalization of his own principles and their application elsewhere.

With the loss, in the spring of 1862, of the Memphis and Charleston Railroad, the Virginia and Tennessee Railroad became the logical route by which major Confederate forces could be moved from one line of operations to another. The Army of Tennessee lay at one end, the Army of Northern Virginia at the other. Between these two strongest Confederate armies lay fairly significant forces deployed adjacent to the railroad, primarily in the Departments of East Tennessee and Southwestern Virginia. Not only was it a natural route for maneuver which lent itself to the application of the pipeline concept, but it was a shorter route than the comparable rail connections available to the Union and far better than the circuitous route between Tennessee and Mississippi which was employed instead. Davis and Seddon saw this opportunity in March and April of 1863. Had Lee been able to perceive this and could he have balanced the exigencies and opportunities in Virginia and Tennessee, then broader and more successful applications could have been made of that basic pattern in Confederate strategy.

Until the Virginia and Tennessee Railroad was lost Lee's advice, however, was conditioned by his ignorance of the western theater, of its physical and economic geography, and of the strength of the enemy there. His judgment was also colored by his recurring conviction that Virginia was to be the scene of the principal Union effort and by his loyalty to and concern for his native state. In addition, all of Lee's Confederate service had been in Virginia, with the exception of a few months at the Charleston defenses. Constantly beset by the problems of his Virginia army, Lee was unable to perceive Confederate strategic problems in their entirety; hence his advice could not be based upon that fine strategic understanding which his operations in Virginia reflected. Perhaps Lee should be criticized for offering advice so freely, for assuming competence in areas about which he was ignorant. And perhaps Davis realized this, for until 1864 he consistently ignored Lee's recommendations about the West and heeded only those about the seaboard, an area about which Lee was better informed and one which Davis had implicitly placed under his jurisdiction.

Any evaluation of Davis' strategic decisions is heavily dependent on that made of Lee and whether one accepts the assumptions on strategy and the East vs. West controversy. If Lee's advice about the primacy of Virginia was correct, then Davis erred in rejecting it; if Lee's advice was incorrect he should receive credit for ignoring it but be criticized for not earlier perceiving the importance of the central corridor to Atlanta and for not sooner adopting offensive and national concentrations.

The roles changed after Davis had overruled Lee and sent Longstreet to Chickamauga. The conflict between Lee and the western concentration bloc was resolved and he became a collaborator in devising western offensives. This remained the essential situation even after Longstreet's return. Lee's urging of a western offensive fitted with Davis' perception of the situation, and Union strategy so immobilized Confederate reserves as to make any east-west shift apparently impossible.

In his combativeness and his long struggle against superior odds, Lee has something in common with Frederick the Great. Unfortunately for the Confederacy, he was only a Virginia Frederick. When Davis asked him to go to the most endangered theater he declined. His greatest service might have been to put his great skill on the battlefield to work by emulating Frederick, who, whenever possible, commanded in person at the point of concentration or the place of greatest danger to the state.

That Davis should seek to employ Lee in this role indicates that the President may have perceived that geography and Federal strength rendered Virginia an unproductive place for an offensive; that its offensive asset was the general commanding there who might be moved where the situation was more propitious. More likely the cause of Davis' desire to use Lee outside of Virginia was a serious command problem which faced the Confederacy.

President Davis' distrust of the abilities of his principal generals ripened with time and constituted a most serious weakness in the Confederate command structure. In 1864, just when Lincoln, by much trial and error, had found capable commanders for both East and West, the Confederate situation became critical. In Lee, J. E. Johnston, and Beauregard, Davis had early found three capable army commanders. In 1862 he had lost confidence in Beauregard and relegated him to a position of secondary importance, one which, though it utilized his engineering talents, failed to use his experience and painfully and expensively acquired skill commanding a field army. The appointment of Bragg had not been successful, something which the President and the Secretary of War had realized in early 1863, but had been unable to remedy because Johnston refused to cooperate in their serpentine efforts to replace Bragg or to nullify that general's ineptitude. Since Davis, in July of 1863, had lost confidence in Johnston and pointed to the loss of Vicksburg as positive evidence of Johnston's incapacity, the President now found the situation reversed—he distrusted Bragg less than he did Johnston. Efforts to resolve the dilemma by sending Lee west foundered on that general's reluctance to leave Virginia.

Unlike Lincoln, Davis had established no tradition of rapid and frequent removals from command. The fact that the Confederacy possessed a hierarchy of lieutenant generals and generals may have made constant shifting of appointments more difficult as did the lack of interior commands, unmenaced by enemy action, as places to lay on the shelf unsuccessful army commanders. Lincoln sent John Pope to Minneapolis; there was no comparable place for Confederate generals, though it is often said that the Trans-Mississippi filled this role. But unemployed full generals were extremely difficult to dispose of, and this may in part account for Bragg's appointment in Richmond. Where else was he to go?

The President was reluctant to change generals because he had a strong appreciation for the difficulties of army command, but he was loath to employ either Johnston or Beauregard. Certainly Davis was at fault in his failure to use those two seasoned men, but they themselves had made a significant contribution to that state of affairs. Unlike Lee, both Beauregard and Johnston were uncommunicative and secretive, often failing to report, much less confide fully, their plans. Later, when at Charleston, Beauregard changed completely and supplied the War Department with full intelligence of enemy action and his own dispositions and plans. This change of habit may explain Davis' later revival of confidence in Beauregard, though after Shiloh and Corinth he never seems to have envisioned Beauregard as commander of a field army. Certainly Davis might have earlier found a way out of the Bragg-Beauregard-Johnston circle and tried Longstreet, or Hardee, though the latter did decline command when proffered. As it was, the Confederacy went through most of the last two years of the war crippled by having only one army commander when at least two were needed.

As generalissimo of the Confederate armies, Davis' own perform-ance seems to have peaked in 1863 and then declined thereafter. In the first two years of the war he had markedly improved his performance—redesigning his departmental system until it was an effective means of implementing what was an extremely aggressive version of the offensive-defensive strategy.[15] He increasingly per-ceived and applied the strategic principles of Jomini and Napoleon to coordinate the departments and Confederate strategy as a whole. Yet in the latter part of the war, the last year in particular, many of these gains were lost. His response to changed circumstances, never very prompt, became quite tardy, disastrously so. He seemed to have a less complete grasp of the whole than he had displayed in 1863.

Yet, since the Trans-Mississippi and the Atlantic seaboard had good unity of command, this deterioration really reflected the perennial problem of the West—how to secure unity while recognizing the diversity of so large an area. During the period between Johnston's and Beauregard's regional commands in the West, the President tried to supply unity from Richmond. Although there were two timely reinforcements from Mississippi for the Army of Tennessee, Davis' distance from the theaters of operations and his laissez faire methods meant that regional unity of command and consolidation of western logistical resources would have markedly improved the situation in the West. When the Military Division of the West was finally created after the fall of Atlanta, it was not a single department but another coordinating command which Beauregard, like Johnston, seemed

[15] Frank Vandiver, "Jefferson Davis and Confederate Strategy," *The American Tragedy* (Hampden-Sydney, Va., 1959), 19–32. 21–26, 30.

unable to implement. The weakness of the division, together with the President's failure to perceive that the seaboard was now a "western" front, meant the change was ineffectual.

Davis' failure to deal adequately with the West had many causes. The lack of a commander to whom he could confidently delegate such large responsibilities undoubtedly was a factor and may explain the limited authority enjoyed by both Johnston and Beauregard. Of course, defeat, manpower losses, and resource depletion limited his opportunities for success as he opposed Union armies which were stronger, increasingly well organized, and skillfully led. Although it was always Davis who made the decisions, there seemed to be no correlation between his performance and his advisers'. James A. Seddon was Secretary of War during the periods of best and worst performance. Lee's advice, too, was constant throughout the period. Bragg's appointment in Richmond only brought into the formal organization the influence of Beauregard and the western bloc which had already long been exercised informally but decisively.

More likely Davis' performance deteriorated because of the strain of the years of overwork without vacations, of bad health, of defeat after defeat, of diplomatic hopes dashed, of the loss of his child, of the debacle of Hood in command, of quarrels with friends and supporters, of news of victories which turned out to be defeats, of the death of valued officers and friends, of captious press criticism and conniving generals and politicians. Even the hot, humid summers in Richmond without the usual relief of sojourns in the country could well have contributed to a performance which so obviously deteriorated during the last year of the war.

His uneven performance makes it difficult to evaluate Davis as military commander in chief. His strategic insight and his command system seem better than his performance in action. His ability to dominate the situation and impose order where chaos might have reigned contrasts with his tardiness, even reluctance, in making decisions. In dealing with people, Davis was neither forebearing nor conciliatory, yet he was often unwilling to dismiss those whom he had appointed; his appreciation of the difficulties of command made him cling to generals who had failed or to those he believed would fail.

Any evaluation of the military performance must take into consideration the great number of important decisions Davis made and also those which he might have made but did not. The varying estimates of Davis' people, of the advice he received, of his appointments and nonappointments, and of removals and nonremovals complicate any judgment. Moreover, Davis was a loser. Compared to a winner, a loser always receives harsher judgment unless he captures the imagination of his contemporaries or historians. The critic seeks reasons for a loser's failure, but the successes of winners are seldom examined for flaws. Further, a military leader who does not command on the battlefield, who always works through intermediaries is more difficult to evaluate. It is difficult to point to tangible achievements. And this difficulty applies to an evaluation of one who had no predecessor or successor. Evaluations of Joe Johnston, for example, would be far different had Hood not failed.

Finally there is the problem of standard of comparison. Few generals compare favorably with Napoleon. A fairer comparison would be between two generals in like situations in long wars. The performance of the Confederacy does not compare unfavorably with any mid–nineteenth-century performance, other than the Prussian, which is the more remarkable considering that the Confederacy inherited from the United States a command and staff system little different from that which prevailed in Marlborough's day. Only the reader can judge the relative weights to assign to the things Davis did right and wrong or even which *were* right and wrong. Yet it must be remembered that the responsibility was finally his for the creation of a viable and extremely effective military machine. This creation did not come about in spite of Davis but because of him. He gave it an active direction, the appointments were his, the distributions of forces were his, and many of the grand maneuvers either were his or were supported by him.

Such a positive and active leader as Davis must be central in any account of an effort to influence decisions so long as the leader was responsive to those efforts. And Davis was responsive; he did change and much which is credited to or blamed on Davis belongs to his generals. Much that he did was in response to their ideas, urgings, and advice. If anything, he leaned too heavily on them, and the image of Davis as the cast-iron man waging a war according to his experiences at Buena Vista, must be superseded by a different picture. Instead of Buena Vista, the predominating influence was the strategic ideas of Jomini and Napoleon as interpreted by Beauregard and best exemplified on a local basis in Lee's early campaigns.

Instead of the image of a rigid autocrat, Davis might well be depicted as a harried leader beset by personnel problems and responding to pressures and ideas generated within his organization. He moved from crisis to crisis, resolving each by choosing among the alternatives presented by his staff, the politicians, the officers in the field, and from his own ideas. The resulting decisions were a complex of the Napoleonic-Jomini influence: the ideas of Lee, the pressures brought to bear by Beauregard, the western concentration bloc and its network of informal associations, and Davis' own changing concept of the departmental command system. Therefore, any serious evaluation of Davis' strategy must also consider those who influenced him, for his key decisions were products of the politics of command.

Appendix:
Some Potential
Prewar Associations
Among Confederate
Leaders

To test the hypothesis that there were many informal connections among the Confederate leadership, some readily available data about the prewar careers of officers, congressmen, and other civil leaders were put on data processing cards. These data included college attendance, legislative and congressional service, and Mexican War service. The computer then found the people who were at the same place and at the same time. The implicit assumption is, of course, that they knew one another well enough and favorably enough for this association to be the basis of wartime contacts or alliances that could have been used to influence policy or decisions. Obviously this assumption will be true in only some of the cases; in others a basis for active enmity will have been uncovered. In many other instances there would have been no association at all.

This exercise in establishing potential prewar associations is intended only to be a representative of what could be done. For this, more complete and detailed data would be needed. For example, it should be indicated whether they were of the same or opposite political party or party faction. In addition the list should be expanded to include important leaders such as John A. Campbell and Jacob Thompson, who did not hold one of the ranks or offices used to develop the original list. Staff officers and influential colonels would be another important group to include. The list of potential prewar associations would be expanded considerably. Among these would be common service in the U.S. Army, genealogy, and other political associations. More difficult to find would be business associations and professional contacts among lawyers and physicians as well as lawyer-client and physician-patient relationships. Some potential social associations might also be developed on the basis of residence in the same town or county, or vacations at the same watering place.

If the number of individuals and potential contacts were thus expanded, it seems, on the basis of this preliminary study, that there would be a fairly complete network of prewar interactions among the members of the Confederate establishment. If common service during the first year of the war were added, the contacts would be increased very significantly. If indirect or second order relationships (that is, having a contact in common) were included, it seems likely that the contacts of many of the political and military leaders would virtually saturate the entire list. Such a study would raise many good questions for historians to investigate. Knowledge of whether these contacts were actual or potential, exploited or dormant, or in friendship or enmity should shed a good deal of additional light on civilian as well as military behavior and might also help explain the differing patterns of action among state government leaders.

General officers, congressmen, cabinet members, war governors, and the President and Vice-President—in all, 605 members of the Confederate establishment—were included. On the basis of college attendance, congressional and legislative experience, and Mexican War service with either Taylor or Scott, each of these 605 individuals had an average of 39.92 potential prewar contacts with others of the group. The median number of contacts was 41. As a result of being a West Pointer who served in both the Buena Vista and Mexico City campaigns, Cadmus M. Wilcox had the largest number of potential prewar contacts—141. P. G. T. Beauregard was well above average with 92 such contacts. Louis T. Wigfall had 45, based on college attendance and legislative and congressional service.

The computer was then asked to develop the indirect relationships or contacts, i.e., the number of people with whom each man on the list had a common potential contact. The average number of these potential relationships was 151.52, the median 164. The high number was 307, shared by Jefferson Davis and Humphrey Marshall, both West Pointers and Mexican War veterans who served in Congress. Beauregard had 228 such contacts and Wigfall 226.

The process was repeated for the wartime period, using contacts developed during the war through June of 1862. The potential contacts used were within and between Congress and the executive branch and some very limited military associations. The latter were developed from tables of organization used at First Manassas and Seven Days', and the period between and the tables of organization for Shiloh and Corinth. Commanders were presumed to have potential contact with their subordinates and with others on the same command level. Since the informal organization was the focus of the study, no contact was shown between the army commanders on the one hand and the President or the Secretary of War on the other. The results were:

	Average	Median	High
Direct	63.29	61	191(Davis)
Indirect	258.65	288	431(Wigfall)

The early wartime associations, like those of the prewar period, provided the basis for many informal organizations and the paths for much unofficial communication. Beauregard had 143 potential direct contacts and Wigfall 185. That such an inveterate wire puller as Wigfall should have the largest number of potential indirect contacts and that Beauregard should be close behind with 410 give added confidence that this computer exercise bears some relationship to reality and that the kind of relationships hypothesized here might well be a fruitful field for historical investigation.

Illustrative Diagrams

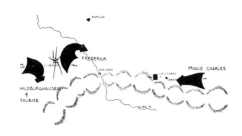

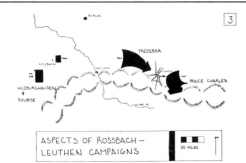

ASPECTS OF ROSSBACH –
LEUTHEN CAMPAIGNS

50 MILES

ASPECTS OF FREDERICK'S
CAMPAIGN OF 1758

47 MILES

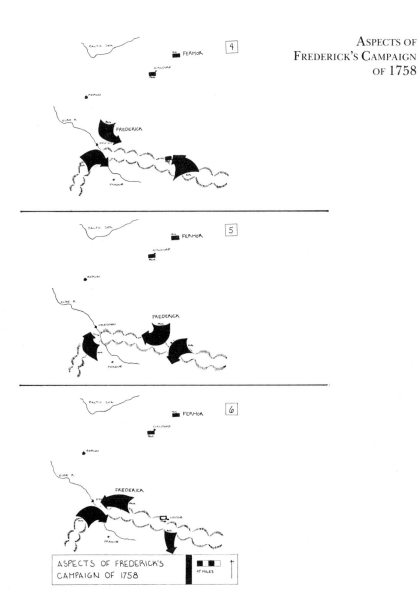

ASPECTS OF FREDERICK'S
CAMPAIGN OF 1758

47 MILES

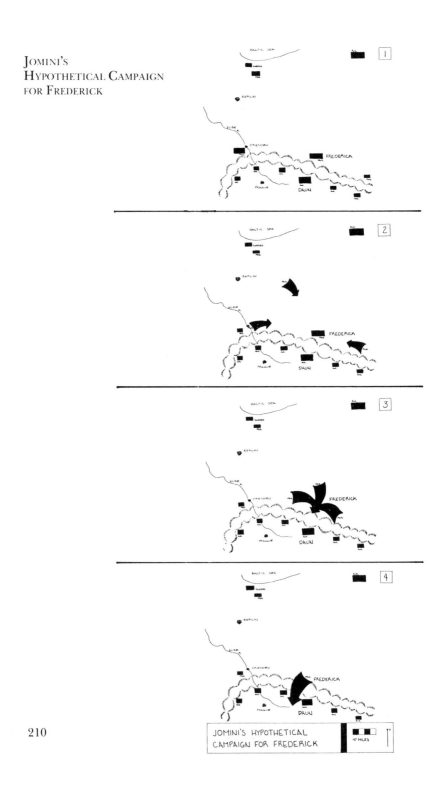

JOMINI'S HYPOTHETICAL
CAMPAIGN FOR FREDERICK

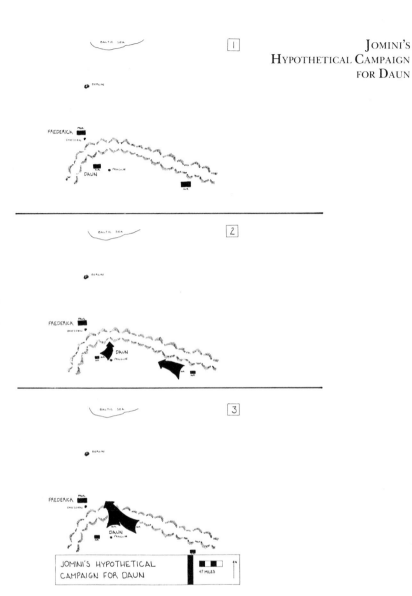

JOMINI'S HYPOTHETICAL
CAMPAIGN FOR DAUN

47 MILES

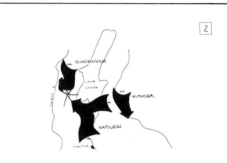

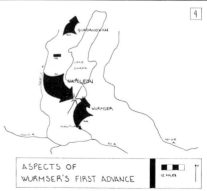

ASPECTS OF
WURMSER'S FIRST ADVANCE

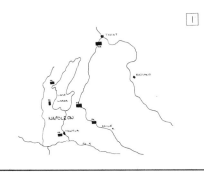

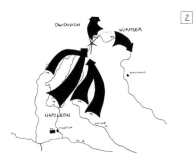

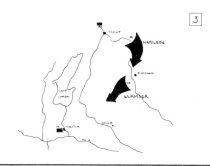

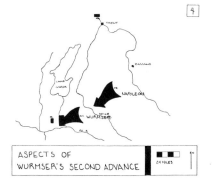

ASPECTS OF
WURMSER'S SECOND ADVANCE

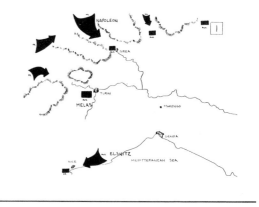

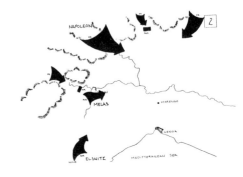

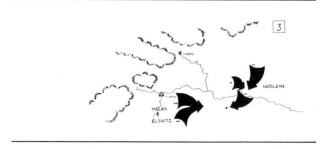

ASPECTS OF THE
MARENGO CAMPAIGN

20 MILES

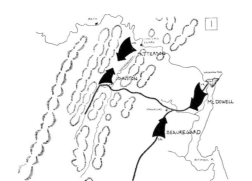

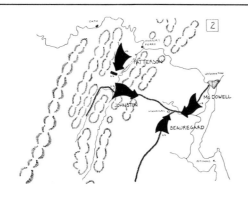

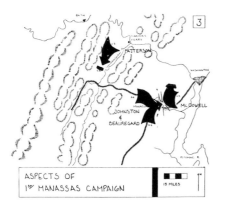

ASPECTS OF
1ˢᵗ MANASSAS CAMPAIGN

15 MILES

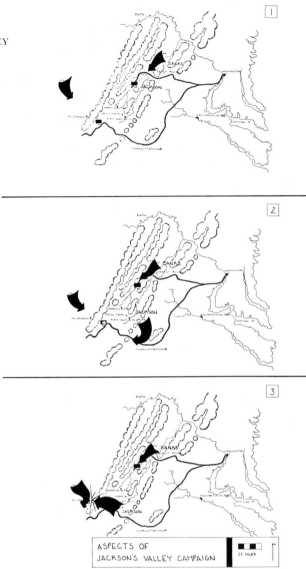

ASPECTS OF
JACKSON'S VALLEY CAMPAIGN

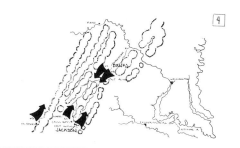

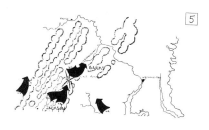

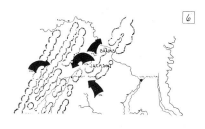

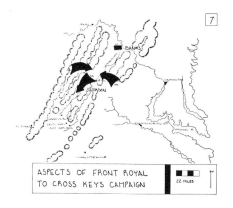

ASPECTS OF FRONT ROYAL
TO CROSS KEYS CAMPAIGN

22 MILES

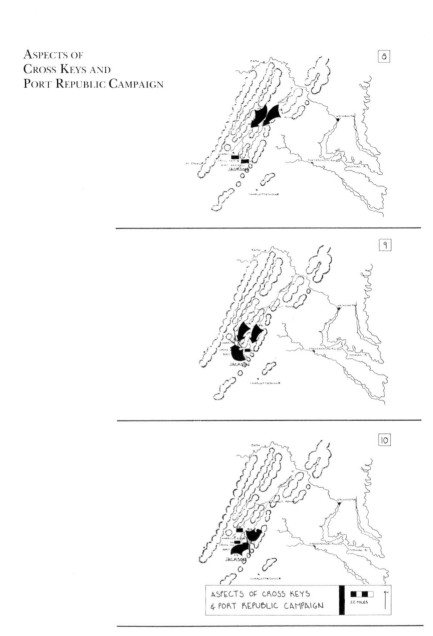

ASPECTS OF CROSS KEYS
& PORT REPUBLIC CAMPAIGN

22 MILES

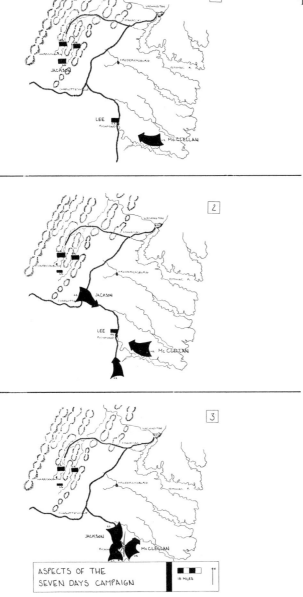

ASPECTS OF THE
SEVEN DAYS CAMPAIGN

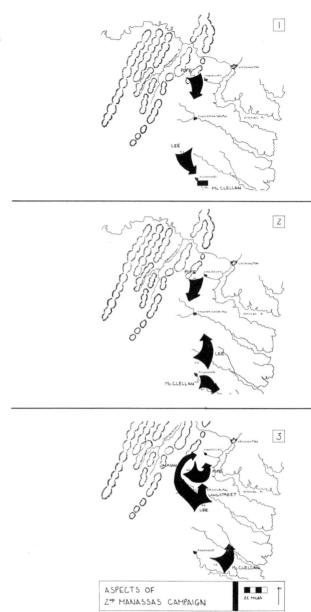

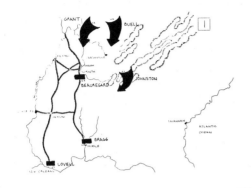

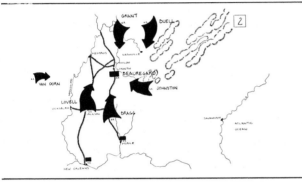

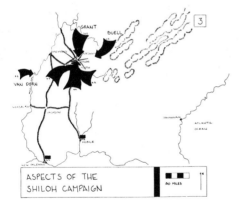

ASPECTS OF THE
SHILOH CAMPAIGN

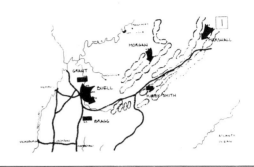

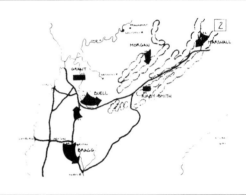

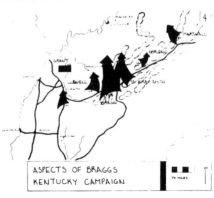

ASPECTS OF BRAGGS
KENTUCKY CAMPAIGN

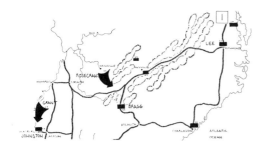

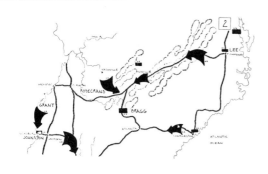

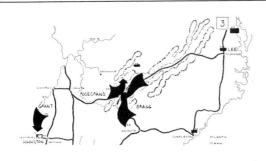

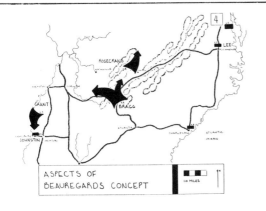

ASPECTS OF
BEAUREGARDS CONCEPT

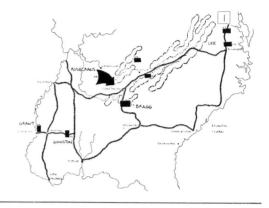

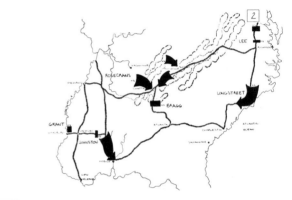

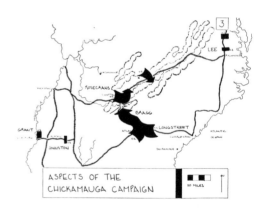

Essay
on Selected Sources

Not all sources cited in the footnotes are mentioned here. The reader is urged to consult each chapter's citations for information.

A large number of manuscript collections, particularly the papers of major Confederate officers, were used by the authors in preparation of this book. Many of these were not cited specifically in the footnotes, but are of great value in any research on the strategy debate within the Confederacy. Important Beauregard correspondence is found in the Beauregard Papers in the Library of Congress, the Beauregard correspondence in the Confederate Records Division of the National Archives, the Wigfall Family Papers and the Alfred Roman Papers in the Library of Congress, the Albert Sidney Johnston–Beauregard correspondence in the Howard-Tilton memorial Library at Tulane University, and in other collections of Beauregard correspondence at Duke University, the Department of Archives, Louisiana State University, and elsewhere.

Important collections of Joseph E. Johnston Papers found useful in this project are located in the Joseph E. Johnston Papers, College of William and Mary Library; the Joseph E. Johnston Letters at Miami (Ohio) University Library; the Joseph E. Johnston Papers at Duke University Library; the Joseph E. Johnston letters in the Century Collection, New York Public Library; the Wigfall Family Papers in the Library of Congress, and elsewhere.

Lee papers are, of course, in abundance. Those which proved especially helpful in this project include the R. E. Lee Papers at Washington and Lee University; the R. E. Lee Papers, Library of Congress, the George Bolling Lee Papers, Virginia Historical Society, the Lee collection in the Mrs. Mason Barret Collection, Howard-Tilton Memorial Library, Tulane; and the R. E. Lee Papers, Virginia Historical Society.

Collections of Braxton Bragg Papers found useful in this project include the Bragg papers in the William Palmer Collection, Western Reserve Historical Society; the Bixby Collection of Bragg Papers, Missouri Historical Society; and other Bragg collections at Duke University, the Houghton Library, Harvard University; the Historical Society of Pennsylvania, and elsewhere. Collections of Jefferson Davis letters found helpful include the Davis Papers in the Howard-Tilton Memorial Library at Tulane, the Duke University Library, the Emory University Library, and elsewhere.

Numerous other collections of papers of Confederate officers were consulted, too many to be listed here, Among those found most useful, for example, were the Albert Sidney Johnston letters in the Mrs. Mason Barret Collection of Albert Sidney and William Preston Johnston Papers, Howard-Tilton Memorial Library, Tulane; the James Longstreet Letters in the Emory University Library; the Leonidas Polk Papers at the University of the South, Duke University, the Library of Congress, and others.

Compared with the extensive publication on other facets of the Civil War, relatively little has been written in recent years on strategy. There is, for example, no extensive study of Confederate strategy. Among the best sources available for such, by modern writers, are T. Harry Williams, "The Military Leadership of North and South," in David Donald (ed.), *Why the North Won the Civil War* (Baton Rouge, 1960); Frank Vandiver, "Jefferson Davis and Confederate Strategy." in *The American Tragedy* (Hampden-Sydney, Va., 1959); David Donald, *Lincoln Reconsidered* (New York, 1956); Grady McWhiney (ed.), *Grant, Lee, Lincoln and the Radicals; Essays on Civil War Leadership* (Evanston, Ill., 1964); Archer Jones, *Confederate Strategy from Shiloh to Vicksburg* (Baton Rouge, 1961); and Frank Vandiver, *Rebel Brass: The Confederate Command System.*

Other recent books useful for some discussion of Confederate strategy are Thomas L. Connelly, *Army of the Heartland: The Army of Tennessee, 1861–1862* (Baton Rouge, 1967) and *Autumn of Glory: The Army of Tennessee, 1862–1865* (Baton Rouge, 1970); Frank Vandiver, *Their Tattered Flags* (New York, 1970); John G. Barrett, *The Civil War in North Carolina* (Chapel Hill, 1963); Grady McWhiney,

Braxton Bragg and Confederate Defeat, Vol. I, *Field Command* (New York, 1969); Gilbert E. Govan and James Livingood, *A Different Valor: The Story of General Joseph E. Johnston, C.S.A.* (New York, 1956); Donald B. Sanger and Thomas R. Hay, *James Longstreet* (Baton Rouge, 1952).

Recent articles on Confederate strategy which may prove useful include: Archer Jones, "The Gettysburg Decision Reassessed," *Virginia Magazine of History and Biography* (January, 1968); Thomas L. Connelly, "Robert E. Lee and the Western Confederacy: A Criticism of Lee's Strategic Ability," *Civil War History* (June, 1969); Archer Jones, "Jomini and the American Civil War, A Reinterpretation," *Military Affairs* (December, 1970); Grady McWhiney, "Who Whipped Whom? Confederate Defeat Re-Examined," *Civil War History,* XI (March, 1965); and Edward Hagerman, "From Jomini to Dennis Hart Mahan: The Evolution of Trench Warfare and the American Civil War," *Civil War History,* XIII (September, 1967).

Other useful material on Lee and the matter of strategy, in addition to that cited above and in the Lee chapter notes, includes Douglas S. Freeman, *R. E. Lee: A Biography* (4 vols.; New York, 1936); Sir Frederick Maurice, *Robert E. Lee the Soldier* (Boston, 1925); Burke Davis, *Gray Fox* (New York, 1956); B. H. Liddell Hart, "Lee: A Psychological Problem," *Saturday Review of Literature,* XI (December 15, 1934), and "Why Lee Lost Gettysburg," *Saturday Review of Literature,* XI (December 15, 1934); Kirkwood Mitchell, "Lee and the Bullet of the Civil War," *William and Mary Quarterly,* XVI, 2nd ser. (January, 1936); T. Harry Williams, "Freeman, Historian of the Civil War: An Appraisal," *Journal of Southern History,* XI (February, 1955); Elbridge Colby and Douglas S. Freeman, "Robert E. Lee: Is His Military Genius Fact or Fiction?" *Current History,* XXIX (October, 1928); J. J. Bowen, *The Strategy of Robert E. Lee* (New York, 1914); Gamaliel Bradford, "Lee and the Confederate Government," *Atlantic,* CVII (February, 1911); and many other sources.

There is no comprehensive study of Jefferson Davis as President of the Confederacy, much less as a war strategist. Davis' role as a strategist is treated in Vandiver's *Rebel Brass* and *Their Tattered Flags,* as well as in his "Jefferson Davis and Unified Army Command,"

Louisiana Historical Quarterly, XXXVIII (1955), and in his "Jefferson Davis and Confederate Strategy." Less sympathetic appraisals of Davis as a strategist might be obtained from Jones's *Confederate Strategy from Shiloh to Vicksburg,* in Williams' "The Military Leadership of North and South," in Thomas R. Hay's "Braxton Bragg and the Southern Confederacy," *Georgia Historical Quarterly,* IX (December, 1925), and "The Davis-Hood-Johnston Controversy of 1864," *Mississippi Valley Historical Review,* XIX (June, 1924), and "Davis, Bragg and Johnston in the Atlanta Campaign," *Georgia Historical Quarterly,* VIII (March, 1924); Connelly, *Autumn of Glory* and *Army of the Heartland;* Archer Jones, "Tennessee and Mississippi: Joe Johnston's Strategic Problem," *Tennessee Historical Quarterly,* XVIII (June, 1959); Sir Frederick Maurice, *Statesmen and Soldiers of the Civil War: A Study in the Conduct of the War* (Boston, 1926); and Allan Nevins, *The War for the Union* (2 vols.; New York, 1959). Despite the lack of a complete biography of Davis, the traditional studies by Hudson Strode, Hamilton Eckenrode, Robert McElroy, and Edward Pollard offer useful, if not differing opinions of Davis.

Foreign observers who witnessed the war and later foreign writers have made a substantial contribution to the modest bibliography of Confederate strategy. The contributions of both groups in the matter of strategic discussion are treated in several excellent works by Jay Luvaas, including his edition of G. F. R. Henderson's *The Civil War: A Soldier's View* (Chicago, 1958); *The Military Legacy of the Civil War* (Chicago, 1959); "G. F. R. Henderson and the American Civil War," *Military Affairs,* XX (Fall, 1956); and *The Education of an Army* (Chicago, 1964).

Among the more important contemporary accounts which touched on Confederate strategy are: Charles Girard, *A Visit to the Confederate States of America in 1863: Memoir Addressed to His Majesty Napoleon III,* trans. and ed. William Stanley Hoole (Tuscaloosa, Ala., 1962); Justus Scheibert, *Seven Months in the Rebel States During the North American War,* ed. William Stanley Hoole, trans. Joseph C. Hayes (Tuscaloosa, Ala., 1958); Fitzgerald Ross, *A Visit to the Cities and Camps of the Confederate States,* ed. Richard Harwell (reprint; Urbana, 1958), published originally in *Blackwood's Edinburgh Magazine;* Viscount Garnet J. Wolseley, *The American Civil War: An English View,* ed. James Rawley (Charlottesville, 1964); see also Wolseley, "A Month's Visit to the Confederate Headquarters," *Blackwood's Edinburgh Magazine,* XCIII (January, 1863); C. C. Chesney, *Campaigns in Virginia, Maryland,* etc. (London, 1865). See also Chesney's "Recent Changes in the Art of War," *Edinburgh Review,* CXXIII (January, 1866), "The Last Campaign in America," *Edinburgh Review,* CXXI (January 1865), and "Memoir of General Robert E. Lee," CXXXVII, *Edinburgh Review* (1873); Walter Lord (ed.), *Fremantle Diary, Being the Journal of Lieutenant Colonel James Arthur Fremantle* (reprint; Boston, 1954). Among the later foreign writings, particularly the extensive English publications, some are more important because of their comments on Confederate strategy. Among these are W. B. Wood and J. E. Edmonds, *A History of the Civil War in the United States, 1861–5* (London, 1905); Cecil W. Battine, *The Crisis of the Confederacy; A History of Gettysburg and the Wilderness* (London, 1905); J. F. C. Fuller, *Grant and Lee* (New York, 1923); B. H. Liddell Hart, "Strategy and the American War," *Quarterly Review,* CCLIII (July, 1929), *Sherman: Soldier, Realist, American* (New York, 1929), and *The Ghost of Napoleon* (London, 1933); see also Liddell Hart's articles in the *Saturday Review of Literature* already mentioned.

For the political-military ties in Confederate policy making, see Williams, "The Military Leadership of the North and South"; McWhiney, *Grant, Lee, Lincoln and the Radicals;* Connelly, *Autumn of Glory;* Vandiver, *Rebel Brass.* See also Wilfred B. Yearns, *The Confederate Congress* (Athens, Ga., 1960); Richard E. Beringer, "A Profile of the Members of the Confederate Congress," *Journal of Southern History,* XXXIII (November, 1967); E. M. Coulter, *The Confederate States of America, 1861–1865* (Baton Rouge, 1950); Edward Pollard, *The Lost Cause; A New Southern History of the War* . . . . (New York, 1866); Rembert Patrick, *Jefferson Davis and His Cabinet* (Baton Rouge, 1944); Frank Owsley, *State Rights in the Confederacy* (reprint; Gloucester, Mass., 1961); May Ringold, *The Role of the State Legislatures in the Confederacy* (Athens, Ga., 1966); Ben Proctor, *Not Without Honor: The Life of John H. Reagan* (Austin, Tex., 1962); and Georgia Lee Tatum, *Disloyalty in the Confederacy* (Chapel Hill, 1934).

Index

DATE DUE

DEMCO 38-297

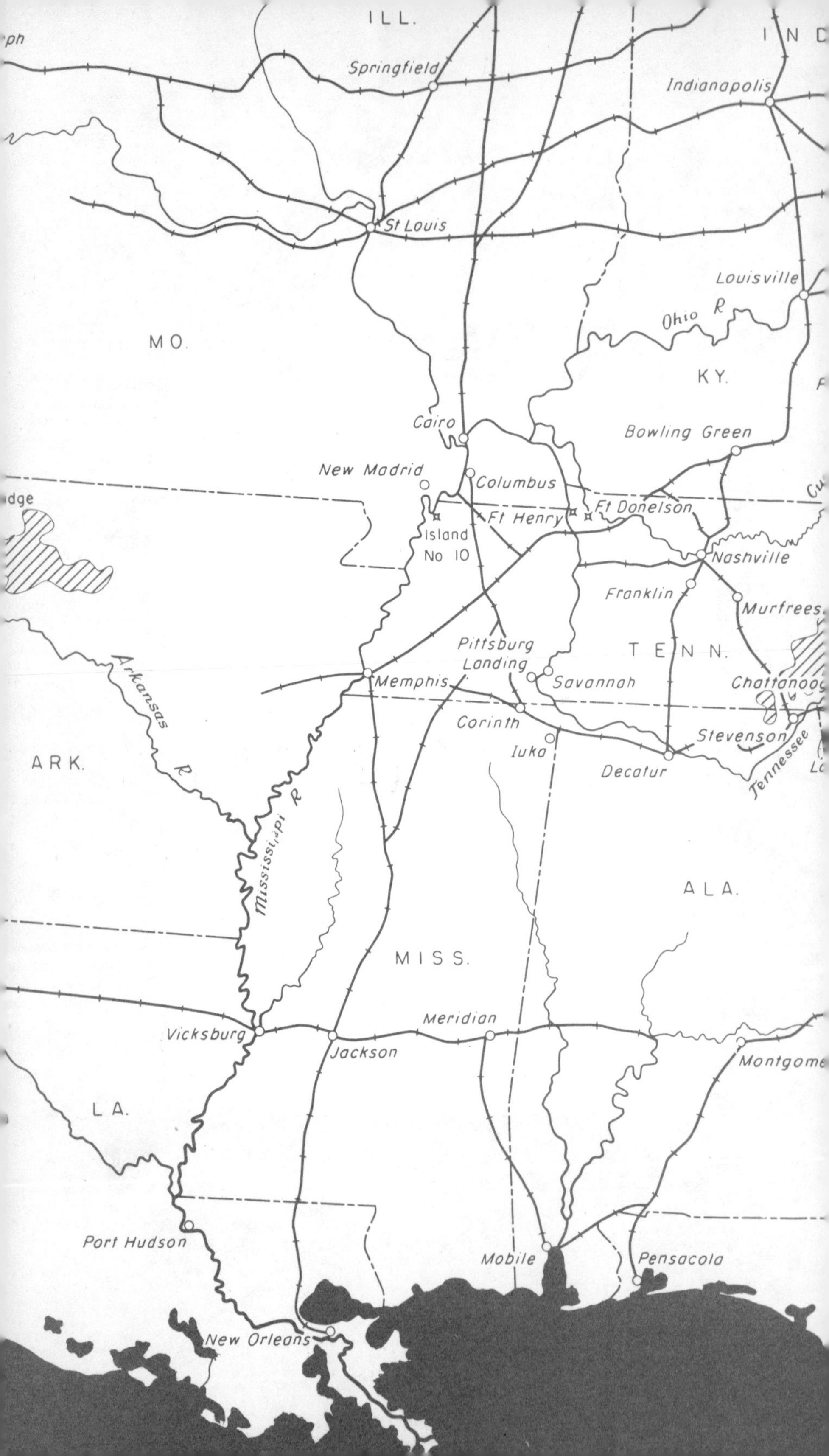

ILL.
IND
Springfield
Indianapolis
St Louis
Louisville
Ohio R
MO.
KY.
Cairo
Bowling Green
New Madrid
Columbus
Ft Donelson
Ft Henry
Island No 10
Nashville
Franklin
Murfrees
Pittsburg Landing
TENN.
Savannah
Memphis
Chattanoog
Corinth
Stevenson
Iuka
Decatur
Tennessee
Arkansas R
ARK.
Mississippi R
ALA.
MISS.
Meridian
Vicksburg
Jackson
Montgome
LA.
Port Hudson
Mobile
Pensacola
New Orleans